HUMAN RESOURCES LEADERSHIP IN

Hospitality

JOHN WALKER

*McKibbon Professor Emeritus and
Fulbright Senior Specialist
University of South Florida*

NICHOLAS THOMAS

*School of Hospitality Leadership
Driehaus College of Business
DePaul University*

Kendall Hunt
publishing company

MW01255925

Cover images © Shutterstock, Inc.

Kendall Hunt
publishing company

www.kendallhunt.com
Send all inquiries to:
4050 Westmark Drive
Dubuque, IA 52004-1840

Copyright © 2018 by Kendall Hunt Publishing Company

ISBN 978-1-5249-5038-5

Published in the United States of America

ACKNOWLEDGMENTS

To Paul and Stefani for making it happen.
—*John Walker*

For Lisa, Hamilton, and Bao Bao.
—*Nick Thomas*

CONTENTS

Chapter 3—Employment and the Law   31

Chapter 4—Workforce Planning and Organizing   55

Chapter 5—Recruiting   77

Chapter 6—Selection   95

Chapter 9—Employee Compensation   157

Chapter 10—Employee Benefits and Services   175

Chapter 11—Leading High-Performing Employees   195

Chapter 12—Employee Relations   213

Chapter 13—Health and Safety   233

Chapter 14—Working with Organized Labor   253

Index   275

INTRODUCTION

Ask any hospitality manager what are some of your greatest challenges and one answer would likely be "finding and retaining great employees." We wrote this text to address this issue and because we strongly believe that we should be leading our human resources not managing them—there is a distinct difference and this text proves it. We also believe that the human hospitality industry is constantly evolving on many different fronts.

From innovations in technology to more exacting customer expectations, the changes that the hospitality industry has undergone seems almost endless. With all these changes one thing has remained constant; the need for well-trained human resources to deliver service in order to meet operations demands. From Shanghai, China to Chicago, Illinois the employees are the core of this industry and, without them, hospitality fails to succeed.

We want this book to have a logical flow. We designed this book exactly how we teach this class in a college-level course. We start with a basic overview of human resources leadership because, without that, there is no sense in diving deep into the content. Next, we touch on the topic of diversity and regulatory issues. This is where we start to deviate from some other texts in the marketplace. You see, we live in a diverse world and the hospitality industry no different. This is an industry that prides itself on employing an extremely diverse workforce in terms of, among other traits, race, gender, and national origin, and we should be an industry that encourages equality.

We felt so strongly that this was important we wanted to discuss it first since a solid understanding of this, combined with the regulatory issues (the law), which is discussed next, will help provide a framework for the other specific human functions discussed in later chapters of the book. For example, when we talk about recruiting or compensation, you not only need to talk about it and develop strategies both in the context of what the law says is "legal," but also develop business practices that are the "right thing to do" and "fair."

Once an introduction, diversity, and regulatory framework have been discussed, the book takes a deep dive into various functions of human resources leaderships. Out of the gate, we tackle workforce planning and organizing—essentially, making sure you have the right number of people in the organization at the right time to meet the needs of your customer. Once that's done, we move on to the next function, recruiting. Recruiting is always fun for some, especially, if they enjoy the process of selling because some think recruiting is like a sales process. Essentially, when you recruit you're trying to convince someone to become an applicant for an open position in your organization. You can find these potential applicants either internally or externally.

Once a person has officially applied for a position, now the real fun, or some may say challenge, begins, you have to pick which one you want to hire! This is where the function of selection starts. Selection is identifying the best applicant and offering them the job. There are a variety of methods to do this and those methods are discussed in detail.

Once you have hired a new employee, you have to give them the knowledge, skills, and abilities to their jobs successfully. This is where the human resources function of training comes into the mix. Some

HR books combine the function of training and development. We have chosen to divide them in to two since we see them as two different functions. Training is designed to provide employees with skills and abilities needed to do their current job, while development is focused on providing employees with skills they need for future jobs they may have within the organization.

As we split training and development, we also decided to split compensation and benefits. We opted to do this for two reasons. First, they are two different functions. Second, there is just so much to talk about.

Moving on from compensation and benefits, we discuss how to manage employee performance, labor relations, and workplace safety and health, and then we conclude with a discussion of working with labor unions. These final four chapters are critical, as you work your way up into senior-level leadership of an organization and begin to develop strategy about how to lead your human resources to meet organization goals.

Throughout the book, we have also included some vignettes that provide insight from industry practitioners and members of the academic community who teach and do research HR. This will give you "real world" at what's really going on in the world of HR.

Thank you for taking the time to read our book. We hope you enjoy this journey to discover what it takes to lead human resources in the hospitality industry.

John Walker
Nicholas Thomas

Dr. John R. Walker, DBA, FMP, CHA, is the McKibbon Professor Emeritus of Hotel and Restaurant Management at the University of South Florida and Fulbright Senior Specialist. He graduated from Ealing Hotel School at Ealing Polythenic University, London and undertook management training at the Savoy Hotel London. This was followed by terms as food and beverage manager; Human Resources Manager at the Selsdon Park Hotel; Assistant Rooms Division Manager at the Royal Garden Hotel, a 550 room five-star hotel; Senior Assistant Conference and Banqueting Manager at the five-star London Hotel InterContinental; and general manager of the prestigious five-star Coral Reef Club, Barbados, West Indies. He has an M.B.A. from the Canadian School of Management, Toronto Canada and a Doctor of Business Administration D.B.A., form the United States International University, San Diego California.

John has taught Human Resources Leadership for several years and received presidential awards for scholarship and has been published in leading journals and newspapers and has been awarded professor emeritus twice. He is an Editorial Board member of the *Journal of Human Resources in Hospitality and Tourism*. He is a past president of the Pacific Chapter of International CHRIE and is a certified hotel administrator, and food service management professional. John is coauthor of *Tourism Concepts and Practices* also published by Kendall Hunt. He can be reached at jwalker@sar.usf.edu

DePaul University/Jeff Carrion

Dr. Nicholas J. Thomas holds the positions of Assistant Professor and Director of the J. Willard and Alice S. Marriott Foundation Center for Student Development and Engagement in the School of Hospitality Leadership at DePaul University. At DePaul, Dr. Thomas teaches innovative and practically focused undergraduate- and graduate-level courses related to human resources, hospitality operations, technology, and customer service. In addition to teaching, he is an active researcher in the areas of human resources and hospitality education. The human resources topics he researches include turnover, job satisfaction, organization social capital, and supervisor gender. The hospitality education topics he focuses on include the use of technology in the classroom and student expectations as they enter hospitality industry careers. He has published in the field's top journals and has been sought out to author textbook chapters and present his research findings in both academic and industry settings.

Outside of DePaul, Dr. Thomas has actively served in board positions for the Council on Hotel, Restaurant, and Institutional Educators, including the role of President for the Central Federation. Before joining DePaul, Dr. Thomas held the position of Chair of Academic Affairs for the University of Nevada, Las Vegas William F. Harrah College of Hotel Administration Singapore Campus and a faculty position at Iowa State University.

Dr. Thomas has held leadership positions in some of the most recognizable and successful hospitality organizations, with the majority of his career focused on human resources and luxury hotel operations. Highlights from his career include being a member of the opening team for two large hospitality resorts.

Dr. Thomas earned a Doctorate of Philosophy in Hospitality Administration, Master in Hospitality Administration, and Bachelor of Science in Hotel Administration from the University of Nevada, Las Vegas. He currently resides in Chicago with his wife Lisa and their two Parson Russell Terriers, Hamilton and Bao Bao.

© Andrey_Popov/Shutterstock.com

Chapter 1

HUMAN RESOURCE LEADERSHIP

From Good to Great: The Case of the Portman Ritz-Carlton, Shanghai, China

Twilight along the Huangpu River in Shanghai, China

© mihaiulia/Shutterstock.com

The Logo for the Ritz-Carlton Hotel Brand

© Leonard Zhukovsky/Shutterstock.com

Shanghai's Portman hotel was good but not great. Employee satisfaction ratings averaged 70–80%. Finances were average (Yeung, 2006). When it took over the hotel recently, the Ritz-Carlton company and the hotel's new general manager Mark DeCocinis set out to make the Portman a premier property. Their strategy in doing so was to dramatically improve guest service. And Mr. DeCocinis knew the hotel's employees were crucial to such an effort. "We're a service business, and service comes only from people." He introduced the Ritz-Carlton company's employee-centric human resource system. Their efforts paid off. Several years later, the Portman Ritz-Carlton was named the "Best Employer in Asia." The hotel now scores 98% in employee satisfaction (Dessler, 2008, p. 1).

This book demonstrates how this "good to great" improvement can be achieved and the importance of human resource leadership.

First, the book introduces current and future hospitality professionals to the important functions necessary to hire and keep a high-achieving workforce. These are the functions that are traditionally thought of as being done by a human resources department. But second—and perhaps more importantly—it helps these professionals understand how, no matter their place in the organization, leading the workforce in their own business unit (department) necessitates knowledge and implementation of these same functions. That is to say, recruiting, training, and safety aren't jobs solely done by the human resources department. They are done by most supervisors and managers in the organization. So when we use the term "human resources leadership," we are not referring to the bosses in the human resources department. We mean each and every person in the organization who leads employees—the human, the most important, resource of the company.

In this first, introductory chapter we cover several topics relating to human resources leadership because, as one successful Food and Beverage Manager told the authors, "we lead our human resources we don't manage them" (B. Weil, personal communication, April 14, 2013). Horst Schulze, the legendary hotelier, former president of Ritz-Carlton, now president of Cappela Hotel Group says, "Cappela is superior to the competition because they hire employees who work in an environment of belonging and purpose. You need superior knowledge and real leadership not management." Because of this, Schulze says "we specifically developed a process for leaders, we don't hire managers" (Forbes, 2013).

After reading and studying this chapter you should be able to

■ Discuss the importance of service leadership.
■ Discuss the changing role of a human resources organization.
■ Identify the functions of HR.
■ Outline the responsibilities of the various roles in a human resource department.

Maya Angelou delivers poem on Bill Clinton's Inauguration Day January 20, 1993 in Washington, DC

© Joseph Sohm/Shutterstock.com

> "I've learned that people will forget what you said, people will forget what you did, but people will never forget how you made them feel."
>
> —Maya Angelou

This text comes with 14 chapters as outlined below.

Chapter 1 Human Resource Leadership
Chapter 2 Leading Diverse Employees
Chapter 3 Employment and the Law
Chapter 4 Workforce Planning and Organizing
Chapter 5 Recruiting
Chapter 6 Selection
Chapter 7 Employee Training
Chapter 8 Employee Career Development
Chapter 9 Employee Compensation
Chapter 10 Employee Benefits and Services
Chapter 11 Leading High-Performing Employees
Chapter 12 Employee Relations
Chapter 13 Health and Safety
Chapter 14 Working with Organized Labor

After this first chapter, each of the remaining chapters will have a section on related legal terms and developments, which we have titled "Legalize," because no area of human resources is immune to compliance with the law. Additionally, a section on human resources Technology is included in each chapter because technology is crucial to all aspects of human resources leadership.

Learning Objective 1: Discuss the importance of service leadership

Hospitality Human Resources Leadership

Service Leadership: Leadership that asks how to help employees reach their goals, personal or professional.

The hospitality industry is unique in that it operates 365 days a year, 24 hours a day, and 7 days a week. It utilizes large number of employees, many of whom are semi-skilled or unskilled. To manage this nonstop industry in the continuously innovating service economy, **service leadership** is required throughout the organization.

From this standpoint, the role of any leader is to get to know your people individually and demonstrate that you care about them. Start by asking yourself some basic questions about your people.

- Why are they here?
  - What do they want to achieve working for our organization (or buying our product)?
  - What are their goals in life, both personal and professional?
  - Where are they in their life's journey?
  - What barriers are they currently facing in life?
  - And lastly, how can I, as the people leader, genuinely help them get where they want to be, be what they want to be, and contribute what they want to contribute?

True leaders inspire others to proactively commit to the vision and mission of the organization

© nd3000/Shutterstock.com

This new leadership role is based on carefully and intentionally collected information about people's agenda, apart from their contextual status as guests or employees. Start looking at people not from the perspective of how they can help you, but how you can help them. Master this single law and your success is likely assured.

As Warren Bennis, a leadership scholar said, "Great leaders make people feel that they are at the very heart of things, that they make a difference to the success of the organization, and that their work has meaning" (Vogel, 2012). Additionally, true leaders inspire others to proactively commit to the vision and mission of the organization—not just to the task at hand or the crisis of the day (Brantley, 2012). Warren Bennis researched visionary leaders and found that visionary leaders (Bennis, 2009 as cited in Andrews, 2009, p. 45).

- Search for ideas, concepts, and ways of thinking until a clear vision crystallizes.
- Articulate the vision in easy-to-grasp philosophy that integrates strategic direction and cultural values.

- Motivate employees to embrace the vision through constant persuasion and setting an example of hard work.
- Make contact with employees at all levels in the organization, attempting to understand their concerns and impact the vision has on them.
- Act in a warm, supportive way, always communicating that, "We are in this together as a family."
- Translate the vision into a reason for existing. It continually relates the vision to each individual's concerns and work.
- Concentrate on the major strengths within the organization that will ensure the success of the vision.
- Remain at the center of the action, positioned as the prime shaper of the vision.
- Look for ways to improve, augment, or further develop the vision by carefully observing changes inside and outside the organization.
- Measure the ultimate success of the organization in terms of its ability to fulfill its vision.

But before one can be a great leader, one has to find <u>and retain</u> outstanding hospitality employees. Traditionally, in comparison to other industries, the hospitality industry suffers from high employee turnover. It is not unusual for employee turnover to be in excess of 100% per year. This represents an enormous cost of doing business. The average cost of turnover at the front desk of a hotel is 30% of salary. Imagine the savings that the Ritz-Carlton, Sarasota has with an employee turnover rate of only 9% a year. It's easy to see that a company that retains a high percentage of its employees could potentially make more money.

In today's competitive marketplace, the name of the game is to delight guests—not just satisfy them—and how do we delight guests? Just ask Kurt Wachtveilt, the former 40-year veteran general manager of the Oriental Hotel in Bangkok, Thailand, considered by many to be one of the best hotels in the world. When he was asked, "What is the secret of being the best? He replied, "Service, service, service!" Outstanding leadership is essential to producing a workforce that gives guests and fellow employees (the internal guest) outstanding service.

Bangkok, Thailand is Home to the Mandarin Oriental Hotel, one of the most luxurious in the world

© Doraemonz32/Shutterstock.com

Learning Objective 2: Discuss the changing role of HR

The Changing Role of the Human Resources Department

Today, human resources functions have a seat at the executive decision-making table

© BlueSkyImage/Shutterstock.com

In the past, the person in charge of a human resources unit was not always a part of the senior management decision-making team in a company. Company presidents mostly came from operations, finance, or marketing and had little or no interest in human resources. Decisions were made by senior leaders of an organization, and then human resources were told "make them happen!" Human resources was seen as a necessary evil as it was not a revenue generator. Human resources personnel, traditionally, did not understand and were therefore not seen as contributing to the complete business, all the essential parts, and how to achieve the key organizational goals.

Ulrich, Younger, Brockbank, and Ulrich (2012) writing in *HR from the Outside* say "If HR professionals are truly to contribute to business performance, then their mindset must center on the goals of the business." Ulrich et al. (2012) continue to say that human resources professionals must practice their craft with an eye to the business as a whole and not just their own department.

Today, thanks to an increasing awareness and appreciation of human resources by corporate executives in most hospitality companies, human resources functions has a seat at the executive decision-making table and human resource professionals are concentrating on the organizational goals deemed to have an input on success (Ulrich et al., 2012). Many executives speak in terms of **return on investment (ROI)**, and the bottom line (BL), so organizations need to present a clear evidence of their impact on the vision, mission, values, culture, and goals of the company including return on investment. To facilitate this process, human resources departments need to measure things that impact these goals. If a human resource professional can be like a consultant who diagnoses and prescribes a remedy for a situation, you will get the president or chief executive officer's (CEO's) attention and be a real enterprise partner.

> **Return on Investment (ROI):** The return gained on an investment.

An example of HR measuring something that impacts the BL is employee turnover. As noted already, the hospitality industry is known for having a high employee turnover of sometimes over 100%, compared to some other industries. Now, if a statistic like turnover can be quantified, the cost of turnover can be determined. An example is a hotel front office where guest service agents' turnover is 100% a year and it is determined that it costs $6,000 to advertise, recruit, interview, orientate, train, and account for mistakes made by the new person. So, if there are 10 front desk guest service agents, then we know that the cost of this turnover is 10 × $6,000 totaling $60,000 a year for just one department. We can also compare our property with local and national industry benchmarks for turnover rates.

Human resources professionals have adopted the concept of talent that recognizes a new breed of employees called **knowledge workers**. The knowledge worker is a highly qualified and competent person who possesses complex information and processes skills to convert it into currency. It is essential for human resources directors and managers to accurately assess the talents required for each position and to hire those who best suit the organization's needs.

Learning Objective 3: Identify the functions of Human Resources

The Functions of the Human Resources Department

Human resource departments, be they large or small, typically perform a variety of functions.

- If not already put in place by senior company management, human resources department may take the lead in strategic planning helping to formulate the vision, mission, and culture of the organization. The vision, mission, and culture of the company are very important not only for their functions, but the entire company because they set the tone or spirit for the whole company and make it the employer of choice and one of the best companies to work at.

- *Workforce planning and organizing*: Due to the high demands of guests 365 24/7, hospitality organizations must ensure that they have employees in the right place at the right time. They also must ensure that all jobs within the organization have clear and easy-to-follow job descriptions.

- *Recruitment*: The process of looking internally and externally for candidates to fill open positions in the organization and then getting them to formally express interest through the application process is vital.

- *Selection*: Based on a pool of applicants identified during the recruitment process, selection identifies, through valid and reliable methods, the candidate who is best suited to fill the role.

- *Training and development*: Training provides employees with the skills and abilities for a job they currently have within the organization. Development, while similar, provides skills that an employee will need in the future with the organization.

- *Compensation and benefits*: Providing compensation and benefits, that is both financial and nonfinancial in nature, for work completed in the organization is a key function. This can also include developing and implementing incentives to encourage outstanding performance and to retain employees.

- *Managing employee performance*: HR takes the lead in measuring and recording employee performance based on standards outlined in organizational policies and procedures.

- *Employee and labor relations*: Maintaining a high morale among employees is critically important. A critical element is having excellent communications so that company policies and regulations are known or accessible to all via the company Intranet, social media, departmental meetings, bulletin boards, and newsletters. Additionally, engaging in a cooperative relationship with unions that represent employees be the best way to conduct labor relations.

- *Workplace safety and health*: Hospitality employees should work in safe working conditions. Additionally, the highly demanding hospitality workspace means that organizations should make an effort to ensure their employees' own health and wellness is a top priority. The overall health and welfare of employees has an impact on the culture of an organization, and most importantly, the financial BL.

As you continue to read this book, each of these HR functions will be discussed in greater detail. Additionally, the study of HR also includes other concepts, such as laws and regulations, ethics, and diversity. These provide the context for all HR functions and underlie both overarching goals and daily implementation of policies and procedures throughout the organization.

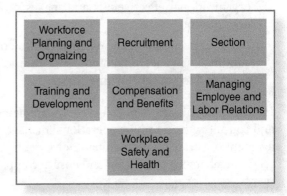

© Kendall Hunt Publishing Company

Learning Objective 4: Identify the responsibilities of various roles in a human resources department

Human Resources Vice President or HR Director

In many large companies, the human resources function is headed by a vice president. In smaller operations, the title might be Director of Human Resources. In either case, the duties and responsibilities are similar although a vice president may have a larger strategic role. The vice president of human resources or the HR director often have a seat at the executive council or committee where key decisions, both strategic and tactical, are made regarding the company.

The vice president of human resources or the director of human resources for a hospitality corporation would be responsible for strategic human resources activities including, but certainly not limited to: compensation, benefits, recruitment, policies and procedures, employee relations, training, employee and labor relations, and regulatory compliance.

In many instances, human resource vice presidents and directors are largely responsible for shaping the values and culture of the organization.

Human Resources Proficiencies

Being the manager of a human resources organization manager is challenging and requires several proficiencies. Dessler (2008, 20 pp) describes four categories of proficiencies for all employees as they manage human resources: HR proficiencies, business proficiencies, leadership proficiencies, and learning proficiencies.

1. *HR proficiencies* represent traditional knowledge and skills in areas such as employee selection, training, and compensation.
2. *Business proficiencies* reflect human resource professionals' new strategic role. For example, to assist the top management in formulating strategies, the human resource leader needs to be familiar with strategic planning, production, service, and finance. They must be able to speak the Chief Financial Officer's (CFO's) language, by explaining human resource activities in measurable terms, such as return on investment, payback period, and cost per unit of service (Wells, 2003, as cited in Dessler, 2008, p. 17).
3. *Leadership proficiencies* encompasses all the skills needed to enable groups and teams to effect organizational effectiveness and makes progress toward the goals to support the mission of the organization.
4. *Learning proficiencies* means that, due to constant and rapid change, the HR manager needs to be continually in a learning mode. New technologies and new laws constantly require the HR manager to stay on top of the learning curve.

HR professionals are responsible for the implementation of the operations of human resources strategy and consult with and advise operational managers on all aspects of human resources. They educate management on strategies to maintain positive employee relations. Additionally, they identify and develop team members for promotion and ensure company's compliance with policies, procedures, and government regulations.

Human Resources Department and HR Specialists

In addition to the director, the larger human resources departments also have specialist positions.

Employment manager: After understating other departments' needs, interviews candidates, obtains references and background checks, and processes documents for employment, including ensuring candidates' eligibility to work in the United States.

Payroll manager: maintains time sheets and payroll records and is responsible for ensuring that employees get paid correctly and on time.

Benefits manager: researches and helps negotiate a range of benefits for employees according to company policy. The benefits manager assists in enrolling employees in the various programs, answers questions regarding benefits, processes claims, and ends benefits for employees who leave.

Labor relations manager: responsible for labor relations, largely responsible for labor policy, responsible for the implementation of labor policy, participates in collective bargaining and labor contracts, and attempts to resolve grievances and disputes.

Training and development manager: assesses training and development needs, then plans, organizes, and offers appropriate training programs.

Depending on the size of the hospitality company there may be all of the above positions or, for smaller operations, there may be just one human resources position who literally does everything.

HR generalist: The HR generalist manages the day-to-day operation of the HR department office and manages the administration of projects, implements plans, and assists HR specialists. They are almost a "Jack of All Trades." A HR generalist has responsibilities relating to the Human Resource Information System (HRIS), departmental development, record-keeping, benefits, compensation, and employment.

All Leader-Managers are Involved with Human Resources

In small hospitality operations, the general manager and other supervisors may take on HR responsibilities if there is no or only a limited number of supporting staff and departments. This type of situation emphasizes the potential importance of the incumbents in all the management positions having good knowledge of human resources leadership.

However, in all organizations, no matter their size, human resources is a vitally important skill set for all managers and supervisors because HR functions, carried out correctly, produce better employees who, in turn, enable a hospitality company to attract and retain guests. At a base level, one hospitality operation is much the same as another, so it is up to the employees to make the difference in delivering exceptional guest service. It's as simple as happy employee's equal happy guests. All line managers and supervisors are or need to be leading the team they work with and ensuring compliance with all laws and contracts. So not just human resources professionals, but all managers have the responsibility to establish and work closely with managers to help maintain an outstanding workplace with empowered and highly engaged employees working to exceed the goals of the company.

The study of hotel operations and human resources experiences makes it clear that one basic premise is tried and true when dealing with people: we are all different, no matter how much we try to look or act like each other.

As one author describes it, when we are born we come into this world with invisible knapsacks on our backs. As we go through life we pick up grains of sand, pebbles, rocks, and sometimes boulders and put them in our knapsacks—these are our life experiences. Some things that come our way are easily handled and absorbed. Things like a speeding ticket, a bad grade in school, an argument with a parent or sibling. Those are the grains of sand. Other things happen in life, which are a bit more burdensome. They can be a bad family situation, an economic setback, or a missed job opportunity. These are the rocks. A tragedy, such as an unexpected loss of an immediate family member, a serious personal violation, or the loss of a home, or accident are life altering experiences and can be a boulder-sized burden to carry. We rarely know what is in someone else's knapsack. But we need to remember that each of us has one.

Ethical Leadership

Ethics: A set of moral principles and values that people use to answer questions about right and wrong.

Ethics is a set of moral principles and values that people use to answer questions about right and wrong. Ethics and morals are an integral part of hospitality decisions, from employment to truth in menus. Many corporations have developed a code of ethics that all employees use to make decisions. This became necessary because too many managers were making decisions without regard for the impact of such decisions on others (Walker, 2013).

Human resources often has a special role to play in being the ethical and moral conscience of an organization. For example, ethical concerns relate to abuse of physical and human resources, practices such as, unscrupulous marketing and, in some organizations, ecology and the environment. Unethical practice of human resources has also raised concern over outsourcing and off-shoring, reneging on company pension agreements, working excessively long hours, increased work stress, and questionable management decision-making.

Companies commit to ethical and moral operations through Corporate Social Responsibility

© Jacob09/Shutterstock.com

One of the ways that companies commit to ethical and moral operations can be via *Corporate Social Responsibility (CSR)*, a concept that refers to the responsibilities and relations between a company, the community, and the whole world. Some companies now include a "social audit" in their annual reports—this shows a commitment to the level of impact on the environment and the community. Having a CSR is good for business as increasingly potential guests are positively influenced by companies with a CSR (Gravett, 2013).

Technology in Human Resources

In the past, most human resources functions were performed exclusively on a face-to-face basis. The application process required individuals to appear in person and physically fill out the application form by hand. Training and development of employees was conducted in either a direct one-on-one or team setting with the department or HR manager. The collection of applicant, employee, and company-wide data was maintained in physical form and was less accessible to employees and managers. A big downside to this person-to-person process was a lack of depth and consistency in what applicants and new employees were told. As a whole, employees were not as knowledgeable about company policies and procedures, compensation and benefits, or laws pertaining to the workplace.

Today, in most organizations, human resources has become web-based resulting in more information being more efficiently and universally accessible for companies' managers and their employees. This new structure is known as electronic human resources or "E-HR" throughout the business world. E-HR combines both personal and technological features with human resource management (Johnson & Gueutal, 2011). This includes, but is not limited to, web-based application forms, job posting sites (such as Indeed, Craigslist, and HCareers), online training programs, and access by both HR personnel and the employees through a company web portal.

The drive to adopt a more technologically savvy approach to human resources stems from the need to cut costs, increase functional effectiveness, and to expand the amount of data accessible. Successful E-HR systems decrease administrative and labor expenses within HR departments, increase the talent pool for potential employees from a local or national level to a global level, and increase the access to personal and company-wide date. As technology continues to develop, we will continue to see a trend toward a more technology-driven workplace.

E-HR combines both personal and technological features with human resource management

© Kzenon/Shutterstock.com

> **E-HR:** The distinctive functions of human resource management combined with personal and technological based features.

Legalize and Following the Law

General managers have been known to tell HR departments that their job is to keep the company out of trouble. That sentiment sums up our litigious society when it costs thousands of dollars just to defend a company from lawsuits, be they legitimate or those with less honorable intentions. However, this can be difficult when managers and supervisors do not know enough about employment laws and the risks of not following them.

A major part of the human resources director's job then is to ensure the company and all managers are in compliance, at all times, with state and federal laws and, if there are union employees, with the Collective Bargaining Agreement (CBA). The human resources director can save the company literally millions of dollars in fines or judgments.

For example, equal employment laws (discussed in Chapter 3) determine the wording for job advertisements and the questions that can and cannot be asked at an interview. Another example would be laws that stipulate workplace requirements for employees' occupational safety and health laws.

Some companies have found it is a good idea to have an ombudsman who can act as an independent arbitrator between management and an employee, or between one employee and another. An ombudsman is a person to whom employees can go to if they feel they have been wrongly treated by management or if one employee has a problem with another employee and they prefer not to go to management. The ombudsman listens to both sides and makes suggestions on how to resolve the situation. Additionally, if there is a union contract and an employee has a problem with a management action they consider unfair, the employee consults the union representative who will consult with management or the HR department.

Key Points

- The hospitality industry is unique in that it operates 365 days a year, 24/7.
- Service leadership is the kind of leadership that starts not from wondering how someone can help you achieve your goals, but from a very basic, active generosity of asking how you can help your people achieve their goals, personal or professional.
- Human resource organizations' roles have evolved to being a strategic partner of top management.
- Human resource professionals need to understand the whole company operation and its organizational goals including return on investment.
- The functions of the HR department can sometimes help to create the corporate vision, mission, and culture, but always to implement them.
- The core HR functions are talent selection, workforce planning and organization, recruitment, selection, training and development, compensation and benefits, managing employee performance, employee and labor relations, and safety and health.
- HR department specialists are employment managers, payroll manager, benefits manager, labor relations manager, and training manager.
- The four main proficiencies that those managing human resources should have are HR proficiencies, business proficiencies, leadership proficiencies, and learning proficiencies.
- All leaders and managers throughout the company are involved in HR.
- Ethics, legal requirements, and diversity concerns are the context for all HR functions.

Key Terms

E-HR	Knowledge workers	Return on investment (ROI)
Ethics	Ombudsman	Service leadership

Discussion Questions

1. What is included in the total cost of employee turnover?
2. List and discuss the various functions of human resources.
3. How does the size of an organization impact the organizational structure of a human resources function?
4. Outline the HR director's needed proficiencies.
5. Discuss the meaning of ethics in a hospitality environment.

Ethical Dilemma

1. You are the manager of a large convention and banquet operation at a five-star hotel. The flowers for the hotel are booked through your office. The account is worth $15,000 per month. The owner of the floral company offers you a 10% kickback. Given that your colleague at a sister hotel receives a bonus and you do not, despite having better guest satisfaction and financial results, do you accept the kickback? If so, whom do you share it with?
2. You are an HR director of a large hospitality company and the owner of the company wants you to hire a relative of his or her for a position that you know the relative is not as qualified for as some possible internal and perhaps some external applicants. What do you do? Be sure to think of the implications of your actions.

Case Study

Marriott International did not suddenly emerge as a leading hospitality corporation with multiple brands and thousands of hotels. They began in the summer of 1927 as a nine stool A&W Root Beer franchise, which was soon called "The Hot Shoppe." The name change came about because root beer sold well in the hot Washington summer but as soon as winter came the Marriott had to come up with something else to satisfy the needs and wants of their guests. So, they added hot Mexican food items to the menu. The Hot Shoppe proved successful and other stores opened up. In 1937, Marriott's airline catering business opened at Hoover Field in Washington, DC. The division was named "In-Flite Catering" and served then Capitol, Eastern, and American Airlines.

Later, in 1957, Marriott opened its first hotel the Twin Bridges Motor Hotel in Arlington, Virginia. As the company grew, in 1967, the corporate name was changed from Hot Shoppes, Inc. to Marriott Corporation. In 1969, the first international Marriott hotel opened in Acapulco, Mexico. A timeline of other important milestones in Marriott's development includes

- In 1981, Marriott opened its 100th hotel.
- In 1983, the first Courtyard hotel opened.
- In 1987, Marriott acquired Residence Inn and by 1989 there were 500 Marriott hotels.
- In 1998, Marriott's 1,500th hotel opened and Marriott's food service and facilities management business was sold to Sodexho Alliance.
- In 1990, Pathways to Independence: Marriott's Welfare-to-Work Program was established.
- Marriott acquires the Renaissance Hotel Group and introduces Towne Place Suites, Fairfield Suites, and Marriott Executive Residence brands.
- In 2002, Marriott had 2,300 hotels and 200,000 employees in 63 countries and territories with annual sales of $20 billion.
- In 2006, all the United States and Canadian hotels go smokeless.
- In 2007, Bill Marriott launches a blog as Marriott celebrates 80 years in business and 50 years in the hotel business.

(It is interesting to note the strategic moves that Marriott has made over the years.)

Question: Imagine being the VP of Human Resources at any one time of this incredible development and outline some of the challenges you would have faced.

Internet Exercise

Organization: Society for Human Resource Management
website: www.shrm.org
Description: The society for Human Resources Management is the largest human resource association in the United States. Their website provides in-depth information for both students and professionals around the world.
Assignment
A. Briefly discuss two of the latest news articles and how they affect the hospitality industry.
B. Discuss the information given in two of the HR disciplines tab near the top of the homepage.

References

Brantley, A. (2012). New leadership imperative – Finding future leaders. *HR Florida Review* (Fall), 7.

Bresler, J. L. (2011, October). Presentation to the Sarasota Human Resources Society, Sarasota, Florida.

Dessler, G. (2008). *Human resource management* (11th ed.). Upper Saddle River, NJ: Pearson.

Forbes. (2013). *Former Ritz Carlton President Horst Schulze talks about the new frontier in luxury hotels.* Retrieved October 26, 2013, from http://www.forbes.com/sites/katiebell/2012/05/03/horst-schulze-on-the-new-frontier-in-luxury-hotels/

Gravett, L. (2013). *How human resources can help build an ethical organization.* Retrieved April 24, 2013, from http://www.e-hresources.com/Articles/August2002.htm

Johnson, R. D., & Gueutal, H. G. (2011). Transforming HR through technology: The use of E-HR and HRIS in organizations. *SHRM Foundation's Effective Practice Guidelines Series* (p. 1–2).

Ulrich, D., Younger, J., Brockbank, W., & Ulrich, M. (2012). HR from the outside. In *Six competences for the future of human resources* (p. 7). New York: McGraw Hill.

Vogel, H. E. (2012). Leadership and succession. *HR Florida Review* (Fall), 6.

Walker, J. R. (2013). *Introduction to hospitality management* (4th ed., p. 485). Upper Saddle River, NJ: Pearson.

Wells, S. (2003, June). From HR to the top. *HR Magazine*, 49.

Yeung, A. (2006). Setting up for success: How the Portman Ritz-Carlton hotel gets the best from its people. *Human Resource Management, 45*(2), 67–75.

© Rawpixel.com/Shutterstock.com

LEADING DIVERSE EMPLOYEES

Introduction

Room Service is a highly sought after amenity in full-service hotels

© Pariyes Arunrat/Shutterstock.com

Human resources directors of most well-known hospitality companies receive applications to fill job openings on a weekly if not daily basis. Their job is to sort through them and then forward the best applicants to various department heads throughout the hotel. Consider this scenario:

You are an HR professional, the head of hiring and training for a large hotel with a wide range of amenities to accompany a variety of hotel room categories, including food and beverage, spa, and several retail outlets. One day, an individual comes to your office unannounced. He explains that he applied for a job as a Room Service Attendant online but wants to talk to you in person. His concern is that he has some limitations in the use of his left hand. He is afraid he will be rejected for that reason. He explains that he has several years of experience as a Room Service Attendant at another hotel, but has heard that your hotel pays higher wages. He says he can provide excellent references and can perform all the necessary functions of the advertised position. He displays a genuinely hospitable and vibrant personality. After reviewing all the applications, you choose the person who came to see you and forward his application and resume to the hiring manger with your recommendation to hire this person.

A few days later, you receive news that the Food and Beverage Manager after in-person interviews promoted one of the bussers from the hotel restaurant to the room service attendant position. This employee did not have any previous experience in room service and had been reprimanded several times over the past year for tardiness. You realize that this situation may have occurred because the Food and Beverage Manager did not look beyond the applicant's disability and did not think he was a capable worker because of his physical challenge.

Unfortunately, this scenario is the reality for certain companies in the hospitality industry. Some managers are unwilling to take a chance on someone with a disability, and others don't want to provide reasonable accommodations for disabled person (which, by the way, is required by the law). However, more and more, we are seeing a changing work environment where an increasing number of individuals with a variety of physical challenges are finding jobs that can accommodate them. In return, many companies are seeing that these individuals are some of their most dedicated and hard-working employees.

After studying this chapter, you should be able to:

1. Identify diversity issues in the workplace
2. Discuss the methods to increase workplace inclusion among employees
3. Explain the challenges of multiculturalism and how they can be overcome
4. Develop an understanding of the methods to encourage a work environment that is both culturally diverse and provides equal treatment of applicants and employees

Learning Objective 1: Identify diversity issues in the workplace

Definition of Diversity

Potentially everyone has their own definition of what diversity means to them and it is impossible to capture every aspect of what diversity is, especially in one or two sentences. In Chapter 3, when discussing regulatory issues, we will give a legal definition related to differences in culture, ethnic group, race, religion, language, physical attributes and qualities, age, gender, and sexual orientation. However, for now, a simple and all-encompassing definition of **diversity** can be the differences that make one person unique from others. This chapter discusses issues one might experience in the workplace related to diversity.

> **Diversity**: The differences that make a person unique from others.

Diversity is important not just as a social issue but as a bottom line issue according to Gerry Fernandez, President of the Multicultural Foodservice and Hospitality Alliance (MFHA) (Walker & Miller, 2017, p. 152–153). He mentions that operators can leverage diversity to positively impact the bottom line. A simple example: companies doing business with government agencies are often asked about the percentage of their business purchases from women- and minority-owned businesses with this being the criteria for awarding a contract (Walker & Miller, 2017, p. 152–153). More broadly, different people bring different experiences, approaches, and attributes to the hospitality industry. Drawing on this, diversity can make a more efficient and effective organization.

Below is a list of characteristics that are commonly considered when discussing diversity. However, it is very important to understand that this list is not meant to be all inclusive, and in many cases, varies by industry and country. Additionally, as we will discuss in Chapter 3, many of these diversity characteristics are impacted by federal, state, and local laws and regulations.

- Race
- Gender
- Ethnicity
- Religion
- Sexual orientation

- Mentally or physically challenged
- Parental status
- Cultural dimensions and background
- Age

Some of the common issues that most managers experience related to diversity are addressed below. Having knowledge of diversity can lead to more positive working conditions and appropriate responses to problems and strategies for using diversity as strength for the company.

Educate yourself as much as possible with issues pertaining to diversity

© kurhan/Shutterstock.com

Physically Challenged

> **Physically Challenged**: Any type of physical disadvantage or impairment that limits the use of mobility or function.

Approximately, 54 million Americans are challenged with a physical disability of some form. The term **physically challenged** can be used to describe any type of physical disadvantage or impairment that limits of mobility or function. At work, people with disabilities may feel that supervisors do not see beyond their disabilities and do not think they are capable workers because of their physical challenges. Another common reaction is that coworkers may seem to patronize them and, because of embarrassment, may avoid speaking directly to them. Many people are afraid to ask questions because they don't want to offend the person and people have a tendency to be afraid of the unknown. However, people with challenges are usually very willing to share their situation with others. The key is education. Educate yourself as much as possible with issues of diversity.

A few words of advice regarding physically challenged employees:

- Look at the differently abled employee in the same way you look at other employees, as a whole person with likes, dislikes, and hobbies and encourage employees to do the same.
- Speak directly to the differently challenged employees.
- Hiring of physically challenged workers has a positive impact on the economy and more importantly on the employee.
- Employees with disabilities can be just as productive as other employees. Managers might have to make some adjustments for disabled employees, but this does not affect the quality of their work.
- People with disabilities do not like to be labeled as "disabled."
- Even with efforts to improve their interaction skills, managers will occasionally do something that will upset an employee. When this happens apologize sincerely. Learn from your experience and don't repeat the mistake.

Mentally Challenged

> **Mentally Challenged**: Any type of mental disability resulting from a cognitive, emotional, or developmental impairment that limits one's ability to function.

The term **mentally challenged** can be used to describe any type of mental disability resulting from a cognitive, emotional, or developmental impairment that limits one's ability to function. There are a few large companies that made great strides in employing the mentally challenged community in early 1980s. Two of these companies were McDonald's and Walmart. Like many large companies they found it difficult to attract a large reliable workforce. These two companies discovered an untapped labor market—mentally challenged people. They discovered that the majority of employees who were mentally challenged were extremely reliable (like showing up time) and were very dedicated to their positions. They had little turnover compared to the majority of employees. The hiring of many mentally challenged employees turned into a win-win situation. The employees were able to be productive citizens and feel good about contributing to society. It was also a win for the companies to have productive employees. In some communities, the government was also willing to subsidize part of the salaries of these employees.

Employers must keep in mind that the employee must be a good fit for the position they are filling. For example, a restaurant would not want to hire a person who has extreme challenges with coordination to cut vegetables. Additionally, managers need to use good judgment in all cases when it comes to the safety of all their mentally challenged employees as well as their coworkers.

Race, Ethnicity, and Culture

Most people's culture and values have been formed by their contact with people they grew up with. Such influence came from parents, friends, geographical location, and many other situations that are different for each of us.

Culture, ethnic group, and race are related terms. **Culture** is a learned behavior consisting of a unique set of beliefs, values, attitudes, habits, customs, traditions, and other forms of behavior. Culture influences the behaviors, beliefs, and characteristics of a particular group, such as an ethnic group. **Ethnic groups** share a common and distinctive culture, including elements such as religion and language. **Race** refers to a group of people related by common descent.

> **Culture**: A learned behavior consisting of a unique set of beliefs, values, attitudes, habits, customs, traditions, and other forms of behavior.

> **Ethnic Groups**: Share a common and distinctive culture, including elements such as religion and language.

> **Race**: A group of people related by common descent.

The population of the United States is becoming more multicultural, and ethnically diverse, every day. Almost one in four Americans has African, Asian, Hispanic, or Native American ancestry. It is estimated that, by 2020, the number will rise to almost one in three, and, by 2050, the number will be almost one in two. The fastest-growing segments of the U.S. population are minority groups (Walton, 1994).

The hospitality industry is one of the largest employers of the U.S. **minority segments**. From a legal and bottom line standpoint, it's a good business decision to have your company's employees reflect the nation's diversity.

The population of the United States is becoming more multicultural, and ethnically diverse, every day

© kurhan/Shutterstock.com

A restaurant's staff often resembles a miniature United Nations, with employees from all around the globe. Foodservice employs many more Hispanics and African Americans than any other industries. Latino workers comprise 25% of the workforce in food preparation and service-related occupations (Bureau of Labor Statistics, 2017), although, in 2016, they were only 17.3% of the overall U.S. population (Bureau of Labor Statistics, 2015). From a legal and bottom line standpoint, it's a good business decision to have your company's employees reflect the nation's diversity. The National Restaurant Association's website states that:

> **Minority Segment**: An outnumbered group that makes up less than half of the population.

- Restaurants employ more minority managers than any other industry.
- More than two-thirds of the supervisors in the foodservice industry are women; 16% are African Americans; and 13% are Hispanic.
- Since 1994, African American spending on food away from home increased by 46%. For Hispanics, that increase was 78.6%.

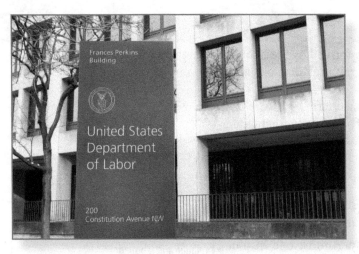

The U.S. Department of Labor tracks changes in workforce demographics

© Mark Van Scyoc/Shutterstock.com

The market-savvy businesses of today are responding to the changing demographics by targeting diverse consumers, employees, and supply partners in ways that build meaningful and reciprocal relationships. If companies' marketers and service providers do not reach out to minority communities in a holistic way, they're setting themselves up for failure in the long run.

For example, smart companies are promoting inclusion in the supply chain by partnering with minority-owned businesses. Partnering with minority-owned firms demonstrates a commitment to inclusion and creates jobs in the very communities that support our businesses as patrons.

© Casimiro PT/Shutterstock.com

ARAMARK is composed of unique individuals who, together, make the company what it is

ARAMARK's definition of diversity is "The mosaic of people who bring a variety of backgrounds, styles, perspectives, values, and beliefs as assets to ARAMARK and our partners." Kaleidoscope Vision states that ARAMARK is composed of unique individuals who, together, make the company what it is and can be in the future. Only when all individuals contribute fully the strength and vision of ARAMARK can be realized. The guiding principles for diversity are: "Because we are committed to being a company where the best people want to work, we champion a comprehensive diversity imitative. Because we thrive on growth, we recruit, retain, and develop a diverse workforce. Because we succeed through performance, we create an environment that allows all employees to contribute to their fullest potential".

Age and Generational Differences

Workplace Generational Differences: A wide range of differences among the generations that are currently employed in our work force.

There will always be workplace generational differences, and these may create certain conflicts or dilemmas between employees. However, workers aged 40 and older are protected by the Age Discrimination in Employment Act (ADEA), which will also be discussed in detail in Chapter 3.

Both younger and older workers want to do their work and be considered a part of the team just like anyone else. They want their managers to listen to them and let them participate in decision-making. Managers need to help facilitate young and older employees working together and learning from each other. For example, an idea to bring two very different generations together is to create a mentor/mentee program. This is a chance for not only the young to learn from the old, but for the old to learn from the young. An older employee may have learned many great strategies for interacting with customers. But, the older employee may not be as familiar with using technology. This is a great opportunity for one generation to learn from another. Encourage this type of collaboration whenever possible.

It is important for managers not to set their expectations of older adults higher or lower than of their younger peers. Be sure to treat all the employees equally.

Religion

The U.S. population reflects many different religious beliefs and that can potentially be a challenging topic in the workplace. The bottom line is that companies must allow all employees, their **religious freedom**, to practice any religion they choose assuming it does not affect the work environment in any negative way.

> **Religious Freedom**: An individual's freedom to practice any religion they choose.

There are ways to limit conflict between employees. Problems usually occur when managers give preferential treatment to one religious group and not to another. For example, it is recommended that companies have a "floating" holiday policy as opposed to having some holidays on set dates, which reflects Christian traditions. A company may want to allow each employee to have three floating holidays a year. The employees can decide when to use the days off to accommodate their particular religious practices. If business levels dictate that most employees work during a "popular" holiday like Christmas, it is recommended to have a religion-neutral policy, such as having the most senior employees allowed to take the holiday before less senior employees. However, there may also be times where no one will be allowed to take time off because of business levels. This may include Sundays, which can be very busy. The policies should be made clear to current and potential employees.

Both younger and older workers want to do their work and be considered a part of the team just like anyone else

© Dmytro Zinkevych/Shutterstock.com

Sexual Orientation

A lot has changed for members of the lesbian, gay, bi-sexual, and transgender (**LGBT**) community over the past 30 years. Years ago, most gay people were not as open about their sexual orientation due to the chance that they may be discriminated against solely based on their sexual orientation.

> **LGBT**: Members of the lesbian, gay, bi-sexual, and transgender community.

As social and legal discrimination has lessened, more individuals have become more open about their orientation. This means that many, perhaps most, people have some type of connection to someone who they know is a member of the LGBT community, whether it is family, friends, neighbors, or coworkers. This has created a more educated and accepting society. According to the UCLA School of Law, there are approximately 9 million Americans who are in the LGBT community However, members of the LGBT community still experience discrimination, as there is still a lack of acceptance in certain people's cultures, philosophies, or religious beliefs.

Managers must ensure, of course, that they follow legal requirements as a simple everyday situation can cause discomfort or conflict. For example, what terminology should be used with the LGBT community? If a manager doesn't use the appropriate terminology, they could easily offend some of their employees or guests and not even know it. Many gay people do not like the use of the word "homosexual." When this term is used, many gay people feel as if they are being "looked down" at. Be aware that being in the LGBT community is NOT a choice. People are born a certain way and then they experience the world in that manner. Hence the use of the term "sexual preference" is also not acceptable to use. The term that the LGBT community uses is sexual orientation, which can be described as the sense of a person's sexual interest toward members of a certain gender.

Sexual Orientation: The sense of a person's sexual interest toward members of a certain gender.

Gender

The representation of women in the hospitality industry varies. In some areas, such as housekeeping, they are overrepresented. In others, such as senior management, they are underrepresented. Industry research by the authors has shown that, in general, women are overrepresented in lower wage occupations and underrepresented in higher wage occupations within the industry. Additionally, for the same work, women are still lagging in pay compared to men. Keep in mind that this is a comparison between a man and woman with the same work experience and educational level doing the same job. Assuming all things are equal (such as experiences), the pay of women is estimated to be less than for men. This is simply not fair. Companies and managers need to be sure not to discriminate against woman simply based on their gender. Administrators need to spend more time making sure that all people are being paid fairly based on their work experience, education, skills, and other factors, and how productive they are in their position. Remember that gender bias applies to women and men. If your company offers benefits to caregivers, for example, men as well as women should be given the opportunities.

In addition to pay, there are additional issues to focus on as a manager concerning the issue of women in the workforce.

- Provide career-enhancing opportunities such as training or responsibilities for a project or team based on gender-neutral evaluation of all your employees.
- Be sure not to show favoritism to males or females. For instance, granting time off more readily or allowing certain employees to come in late or leave early.
- Show the same amount of respect and listen actively to both genders.
- Know the company's policy on sexual harassment and take seriously any charge of misconduct.

Learning Objective 2: Discuss the methods to increase workplace inclusion amongst employees

Workplace Inclusion

Let us now turn our discussion to how HR departments can help to make diversity a strength for the company and limit conflict and potentially illegal actions.

Many people don't feel comfortable or welcome in the workplace due to their differences. Managers in the hospitality industry, especially those in HR, have the initial responsibility to help facilitate the welcoming process to their company.

How does a manager accomplish successful inclusion? This may seem like a common-sense answer and in many ways it is. However, there are many managers that don't understand the importance of making their employees feel welcome and comfortable. A few ideas for making your new employees feel welcome and a part of the company are

Managers in the hospitality industry, especially those in HR, have the initial responsibility to help facilitate the welcoming process to their company

© lightwavemedia/Shutterstock.com

- Make a welcome call or email prior to the employee's first day to answer any additional questions before they start.
- Pair the new employee with an employee mentor—but don't automatically pair people just because they are of the same race, gender, and so on.
- *Personally,* introduce the new employee to other employees they will frequently be working with.
- Physically sit down with the new employee after the first or second day and ask them if they are feeling comfortable. They are likely not going to tell you unless you ask.
- You can start with a simple "how is it going?" then listen. Follow up with "what can I do to help you succeed and look forward to working here each day?" Then listen and, if you can, act on their comments.
- Physically sit down again after a week or two after they have had the opportunity to understand their work environment a little better. Additional follow up may be necessary depending on the situation and the employee.

Workplace inclusion means exactly what it says to include everyone regardless of gender, marital status, race, national origin, religion, age, physical abilities, sexual orientation,

> **Workplace Inclusion:** To include everyone regardless of gender, marital status, race, national origin, religion, age, physical abilities, sexual orientation, weight, and looks or whatever difference you can think of.

Cultural or other types of diversity matters to every single one of us, both professionally and personally

© Ikonoklast Fotgorafie/Shutterstock.com

weight, and looks or whatever difference you can think of (Dr. C. Gruhl, personal communication, February 16, 2018). For example, people's physical appearance is generally irrelevant to how they should be treated except in extreme cases that affect the work environment (such as lack of cleanliness). The ability to do the job should be the employment criteria.

Cultural or other types of diversity matters to every single one of us, both professionally and personally. When a group or segment of the population is excluded or oppressed, all of us are denied. For businesses and communities not only to survive but also to thrive each of us needs to be aware and sensitive to all members of the community. Our communities are rich in resources. When all segments are respected and utilized it benefits everyone involved.

Learning Objective 3: Explain examples of challenges faced regarding multiculturalism and how they can be overcome

Barriers to Communication

A person's nationality, culture, race, gender, and other "differences" can affect how he or she communicates. This communication between people of different cultures can often be difficult and sometimes create challenges when neither person is familiar with the other's style of communicating. Three specific problem areas are common.

1. The tendency not to listen carefully or pay attention to what others are saying,
2. Speaking or addressing others in ways that alienate them or make them feel uncomfortable, and
3. Using or falling back on inappropriate stereotypes to communicate with people who are different than the speaker.

> **Barriers to Multiculturalism**: Communication between people who are different can often be difficult and sometimes create challenges when neither person is familiar with the other's style of communicating.

> **Nonverbal Communication**: A form of behavior that transmits a message or signal, whether intentional or unintentional, as well as a way to exchange information with another individual without the use of speech.

To be an effective manager in a culturally diverse workforce, one must be able to recognize the different ways that people communicate, be sensitive to your own employees' cultural values, and adapt your own supervisory style accordingly. For example, in some cultures, people rely primarily on verbal communication. In other cultures, the spoken word is only part of communication, and there are many different forms of nonverbal communication, which can differ significantly between cultures. The term nonverbal communication describes a form of behavior that transmits a message or signal, whether intentional or unintentional, as well as a way to exchange information with another individual without the use of speech. People express themselves "in context"—language, tone of voice, body language, and the physical setting, are all parts of communication.

The use of personal space is another important cultural difference. If a person steps into someone's personal space, that they will often step back, in order to maintain their space. People from Latin America, Africa, the Middle East, and South America often prefer to communicate at much closer distances than would seem comfortable for people from Canada or the United States. Asians, by contrast, sometimes prefer even more personal space. As a manager, if an employee steps into your personal space and you step back, your action may be seen as being aloof or not wanting to talk. To adjust to situations when talking with someone, stay put and let the other person stand where he or she is comfortable.

Eye contact and facial expressions are two other nonverbal communication techniques that vary among cultures. Whereas in North America it is common to maintain good eye contact and employ facial cues such as nodding the head when listening to someone speak, not all cultures share those practices. In many Asian and African cultures, people will make greater eye contact when speaking, but when listening, make infrequent eye contact. They also might not use facial expressions when listening to others. These nonverbal communication differences may lead to misunderstanding. A manager may wrongly misinterpret that an employee who does not make eye contact or nod in response is simply not listening or doesn't care, when in fact, the employee is listening in a respectful manner.

Cultural differences also affect other areas of communication, such as the rate at which people speak, the volume, speech inflections, and the use of pauses and silence when speaking. It is common

A person's nationality, culture, race, gender, and other "differences" can affect how he or she communicates

© Andrei_R/Shutterstock.com

in Europe and North America to speak whenever there is silence in a conversation, and to speak loudly. This is not always the case in other cultures. In Asian cultures, silence is not regarded as an interruption or indication that the conversation has ended but is often considered as much a part of conversation, as speaking is. Silence is also often used as a sign of politeness and respect for elders rather than a lack of desire to keep talking. Whereas a North American's loud speech in many Asian countries is often interpreted as being aggressive or even angry, an Asian's soft-spoken voice in the United States might be seen as a sign of weakness or shyness.

Another communication difference is the tendency in Europe and the United States to be direct in conversation and get to the point. In many other cultures, this practice is considered impolite and rude. To an Asian American, being direct might be interpreted as being insensitive to the feelings of others. Native Americans, Asian Americans, and some Hispanic Americans value respect and harmony and will use indirect speaking methods to achieve those ends.

It is also important to remember that not everyone from one culture will act the same. Even though it is a common perception that Asian people are soft-spoken, it is not uncommon for Asian people to speak loudly. Don't assume that someone has certain values, experiences, traits, and so on because they "look" like a certain racial or ethnic group.

> **Cross-Cultural Interaction Skills:** Skills in communication across lines of difference.

1. Increase personal awareness.
2. Learn about other cultures.
3. Recognize and practice cross-cultural interaction skills.
4. Maintain awareness, knowledge, and skills.

Figure 2.1 Developing Cross-Cultural Interaction Skills

By developing **cross-cultural interaction skills**, you will be better equipped to do your job and to motivate diverse employees to accomplish company goals. But don't think you will be able to develop these skills overnight or, for that matter, even over a few months. By considering the major steps shown in the Figure 2.1, you will better appreciate that this process is complex and will take time to master. The effective manager is aware that employees come from different cultural backgrounds, learns about how their cultures differ, and works with employees without passing judgment about their cultures. Guests of a different culture such as Europeans, who are not accustomed to tipping, can cause resentment unless they are advised of American custom and servers advised of European custom.

Learning Objective 4: Develop understanding of the methods to encourage a work environment that is both culturally diverse and provides equal treatment of employees

Diversity Statements and Programs

There are many companies in the hospitality industry that truly attempt to embrace diversity into their cultures. It is usually true that, inclusion starts at the top. It is recommended that all companies have a formal diversity statement that is truly all inclusive, shared, and practiced. Statements about how to treat a diverse guest population are a good idea. See the Marriott example adjacent this text.

© Rawpixel.com/Shutterstock.com

Workplace inclusion is an ongoing process that everyone needs to be involved with

Serving a Diverse World

Our employees are trained to go above and beyond for our guests. It's our job to make sure you have the best possible experience while staying in our hotels. As a global company, we have guests from around the world who vary in backgrounds, language, tradition, religion, and cultures. And as our guests, we want to make you feel as at home as we possibly can.

Once a diversity statement is in place, it needs to be read and executed continuously.

Additionally, inclusivity is an ongoing process that everyone needs to be involved with. It cannot just be executed at one level in a company and expected to work. Unfortunately, many CEO's of companies send all of their employees through a 3-hour mandatory diversity training and at the end they believe that their employees appreciate diversity. There nothing more from the truth. Training and cultural practices continually need to be practiced through a **diversity and inclusion program** to engrain this belief in the company culture. It is important for companies to establish a program that encourages ongoing diversity initiatives and inclusivity.

> **Diversity and Inclusion Program**: A program that encourages ongoing diversity initiatives and inclusivity.

The following six steps are the "how-to's" for establishing a diversity and inclusion program:

1. Develop a company mission statement that includes diversity and inclusion.
2. Develop a separate diversity statement from the company's mission statement.
3. Develop goals for diversity and inclusion for each key operating area.
4. Develop objectives/strategies to show how the goals will be met.
5. Develop measurements to monitor progress toward the goals.
6. Monitor progress toward goal accomplishment.

> *Sodexho strives to be the best in class in the hospitality industry and is rapidly becoming a benchmark for corporate America. This is being achieved by six strategic imperatives, diversity being one of them. Alongside financial results they report on how they are doing on diversity and inclusion. The second is an incentive program where bonuses of 10%–15% are linked to the diversity scorecard. Twenty-five percent of the executive team's bonus is linked and the CEO has guaranteed that this bonus will be paid out regardless of the financial performance of the company.*

In larger organizations, it is best to have someone whose sole job is to attend to the diversity and inclusion. It really shows the commitment. This person may be part of the HR team or function separately but the person should report to senior leadership. Given the diverse nature of the hospitality industry workforce, it is more important to create a harmonious work environment where employees can thrive and contribute for the benefit of everyone. Senior management should ensure that all programs and decisions take diversity into account in a similar way as financial implications are taken into account.

> According to Rohini Anand, "There are so many pieces included in a diversity effort. It ranges from recruiting and sourcing to retention . . . my recommendation is that somebody be responsible for diversity and inclusion and report to senior management—preferably the president. You want to have influence at the top. A diversity effort can only be successful if you get top level buy-in along with grass roots efforts."
>
> *Walker & Miller, 2017*

Technology in HR

A company needs to be clear in its expectations for employee-to-employer interactions

The technology used in regard to leading diverse employees is part of a human resources information system (HRIS). The system can track various aspects of diversity so that a hospitality business can determine if they are meeting diversity employment requirements. For example, when a government agency calls the hotel to ask the percentage of minority employees, someone needs to have an answer. Similarly, diversity and sexual harassment training can be provided and then monitored online. Ensuring all employees undergo this training, companies may lessen the chance of losing a lawsuit.

Legalize

A company needs to be clear in its expectations for employee-to-employer interactions. In the best firms, guidance in this area starts at the top of the structure. Many hospitality firms, like Four Seasons, also follow the Golden Rule Approach. Treat other like you want to be treated.

Key Points

- Diversity is not easy to define. Diversity is very complex.
- Diversity includes many issues and is endless.
- Managers need to know what is included and not included in the ADA as much as possible.
- Managers need to be very careful to be as fair as possible with everyone no matter who a person is. Employees need to be judged based on their performance at work.
- Be aware of the different types of discrimination that can take place in the work environment. Examples: Age discrimination, religious issues, sexual orientation, and gender issues.
- Managers need to create an environment of inclusion for all employees.
- There are many barriers to cultures. Managers need to be aware of these challenges and face them head on.
- Earning respect is not always an easy to earn. Managers need to be aware of this aspect of leadership.
- Being aware of one's own biases is half the battle of understanding others.
- Diversity statements are a must in any company no matter what size.
- Create a diversity program where ever you work if the company doesn't already have one.
- Managing conflict in a diverse environment is easier said than done. Managers need to take care of any issues that arise as quickly as possible.

Key Terms

Barriers to multiculturalism
Cross-cultural interaction skills
Culture
Diversity
Diversity and inclusion
    program

Ethnic groups
LGBT
Mentally challenged
Minority segment
Nonverbal communication
Physically challenged

Race
Religious freedom
Sexual orientation
Workplace generational
    differences
Workplace inclusion

Discussion Questions

1. What does diversity in the workplace mean to you?
2. How can you as a manager or a member of the HR organization help facilitate diversity in the workplace?
3. What is stereotyping mean to you? Do you stereotype people today?
4. What are your biases? What can you do to change your biases?
5. How can you earn respect with your employees?
6. How can you manage conflict amongst your employees?
7. Discuss the most common forms of forms of discrimination that take place in the hiring process. What can be done to stop the inappropriate practices?

Ethical Dilemma

Jimmy is an Assistant Front Office manager at a large downtown hotel. His boss Becky is currently looking for a night auditor to fill a vacant position. An older lady, Dianne, came in yesterday and applied for the position. Dianne is the most qualified person to apply for the position. Becky had Jimmy interview all the potential employees. Jimmy told Becky that he thought that Dianne was the most qualified and would fit into the front office perfectly. Becky told Jimmy that she was thinking of not hiring Dianne because she would be working alone at night and Becky didn't think that a woman should be working at the front desk in the middle of the night alone. Becky also told Jimmy that she thought that Dianne is too old to be working the night audit position.

1. What type of discrimination happened in the situation?
2. What should Jimmy do? Should he talk to Becky about the situation?
3. What do you think the General Manager should do if he or she found about the situation?

Internet Exercise

Be yourself! Draft a set of interview questions that would be appropriate for position for Human Resources Director for a large hospitality company. Search the Internet for various sample interview questions regarding diversity and other key issues. Share your draft with a small group and, together, develop a final list of questions.

References

Bureau of Labor Statistics. (2015). Hispanics and Latinos in industries and occupations. *The Economics Daily* (U.S. Department of Labor). Available from https://www.bls.gov/opub/ted/2015/hispanics-and-latinos-in-industries-and-occupations.htm Accessed June 23, 2017.

Bureau of Labor Statistics. (2017). *Labor force statistics from the current population survey*. Retrieved October 31, 2017, from https://www.bls.gov/cps/cpsaat18.htm

Walker, J. R., & Miller, J. E. (2017). *Supervision in the hospitality industry* (8 th ed.). Hoboken, NJ: Wiley.

© Andrey_Popov/Shutterstock.com

Chapter **3**

EMPLOYMENT AND THE LAW

A Scenario

Michael, the manager of a high-end hotel spa in California, is in the process of hiring a women's locker room attendant. While he has a job description for the position and list of ideal qualifications, he is still unsure how to proceed with recruiting and selecting a candidate in a legally defensible manner.

Introduction

Claims of discrimination are difficult for companies to avoid, which is why both human resource professionals and managers company wide need to remain on top of current incidents and trends. Consider Walt Disney World, who was sued by a guest contact person, called a Cast Member, for disallowing her to wear for wearing a hijab, a headscarf commonly worn by individuals of the Muslim faith. Does this employee have grounds for suing the employer for religious discrimination? In another situation, a female employee refused to wear makeup as required by her employer. The employee alleged that the employer was engaging in gender stereotyping by requiring female beverage servers to wear makeup. Although the employee was unable to provide enough evidence to prevail in this case, in other legal jurisdictions, such as Madison, Wisconsin, city laws forbid discrimination based on physical appearance (Gomez-Mejia, Balkin, & Cardy, 2010, p. 87). The display of religious symbols, such as religious jewelry, is another area related to appearance where employers need to be aware of legal trends.

> **Discrimination**: Making a distinction in favor or against a person based not on individual merit but on the class or category that a person belongs—as in racial, sex, age, or other type of discrimination.

Employers can avoid legal actions by having clear policies and practices that avoid discriminatory treatment of employees. For example, appearance policies should not place an undue burden on one gender and not the other one.

Discrimination lawsuits are costly to defend against, and even more costly if the judgment goes against the employer as it did in the highly publicized case of Denny's restaurant chain where several individual store managers and employees of Denny's restaurant chain were alleged to have discriminated against African American guests. Not only did the company subsequently have to pay $46 million to African American patrons and $8.7 million as legal fees to settle these complaints, but the company's image with customers was damaged as well (Faircloth, 1998, as cited in Gomez-Mejia, Balkin, & Cardy, 2010, p. 89). But recovery is possible. Since the loss of the court case, Denny's has transformed itself into a company that has a 43% minority ownership of Denny's franchised restaurants. Additionally, Denny's has been ranked by *Fortune* as one of the top companies for minorities to work at.

Claims of discrimination are difficult for companies to avoid, which is why both human resource professionals and managers company wide need to remain on top of current incidents and trends

© Billion Photos/Shutterstock.com

There is a large body of laws germane to human resources at the federal, state, and local levels. Because of the variety and often significant differences at the state and local levels, this textbook addresses only federal laws and regulations. This chapter discusses specifically laws related to equal employment opportunity (EEO). Laws on other topics are addressed as appropriate in other chapters.

The complexity of human resources law is compounded by lengthy acts such as the Americans with Disabilities Act (1990), which has a technical manual of several hundred pages. To make matters even more complicated, one analysis has concluded that there are as many as 1,000 different disabilities affecting over 43 million Americans (Hall & Hall, 1994).

After studying this chapter, you should be able to:

1. Explain some of the major laws affecting employment.

2. Define what constitutes sexual harassment and how to handle sexual harassment complaints.

3. Follow the steps necessary to ensure EEO enforcement and compliance.

Learning Objective 1: Explain the laws affecting employment

Federal Laws Affecting Discriminatory Practices

For years, despite the Fifth, Thirteenth, and Fourteenth Amendments of the U.S. Constitution, which guarantee individuals the right of equal protection under the law, employers were able to get away with rampant illegal discrimination in the workplace. However, women and minorities were not, and, in some cases, are still not treated equally. In the early 1960s, *Civil Rights* became a national priority, which prompted President Kennedy to send comprehensive civil rights legislation to Congress. Later that summer, in front of the Lincoln Memorial, Dr. Martin Luther King Jr. gave his famous "I Have a Dream" speech that came to symbolize the insistence for meaningful legislation to address the demand for racial equality and justice (EEOC, 2017).

The memorial to the civil rights leader Martin Luther King, Jr.

© Sean Pavone/Shutterstock.com

The first of the EEO laws was the Equal Pay Act of 1963. This chapter describes those laws and how they affect today's workplace. The importance of these laws is realized as all human resource decisions from selection to separation are affected by equal employment implications (Dessler, 2011, p. 31).

Many of these laws discussed in this chapter also outline, very specially, the topic of retaliation. It is illegal to retaliate against any employee who files a lawsuit under the protection EEO laws. The law forbids retaliation when it comes to any aspect of employment, such as hiring, firing, compensating, job duties, promotions, termination, and training.

Equal Pay Act

The Equal Pay Act of 1963 makes it unlawful to discriminate in pay on the basis of sex when jobs involve equal work; require equivalent skills, effort, and responsibility; and are performed under similar working conditions

© Dimitry Kalinovsky/Shutterstock.com

> **The Equal Pay Act of 1963 (Amended in 1972):** This act makes it unlawful to discriminate in pay on the basis of sex when jobs involve equal work; require equivalent skills, effort, and responsibility; and are performed under similar working conditions.

The Equal Pay Act of 1963 (amended in 1972) makes it unlawful to discriminate in pay on the basis of sex when: (1) jobs involve equal work; (2) require equivalent skills, effort, and responsibility; and (3) are performed under similar working conditions. Pay differences derived from seniority systems, merit systems, and systems that measure earnings by production quantity or quality or from any factor other than sex do not violate the act (Cornell Law School, 2012). Pay can be different for different work shifts—the graveyard shift is traditionally paid more in the hospitality industry because it is more difficult to find employees to work during the night and early into the morning. The law also specifies that equal pay is required only for jobs held in the same geographic region. This allows an organization to make allowances for the local cost of living and the fact that it might be harder to find qualified employees in some areas. For example, restaurant servers may be paid $8.00 per hour in California and $2.13 per hour in Virginia. Housekeepers might be paid in high twenties to $30 per hour in New York City and $8.30 in Kansas City.

Title VII of the Civil Rights Act

Federal Laws exist in the United States to protect employees from discrimination

© f11photo/Shutterstock.com

In 1964, the Congress amended the original Civil Rights Act under Title VII and prohibited discrimination based on race, color, religion, sex, and national origin. Title VII applies to employers who have 15 or more employees, labor unions, and employment agencies. Note that employment decisions include "compensation, terms, conditions, or privileges of employment." So not just pay is covered but also things like health benefits and work hours.

Title VII clearly covers persons of any race, color, religion, sex, and national origin. However, as court cases and regulations have grown up around this law, so has the legal theory of a **protected class**. This theory states that groups of people who suffered discrimination in the past require, and should be given, special protection by the judicial system. Under Title VII, examples of protected classes are African Americans, Asian Americans, Latinos, Native Americans, and women.

Discrimination actually means making distinctions among employees. For example, even the most progressive companies can be open to accusations of discriminating when they decide who should be hired, who should be promoted, who should receive a merit raise, and who should be laid off. But the act defines two basic areas of illegal discrimination: disparate treatment and **disparate impact**.

Disparate treatment refers to intentional discrimination. Disparate treatment occurs when protected classes are treated unequally or are evaluated by different standards. Title V11 prohibits employers from treating applicants or employees differently due to their being in a protected class.

Additionally, if the outcome of the company standards or decisions is such that a protected class suffers from adverse impact, then the organization may be required to demonstrate that the standards used in the decision process were related to the job. In October of 1993, Domino's Pizza lost a case in which it attempted to defend a "no-beard policy." The appellate court ruled that the policy has an adverse effect on African Americans because almost half of male African Americans suffer from a generic condition that makes shaving very painful or impossible.

> **Title VII of the 1964 Civil Rights Act**: This act prohibits discrimination based on race, color, religion, sex, and national origin.

> **Protected Class**: This theory states that groups of people who suffered discrimination in the past require, and should be given, special protection by the judicial system under Title VII.

> **Disparate Impact**: This involves employment practices that appear to be neutral; however, policies that have an adverse effect on a group can be considered discriminatory on a protected class based on race, color, religion or sex.

> **Disparate Treatment**: This treatment refers to intentional discrimination. Disparate treatment occurs when classes are treated unequally or are evaluated by different standards.

Should a discrimination case make its way to a court (there are steps to avoid costly court cases such as arbitration), it is up to the plaintiff (the person bringing the case to court) to show reasonable evidence that discrimination has occurred. Legally this is called *prima facie*, meaning "on its face." In a disparate treatment lawsuit, to establish a prima facie case the plaintiff only needs to show that the organization did not hire her (or him), that she appeared to be qualified for the job, and that the company continued to try to hire someone else for the position after rejecting her (Gomez-Mejia, Balkin, & Cardy, 2010, p. 94).

Adverse Impact

Adverse impact is also an important part of diversity. An important provision for establishing a prima facie case that an HR practice may be discriminatory and has an adverse impact is the **four-fifths rule**. The four-fifths rule comes from the EEOC's *Uniform Guidelines on Employee Selection Procedures*, an important document that informs employers how to establish selection procedures that are valid and, therefore legal (Equal Employment Opportunity Commission, 1978). With the four-fifths rule the hiring rates of protected classes are compared to those of the majority. If the hiring rate

> **Adverse Impact**: is a substantially different rate of selection in hiring, promotion or other decision, which works to the disadvantage of a race, sex, or ethnic group.

> **Four-fifths Rule**: Under the four-fifths rule, the hiring rates of protected classes are compared to those of the majority. If the hiring rate of protected classes is less than four-fifths of the majority then HR practices have an adverse impact on the protected classes.

of protected classes is less than four-fifths of the majority then HR practices may have an adverse impact on the protected classes.

Employers can and do defend themselves from claims of discrimination. There are four defenses:

Job relatedness: Employers need to show that the decision was made solely for job-related reasons, hence the importance of good job descriptions.

> **A Bona Fide Occupational Qualification (BFOQ):** This is a characteristic that must be present in all employees for a particular job.

Bona fide occupational qualification: A bona fide occupational qualification (BFOQ) is a characteristic that must be present in all employees for a particular job. The idea of a BFOQ came about because certain jobs require specific characteristics of an employee due to the unique nature of tasks involved. To establish that an employee characteristic is, in fact, a BFOQ, you must prove that a class of employees would be unable to perform the job safely or adequately and that the BFOQ is reasonably necessary to the operation of the business. An example in the hospitality industry would be the gender of a spa attendant at a resort. Privacy concerns would require the spa attendant be the same gender as the person using that particular service or facility.

Seniority: Seniority employment decisions are allowed if there is a well-established formal seniority system in place and if it is universally applied not just on occasions. If the company has a history of not hiring ethnic minorities and women, this defense may not be sufficient. A history of hiring only White males would mean that these employees would have seniority. Past discrimination practices can't protect a company from present claims.

Business necessity: If the practice is necessary for a safe and efficient operation then there is an overriding purpose for the discriminatory practice.

> **Equal Employment Opportunity Commission (EEOC):** EEOC is to administer and enforce EEO laws. The EEOC has five members appointed by the president of the United States.

Title VII also established the Equal Employment Opportunity Commission (EEOC) to administer and enforce EEO laws. The EEOC has five members appointed by the president of the United States and thousands of EEOC staff at 53 offices around the United States. The commission investigates claims of workplace discrimination. If just cause is found, the EEOC first tries to bring about reconciliation between the employee and employer. If this is not possible, the commission will go directly to the court system to enforce Title VII (Dessler, 2011, p. 32).

Executive Orders

> **Affirmative Action:** These programs are established to ensure EEO for those (especially minorities) who may have experienced discrimination in the past.

> **Office of Federal Contract Compliance Program (OFCCP):** OFCCP implements the executive orders and ensures that all federal contractors and subcontractors do not engage in discriminatory practices.

President Johnson signed executive orders 11246, 11375, and 11478 in 1965. These executive orders insist that employers and their subcontractors who do business with the federal government on contracts of over $50,000 and with 50 or more employees develop affirmative action programs to ensure EEO for those (especially minorities) who may have experienced discrimination in the past. The orders established the Office of Federal Contract Compliance Program (OFCCP) to implement the executive orders and ensure that all federal contractors and subcontractors do not engage in discriminatory practices. Affirmative action aims to redress the injustices caused by a long history of discrimination against people of color and women. African Americans are more likely than white Americans be unemployed—8.4% versus 4.3%. The unemployment rate for Hispanics is also higher than for white Americans—5.8% versus 4.3% (BLS, 2017).

With the four-fifths rule the hiring rates of protected classes are compared to those of the majority

Age Discrimination in Employment Act

The **Age Discrimination in Employment Act of 1967 (ADEA)** amended in 1978 prohibits employment discrimination against individuals (employees or applicants) who are at least 40 years old. Employers must not refuse to employ or promote an individual because they think that they are too old to do the job and mandatory retirements (with some exceptions) are prohibited. However, an individual has to be otherwise qualified and able to do the job. The ADEA does not apply where age is a BFOQ reasonably necessary to the normal operation of the particular business.

The Age Discrimination in Employment Act of 1967 (ADEA) amended in 1978 prohibits employment discrimination against individuals (employees or applicants) who are at least 40 years old

© ESB Professional/Shutterstock.com

Age Discrimination in Employment Act (ADEA): ADEA prohibits employment discrimination against individuals (employees or applicants) who are 40 and older.

Vocational Rehabilitation Act

The **Vocational Rehabilitation Act of 1973** was passed in order to rectify the discrimination against disabled individuals. The act

Vocational Rehabilitation Act of 1973: This act was passed in order to rectify the discrimination against disabled individuals.

requires employers with federal contracts of more than $2,500 and recipients of federal assistance, such as educational institutions, to institute an affirmative action plan to employ and promote differently abled persons with mental or physical disabilities. Additionally, the act calls for employers to provide reasonable accommodation for disabilities unless doing so would cause undue hardship for the employer. What constitutes "reasonable" is discussed under the description of the Americans with Disabilities Act.

Pregnancy Discrimination Act

> **Pregnancy Discrimination Act of 1978**: This act prohibits discrimination against pregnancy, child birth, and related medical conditions in hiring, promotion, suspension, and discharge, or in any term or condition of employment (EEOC, 2018).

The **Pregnancy Discrimination Act of 1978** prohibits discrimination against employees due to pregnancy, child birth, and related medical conditions in hiring, promotion, suspension, and discharge, or in any term or condition of employment (EEOC, 2011). The act protects the rights of pregnant women by stating that pregnancy and childbirth is a disability and by requiring employers to offer the same benefits and leave policies for pregnant employees as for employees with any other medical condition. Thus, it would be illegal for employers to deny sick leave for a pregnancy-related illness, such as morning sickness or other complication, if sick leave were permitted for other medical conditions such as surgery for back injuries. Women must be evaluated on their ability to perform the job, and employers are to base leave dates on the individual pregnant employee's ability to work. If an employer has a concern about an employee's ability to work, the employer can request the employee to provide medical documentation.

The Pregnancy Discrimination Act of 1978 prohibits discrimination against employees due to pregnancy, child birth, and related medical conditions in hiring, promotion, suspension, and discharge, or in any term or condition of employment

© VGstockstudio/Shutterstock.com

- Employers must provide pregnant workers with paid leave for the time they are disabled due to pregnancy and childbirth if paid leave is given to employees for illnesses or other disabilities.
- If unpaid leave is given to pregnant women, it must also be given to fathers and to those who adopt.
- Employees cannot refuse to hire or promote an applicant because they are pregnant.

Kristen Zagozdon HR Director Cooper's Hawk Winery and Restaurants

The importance of Equal Opportunity in the Workplace cannot be overemphasized. Diversity in the workplace is a necessity for a successful hospitality operation. While it can be tempting to focus on the restrictions created by the laws in this chapter, I challenge you to look at the opportunities they create.

As an HR Director, the content of this chapter acts as the foundation for many of the decisions I make on a daily basis. I am constantly analyzing our programs and practices to ensure that our methods are fair and encourage excellent performance for all employees. Whether I am making changes to the questions we ask in an interview, implementing a new performance management system, or reviewing disciplinary procedures for our employees, I must always ask myself whether we are acting fairly and equitably to all employees.

This is important not only because there are laws in place requiring it but also it is truly the foundation of a great workplace. At Cooper's Hawk Winery & Restaurants, we strive to be the Best Place to Work. We understand that at the foundation of every great workplace there must be equality. When employees trust that they will be treated fairly, they can focus on their performance and focus on the guest. When fair treatment is not consistently provided, employees may be less trusting, less engaged, and less willing to go the extra mile. This is true for not just the employees that feel they are being treated unfairly, but for their co-workers as well. Great employees do not want to benefit from a workplace system where only some employees are treated fairly—they want to see equal treatment for all employees and know that their own accomplishments are the result of their hard work rather than an unequal system.

When you create an environment where job-related performance is truly the only criterion that matters, you create a workplace where your employees can shine. The path to success becomes evident and your employees will drive for results. You will see that teamwork is cohesive and the guest ultimately benefits from the workplace you have created.

When the workplace rewards individuals in a discriminatory fashion, you will see employees slacking off and expecting others to pick up their slack. You may notice that your workplace diversity disappears over time and your guests may start to disappear too. Consider the best place you have worked, or the best class you have attended. Were individuals recognized based on preferential, discriminatory criteria, or did excellence drive recognition?

As you read this chapter, consider how the laws discussed within it can create an inclusive workplace where employee performance drives the organization. Think not only about what these laws require from you in your future leadership roles, but how you will go beyond the regulations to create the Best Place to Work.

Americans with Disabilities Act (ADA)

The **Americans with Disabilities Act of 1990 (ADA)** was passed to protect persons with disabilities who are otherwise qualified. The act says that all employment decisions regarding disabled persons must only relate to the person's ability to do the

> **Americans with Disabilities Act of 1990 (ADA):** This act was passed to protect qualified disabled persons.

job. Employers may not inquire whether an applicant has a disability, but may ask about his or her ability to perform the job. Employers are prohibited from using tests or job requirements that tend to screen out people with disabilities and from participating in contractual arrangements that discriminate against qualified disabled people. However, the Act does not clearly explain about a reasonable accommodation.

The ADA applies to people who:

1. Have a physical or mental impairment that substantially limits one or more major life activities that an average person can perform with little or no difficulty. There is no specific list of impairments, but the ADA includes examples of people with AIDS, HIV, alcoholism, cancer, cerebral palsy, diabetes, emotional illness, epilepsy, hearing and speech disorders, heart disease, dyslexia, mental retardation, muscular dystrophy, and visual impairments.

2. Has a record of impairment. This refers to someone who was disabled or ill in the past, for example, someone who has cancer or back injuries.

3. Is regarded as having impairment. This includes people who are viewed by others as disabled although they may have no actual impairment. For example, burn victims or those with severe scarring may create an impression of disability.

The ADA also says that employers must make "reasonable accommodations" for mental or physical limitations unless it would cause "undue hardship" on the business. For example, recent cases make it clear that businesses must make "reasonable accommodations" for disabled employees who require additional medical leave beyond the company's short-term disability leave policy. Terminating disabled employees without providing reasonable accommodations can result in liability. This appears to be true even if it might cause "undue hardship" to the business.

Just because a person is disabled it does not mean they should get a job. The act prohibits discrimination against *qualified individuals*—those who can with reasonable accommodation carry out the essential job functions. Reasonable accommodation, for example, might require means that a job schedule may need to be slightly changed or additional equipment such as voice recognition software is provided.

Attorneys, employers, and the courts continue to work through what "reasonable accommodation" means (McQueen, 2007, as cited in Dessler, 2011, p. 37). For example, an employee with a bad back who worked as a door greeter at Walmart asked if she could sit down on a stool while on duty. The store said no. She sued. The federal district court agreed with Walmart that door greeters must act in an "aggressively hospitable manner," which can't be done sitting on a stool (Bloomberg BNA, 1995). In another case, the court held that the employer did not discriminate against a blind bartender by requiring her to transfer to another job because she was unable to spot underage or intoxicated customers (Bloomberg BNA, 1999a).

The Civil Rights Act of 1991 (CRA 1991)

The Civil Rights Act of 1991 (CRA 1991) was passed by Congress because several Supreme Court decisions had the effect of limiting the protection of women and minority groups under the equal employment laws. These limitations were an increase in the plaintiff's (generally the employee's) burden of proof.

Burden of proof: Once an employee claims discrimination, the burden of proof shifts to the employer. For example, if a particular job calls for lifting 70 lb then the employer must prove that this is an essential part of the job and that the business could not function properly without the lifting requirement. But what if a hotel that traditionally requires a security officer to have prior work experience as a police officer or firefighter? That requirement could have a disparate impact on, or unintentionally discriminate against women applicants because women are still underrepresented in these fields (Jerris, 1999, pp. 53–54).

Monetary damages: Before the CRA 1991, victims of *intentional* discrimination (which lawyers call *disparate treatment*) who had not suffered financial loss and who sued under Title VII could not then sue for compensatory or punitive damages. All they could expect was to have their jobs reinstated (or to get a particular job). They were also now eligible for back pay, attorney's fees, and court costs (Dessler, 2011, p. 36).

CRA 1991 now makes it easier to sue for other *money damages* in such cases. It provides that an employee who is claiming intentional discrimination can ask for: (1) compensatory damages (fines awarded to the plaintiff to compensate for the financial or psychological harm the plaintiff has suffered as a result of the discrimination and (2) punitive damages (fines awarded to a plaintiff to punish the defendant), if he or she can show the employer engaged in discrimination "with or reckless indifference to the federally protected rights of an aggrieved individual" (Commerce Clearing House, 1991).

Quotas: In order to avoid adverse impact, many organizations (including the Department of Labor) had developed a policy of adjusting scores on employment tests so that a certain percentage of protected-class applicants would be hired. The 1991 law amending Title VII prohibits *quotas*. Employers who have an affirmative action program giving preference to protected-class candidates have to walk a very fine line between "giving preference" (which is permissible) and "meeting a quota" (which is forbidden) (Gomez-Mejia, Balkin, & Cardy, 2010, p. 100).

Learning Objective 2: Explain what constitutes sexual harassment and how to handle sexual harassment complaints

Sexual Harassment

The EEO states "It is unlawful to harass a person (an applicant or employee) because of that person's sex. Harassment can include 'sexual harassment' or unwelcome sexual advances, requests for sexual favors, and other verbal or physical harassment of a sexual nature. Harassment does not have to be of a sexual nature, however, and can include offensive remarks about a person's sex. For example, it is illegal to harass a woman by making offensive comments about women in general. Both victim and the harasser can be either a woman or a man, and the victim and harasser can be the same sex. Although the law doesn't prohibit simple teasing, offhand comments, or isolated incidents that are not very serious, harassment is illegal when it is so frequent or severe that it creates a hostile or offensive work environment or when it results in an adverse employment decision (such as the victim being fired or demoted). The harasser can be the victim's supervisor, a supervisor in another area, a coworker, or someone who is not an employee of the employer, such as a client or customer." (EEOC, 2018).

One of the most common types of sexual harassment is **quid pro quo** (something for something) which usually happens when a manager or supervisor expects sexual favors, directly or indirectly, in exchange for preferential treatment such as promotion or even keeping a job. Employers are always held responsible for *quid pro quo* harassment, even if they don't know about it.

The other main type of sexual harassment is **hostile work environment caused by managers or supervisors,** which exists when an employees supervisor has authority over them and they use gestures, bad language or other inappropriate behavior.

A third type of **hostile work environment caused by coworkers or nonemployees** this kind of sexual harassment happens when, for example, a female cocktail server is required to wear a scanty and provocative uniform. One court held that a mandatory sexually provocative uniform led to lewd comments by customers. When the employee said she would no longer wear the uniform, they fired her. The employer couldn't

Even if conduct isn't obviously sexual in nature, it can still be considered sexual harassment if it is offensive and aimed at someone because of his or her gender

© Dusan Petkovic/Shutterstock.com

show there was a job-related necessity for the uniform, and only female employees had to wear it. The court thus ruled that the employer, in effect, was responsible for the sexually harassing behavior. Such abhorrent customer behavior is more likely when the customers are in positions of power, and when they think no one will penalize them (Gettman & Gelfand, 2007). EEOC guidelines also state that an employer is liable for the sexually harassing behavior of nonemployees such as guests and vendors.

Employers can protect themselves, to some extent, by having a sexual harassment policy that includes (Garland, 1998):

- A clear statement that sexual harassment is unlawful, against company policy, and if violation of policy occurs, discipline and possibly discharge will result.

- A statement that no one has the right to sexually harass any other employee and that everyone within the company must adhere to policy regarding this from the CEO on down.

- Letting all employees and managers know what behaviors constitute sexual harassment. This should be communicated in writing, in employee handbooks, and also in training programs.

- Assurance that all complaints will be investigated confidentially and without retaliation.

Court decisions regarding sexual harassment have implications for employers. In *quid pro quo* cases, it is not necessary for employees to suffer a tangible job action such as demotion to win the case. The court also laid out an important defense against harassment lawsuits. It said the employer must show that it took "reasonable care" to prevent and promptly correct any sexually harassing behavior *and* that the employee unreasonably failed to take advantage of the employer's policy. The implication is that an employer can defend itself against sexual harassment liability by showing two things (Dessler, 2011, p. 42):

- First, it must show "that the employer exercised reasonable care to prevent and correct promptly and sexually harassing behavior. For example, a server/bartender at Chili's Bar and Grill claimed that her former boyfriend, also a restaurant employee, had harassed her. The court ruled that the restaurant's prompt response warranted ruling in favor of it (Bloomberg BNA, 2008b).

- Second, it must demonstrate that the plaintiff "unreasonably failed to take advantage of any preventative or corrective opportunities provided by the employer" (Dessler, 2011, p. 42).

Immigration Reform and Control Act

Immigration Reform and Control Act of 1986: This act was passed in order to control illegal immigration to the United States.

The Immigration Reform and Control Act (IRCA) of 1986 **(Amended in 1990)** was passed in order to control illegal immigration to the United States. The Act makes it illegal for an employer to knowingly hire, recruit, or refer for employment anyone who does not have the legal right to work in the United States. Employers must also verify that individuals they have hired are not illegal aliens by examining and maintaining on file copies of the following documents (Dessler, 2011, p. 42):

OMB No. 1615-0047; Expires 08/31/12

Department of Homeland Security
U.S. Citizenship and Immigration Services

**Form I-9, Employment
Eligibility Verification**

Read instructions carefully before completing this form. The instructions must be available during completion of this form.

ANTI-DISCRIMINATION NOTICE: It is illegal to discriminate against work-authorized individuals. Employers CANNOT specify which document(s) they will accept from an employee. The refusal to hire an individual because the documents have a future expiration date may also constitute illegal discrimination.

Section 1. Employee Information and Verification *(To be completed and signed by employee at the time employment begins.)*

Print Name: Last	First	Middle Initial	Maiden Name

Address *(Street Name and Number)*	Apt. #	Date of Birth *(month/day/year)*

City	State	Zip Code	Social Security #

I am aware that federal law provides for imprisonment and/or fines for false statements or use of false documents in connection with the completion of this form.

I attest, under penalty of perjury, that I am (check one of the following):

☐ A citizen of the United States

☐ A noncitizen national of the United States (see instructions)

☐ A lawful permanent resident (Alien #) _____

☐ An alien authorized to work (Alien # or Admission #) _____
until (expiration date, if applicable - *month/day/year*) _____

Employee's Signature	Date *(month/day/year)*

Preparer and/or Translator Certification *(To be completed and signed if Section 1 is prepared by a person other than the employee.) I attest, under penalty of perjury, that I have assisted in the completion of this form and that to the best of my knowledge the information is true and correct.*

Preparer's/Translator's Signature	Print Name

Address *(Street Name and Number, City, State, Zip Code)*	Date *(month/day/year)*

Section 2. Employer Review and Verification *(To be completed and signed by employer. Examine one document from List A OR examine one document from List B and one from List C, as listed on the reverse of this form, and record the title, number, and expiration date, if any, of the document(s).)*

List A	**OR**	**List B**	**AND**	**List C**
Document title:				
Issuing authority:				
Document #:				
Expiration Date *(if any)*:				
Document #:				
Expiration Date *(if any)*:				

CERTIFICATION: I attest, under penalty of perjury, that I have examined the document(s) presented by the above-named employee, that the above-listed document(s) appear to be genuine and to relate to the employee named, that the employee began employment on *(month/day/year)* _____ **and that to the best of my knowledge the employee is authorized to work in the United States.   (State employment agencies may omit the date the employee began employment.)**

Signature of Employer or Authorized Representative	Print Name	Title

Business or Organization Name and Address *(Street Name and Number, City, State, Zip Code)*	Date *(month/day/year)*

Section 3. Updating and Reverification *(To be completed and signed by employer.)*

A. New Name *(if applicable)*	B. Date of Rehire *(month/day/year) (if applicable)*

C. If employee's previous grant of work authorization has expired, provide the information below for the document that establishes current employment authorization.

Document Title:	Document #:	Expiration Date *(if any)*:

I attest, under penalty of perjury, that to the best of my knowledge, this employee is authorized to work in the United States, and if the employee presented document(s), the document(s) I have examined appear to be genuine and to relate to the individual.

Signature of Employer or Authorized Representative	Date *(month/day/year)*

Form I-9 (Rev. 08/07/09) Y Page 4

The I-9 Form is used to document that each new employee (both citizen and noncitizen) hired after November 6, 1986 is authorized to work in the United States

LISTS OF ACCEPTABLE DOCUMENTS
All documents must be unexpired

LIST A	LIST B	LIST C
Documents that Establish Both Identity and Employment Authorization	**Documents that Establish Identity**	**Documents that Establish Employment Authorization**
OR	**AND**	
1. U.S. Passport or U.S. Passport Card	1. Driver's license or ID card issued by a State or outlying possession of the United States provided it contains a photograph or information such as name, date of birth, gender, height, eye color, and address	1. Social Security Account Number card other than one that specifies on the face that the issuance of the card does not authorize employment in the United States
2. Permanent Resident Card or Alien Registration Receipt Card (Form I-551)	2. ID card issued by federal, state or local government agencies or entities, provided it contains a photograph or information such as name, date of birth, gender, height, eye color, and address	2. Certification of Birth Abroad issued by the Department of State (Form FS-545)
3. Foreign passport that contains a temporary I-551 stamp or temporary I-551 printed notation on a machine-readable immigrant visa		3. Certification of Report of Birth issued by the Department of State (Form DS-1350)
4. Employment Authorization Document that contains a photograph (Form I-766)	3. School ID card with a photograph	
	4. Voter's registration card	4. Original or certified copy of birth certificate issued by a State, county, municipal authority, or territory of the United States bearing an official seal
5. In the case of a nonimmigrant alien authorized to work for a specific employer incident to status, a foreign passport with Form I-94 or Form I-94A bearing the same name as the passport and containing an endorsement of the alien's nonimmigrant status, as long as the period of endorsement has not yet expired and the proposed employment is not in conflict with any restrictions or limitations identified on the form	5. U.S. Military card or draft record	
	6. Military dependent's ID card	5. Native American tribal document
	7. U.S. Coast Guard Merchant Mariner Card	
	8. Native American tribal document	6. U.S. Citizen ID Card (Form I-197)
	9. Driver's license issued by a Canadian government authority	
	For persons under age 18 who are unable to present a document listed above:	7. Identification Card for Use of Resident Citizen in the United States (Form I-179)
6. Passport from the Federated States of Micronesia (FSM) or the Republic of the Marshall Islands (RMI) with Form I-94 or Form I-94A indicating nonimmigrant admission under the Compact of Free Association Between the United States and the FSM or RMI	10. School record or report card	8. Employment authorization document issued by the Department of Homeland Security
	11. Clinic, doctor, or hospital record	
	12. Day-care or nursery school record	

Illustrations of many of these documents appear in Part 8 of the Handbook for Employers (M-274)

Form I-9 (Rev. 08/07/09) Y Page 5

The I-9 Form is used to document that each new employee (both citizen and noncitizen) hired after November 6, 1986 is authorized to work in the United States

- A U.S. passport; certificate of U.S. citizenship; certificate of naturalization; unexpired foreign passport, if the passport has an appropriate, unexpired endorsement of the attorney general authorizing the individual's employment in the U.S.; or resident alien card.

- Social security card, birth certificate, or other documentation that the attorney general deems acceptable as proof.

- State driver's license with a photograph or other documentation that the attorney general deems acceptable as proof.

But the IRCA also makes it illegal to discriminate in recruiting, hiring, or terminating based on a person's national origin or citizenship status. To avoid discrimination based on an individual's immigration status or citizenship, the employer should treat all people equally when announcing a job, taking applications, performing interviews, making job offers, verifying the individual's eligibility to work, hiring of the individual, and termination of the individual's employment. The U.S. Immigration law prohibits discrimination, on the basis of citizenship, against protected individuals. Protected individuals include citizens or nationals of the United States, lawful permanent residents, temporary residents, and persons who have been granted refugee or asylum status.

The Family and Medical Leave Act

The Family and Medical Leave Act of 1993 (FLMA) requires (Bloomberg BNA, as cited in Dessler, 2011, p. 470):[1]

> **The Family and Medical Leave Act of 1993**: Private employers of 50 or more employees must provide eligible employees (women and men) up to 12 weeks of unpaid leave for their own serious illness, the birth or adoption of a child, or the care of a seriously ill child, spouse, or parent.

1. Private employers of 50 or more employees must provide eligible employees (women and men) up to 12 weeks of unpaid leave for their own serious illness, the birth or adoption of a child, or the care of a seriously ill child, spouse, or parent.

2. Employers may require employees to take any unused paid sick leave or annual leave as part of the 12-week leave provided in the law.

3. Employees taking leave are entitled to receive health benefits while they are on unpaid leave, under the same terms and conditions as when they were on the job.

4. Employers must guarantee most employees the right to return to their previous or equivalent position with no loss of benefits at the end of the leave.

FLMA leaves are normally unpaid but there is a cost to employers for finding replacements, for training them, and for a possible loss of productivity during the training period. Employers must comply not only with FLMA but also with state and local laws that might grant more rights, as in longer leaves and shorter notification—in these cases the state and local laws trump the FLMA.

The National Defense Authorization Act for Fiscal Year 2008 (2008 NDAA), Public Law 110-181, amended the FMLA to allow eligible employees to take up to 12 workweeks of job-protected leave in the applicable 12-month period for any "qualifying exigency" arising out of the active duty or call to active duty status of a spouse, son, daughter, or parent. The 2008 NDAA also amended the FMLA to allow eligible employees to take up to 26 workweeks of job-protected leave in a "single 12-month period" to care for a covered service member with a serious injury or illness. These two types of FMLA leave are known as the military family leave entitlements.

---

[1] The Department of Labor updated its revised regulations for administering the Family and Medical Leave Act in November 2008.

A Brief History of Domestic Partnerships

In 1982, the *Village Voice* newspaper became the first private company to offer its employees domestic partnership benefits. The City of Berkeley was the first municipality to do so in 1984. In 1995, Vermont became the first state to extend domestic partnership benefits to its public employees. In 1997, Hawaii became the first state to extend domestic partnership benefits to all same-sex couples throughout the state. Now many states offer domestic partnership benefits to state employees, while a handful of other states offer domestic partnership registration to same-sex couples who want the same rights and responsibilities of married couples.

Domestic Partnerships

Domestic partners are unmarried couples, of the same or opposite sex, who live together and seek economic and noneconomic benefits comparable to those granted their married counterparts

© Sydia Productions/Shutterstock.com

Domestic partners are unmarried couples, of the same or opposite sex, who live together and seek economic and noneconomic benefits comparable to those granted their married counterparts. Domestic partnerships were born in the early 1980s, when lesbian and gay activists sought recognition of their relationships and new definitions of family. Advocates for domestic partner rights pointed out that only an estimated 10% of American families comprise a working husband, a stay-at-home wife, and children; however, the legal and social systems still provided benefits and protections based on that model.

Learning Objective 3: Follow the steps necessary to ensure EEO enforcement and compliance

EEO Enforcement and Compliance

Given that many employers will, at one time or another, be in receipt of discrimination claims it is imperative that all managers, not just HR managers, know the EEOC claim and enforcement process.[2] The process consists of these steps:

- *File charge:* The process begins when a claim is filed at an EEOC office. Under CRA 1991, the discrimination claim must be filed within 300 days (when there is a similar state law) or 180 days (where there is no similar state law) after the alleged incident took place (2 years for the Equal Pay Act) (Dessler, 2011, p. 53).[3]

---

[2] Prudent employers often purchase employment practices liability insurance to insure against some or all of the employers' expenses involved with defending against discrimination, sexual harassment, and wrongful termination-type claims.

[3] In 2007, the U.S. Supreme Court, in *Ledbetter v. Goodyear Tire & Rubber Company,* held that employees claiming Title VII pay discrimination must file their claims within 180 days of when they first receive the allegedly discriminatory pay.

Either the aggrieved person or a member of the EEOC who has reasonable cause to believe that a violation occurred must file the claim in writing and under oath. The number of private-sector discrimination charges filed with the EEOC climbed to 95,402 in 2008 (Bloomberg BNA, 2008a).

- *Charge acceptance:* The EEOC's common practice is to accept a charge and orally refer to it to the state or local agency on behalf of the charging party. If the agency waives jurisdiction or cannot obtain a satisfactory solution, the EEOC processes it upon expiration of the deferral period. It does not require filing a new charge.[4]

- *Serve notice:* Once a charge has been filed, the EEOC has 10 days to serve notice on the employer.

- *Investigation/fact-finding conference*: The EEOC then investigates the charge to determine whether there is reasonable cause to believe it is true; it has 120 days to make this determination. Early in the investigation, the EEOC holds an initial *fact-finding conference.* The EEOC calls these "informal meetings" for defining issues and determining whether there's a bias for negotiation. However, the EEOC's real focus here is often on settlement. Its investigators use conferences to find weak points in each party's position. They use these as a leverage to push for a settlement (Dessler, 2011, p. 53).

- *Cause/no cause:* If the EEOC finds no reasonable cause, it dismisses the charge and must issue the charging party a Notice of right to Sue. The person then has 90 days to file a suite on his or her own behalf.

- *Conciliation:* If the EEOC does find cause, it has 30 days to work out a conciliation agreement. The EEOC conciliator meets with the employee to determine what remedy would be satisfactory. It then tries to negotiate a settlement with the employer. If both parties accept the remedy, they sign and submit a reconciliation agreement for EEOC approval. If the EEOC cannot obtain an acceptable conciliation agreement it may sue the employer in a federal district court.

- *Notice to sue:* If the conciliation is not satisfactory, the EEOC may bring a civil suit in a federal district court, or issue a Notice of right to Sue to the person who filed the charge. If the plaintiff and the employer both agree to mediation, the mediation session usually lasts up to 4 hours. If the parties don't reach agreement (or one of the parties rejects participation), the EEOC processes the charge through its usual mechanisms (Bloomberg BNA, 1999b).

Legalize

It is critical to train managers, supervisors, and employees on its contents, enforce it and hold them accountable

© Rawpixel.com/Shutterstock.com

Some of the best practices in employment relate to avoiding problems and avoiding racism. The U.S. EEOC recommends these best practices (EEOC, 2015).

- Train HR leaders and all employees on EEO laws. Implant a strong EEO policy that is embraced at the top levels of the organization. Train managers, supervisors, and employees on its contents, enforce it and hold them accountable.

---

[4] If the charge was filed initially with a state or local agency within 180 days after the alleged unlawful practice occurred, the charge may then be filed with the EEOC within 30 days after the person received notice the state or local agency has ended its proceedings.

- Promote an inclusive culture in the workplace by fostering an environment of professionalism and respect for personal differences.

- Establish neutral and objective criteria to avoid subjective employment decisions based on personal stereotypes or hidden bias.

- Recruit, hire, and promote with EEO principles in mind, by installing practices designed to widen and diversify the pool of candidates considered for employment openings, including openings in upper-level management.

- Monitor for EEO compliance by conducting self-analysis to determine whether current employment practices disadvantage people of color, treat them differently, or leave uncorrected. The effects of institutional discrimination in the company.

- Analyze the duties, functions, and competencies. Make sure they are consistently applied when choosing among candidates.

- Ensure selection criteria do not disproportionately exclude certain racial groups unless the criteria are valid predictors of successful job performance and meet the employer's business needs. For example, if educational requirements disproportionately exclude certain minority or racial group, they may be illegal if not important for job performance or business needs.

- Make sure that promotion criteria are made known and that job openings are communicated to all eligible employees.

- When using an outside agency for recruitment, make sure the agency does not search for candidates of a particular race or color. Both the employer that made the request and the employment agency that honored it would be liable.

- Monitor compensation practices and performance appraisal systems for patterns of potential discrimination. Make sure performance appraisals are based on employees' actual job performance. Ensure consistency, that is, that comparable job performances receive comparable ratings regardless of the evaluator, and that appraisals are neither artificially low nor artificially high.

- Develop the potential of employees, supervisors, and managers with EEO in mind, by providing training and mentoring that provides workers of all backgrounds the opportunity, skill, experience, and information necessary to perform well, and to ascend to upper-level jobs. In addition, employees of all backgrounds should have equal access to workplace networks.

- Protect against retaliation. Provide clear and credible assurances that if employees make complaints or provide information related to complaints, the employer will protect employees from retaliation, and consistently follow through on this guarantee.

When these practices are adopted and enforced along with a climate of openness and acceptance a culture of excellence will likely pervade the company.

Technology in HR

Human resource directors work with lawyers either in the corporate office or locally to ensure compliance with the many regulations and laws and to "keep the boss out of jail!" as one HR director said (M. Lucido, personal communication, July 10, 2013). The technology they often use is connectivity via the Internet or email. Many HR offices are now paperless and use technology to assist with various human resources functions. For example, E-verify is a free Internet-based system created by the

Many HR offices are now paperless and use technology to assist with various human resources functions

© GaudiLab/Shutterstock.com

federal government to ensure that an individual has the legal authorization to work in the United States. Created as a result of the Immigration Reform and Control Act, this system makes the selection process much more efficient and ensure that only legal workers are employed by an organization.

Many hospitality organizations also utilize technology to request and fulfill background checks on applicants. In order to save time (and human resources) electronic requests for references are commonly done by a third-party company.

Key Points

- Discrimination lawsuits are costly to defend against, and even more costly if the judgment goes against the employer.
- The Equal Pay Act of 1963, amended in 1972, makes it unlawful to discriminate in pay on the basis of sex when jobs involve equal work; require equivalent skills, effort, and responsibility; and are performed under similar working conditions.
- Title VII of The Civil Rights Act of 1964 prohibits discrimination based on race, color, religion, sex, and national origin. Title VII applied to employers who have 15 or more employees.
- The protected class theory states that groups of people who suffered discrimination in the past require, and should be given, special protection by the judicial system. Under Title VII of the Civil Rights Act, the protected classes are African Americans, Asian Americans, Latinos, Native Americans, and women.
- Disparate treatment refers to intentional discrimination. Disparate treatment occurs when protected classes are treated unequally or are evaluated by different standards.
- Disparate impact involves employment practices that appear to be neutral; however, they result in a protected class being intentionally treated differently, which creates an adverse effect on the workplace (Jerris, 1999, pp. 48–49).
- The four-fifths rule says that the hiring rates of protected classes are compared to those of the majority, if the hiring rate of protected classes is less than four-fifths of the majority then it is assumed that HR practices have an adverse impact on the protected classes.
- A bona fide occupational qualification (BFOQ) is a characteristic that must be present in all employees for a particular job.
- The Age Discrimination Act of 1967 (ADEA) amended in 1978 prohibits employment discrimination against individuals (employees or applicants) who are 40 years of age or older.
- The Vocational Rehabilitation Act of 1973 was passed in order to rectify the discrimination against disabled individuals. The act requires employers with federal contracts of more than $2,500 and recipients of federal assistance, such as educational institutions, to institute an affirmative action plan to employ and promote differently abled people with mental or physical disabilities.

- The Pregnancy Discrimination Act of 1978 prohibits discrimination against pregnancy, child birth, and related medical conditions in hiring, promotion, suspension, and discharge, or in any term or condition of employment (EEOC, 2011).
- The Americans with Disabilities Act of 1990 (ADA), which was passed to protect qualified disabled persons. The act says that all employment decisions regarding disabled persons must only relate to the person's ability to do the job.
- The Title VII prohibition of sex-based discrimination has also been interpreted to prohibit sexual harassment to the person's ability to do the job.
- One of the most common types of sexual harassment is *quid pro quo* (something for something), which usually happens when a manager or supervisor expects sexual favors, directly or indirectly, in exchange for preferential treatment such as promotion or even keeping a job.
- The other main type of sexual harassment is *hostile work environment sexual harassment (caused by managers, supervisors*, coworkers, or nonemployed) which exists when various types of insults are made such as offensive jokes, sexually explicit gestures, language or photos, and inappropriate touching.
- The Immigration Reform and Control Act of 1986 makes it illegal for an employer to knowingly hire, recruit, or refer for employment anyone who does not have the legal right to work in the United States.
- The Family and Medical Leave Act of 1993 (FLMA) requires private employers of 50 or more employees to provide eligible employees (women or men) up to 12 weeks of unpaid leave for their own serious illness, the birth or adoption of a child, or the care of a seriously ill child, spouse, or parent.

Key Terms

Adverse impact
Affirmative action
Age Discrimination in Employment Act (ADEA)
Americans with Disabilities Act of 1990 (ADA)
Bona fide occupational qualification (BFOQ)
Discrimination
Disparate impact

Disparate treatment
Equal Employment Opportunity Commission (EEOC)
Four-fifths rule
Immigration Reform and Control Act of 1986
Office of Federal Contract Compliance Program (OFCCP)
Pregnancy Discrimination Act of 1978

Protected class
The Equal Pay Act of 1963 (amended in 1972)
The Family and Medical Leave Act of 1993
Title VII of the 1964 Civil Rights Act
Vocational Rehabilitation Act of 1973

Discussion Questions

1. What is discrimination?
2. What did the first EEO law do?
3. What did Title VII of the 1964 Civil rights Act do?
4. Describe disparate treatment.
5. Explain what the EEOC does.

6. What does the Pregnancy Discrimination Act of 1978 prohibit?
7. Describe the elements of the Americans with Disabilities Act of 1990.
8. What is sexual harassment?
9. What is the purpose of the Family and Medical Leave Act of 1993?

Ethical Dilemma

According to the Society for Human Resource Management (SHRM) some of the ethical mistakes that HR makes are

1. Placing misleading advertisements for jobs.
2. Misrepresenting the requirements of a particular position.
3. Responding to a hiring manager who has asked you to find a way "around" not hiring a qualified candidate for discriminatory purposes.
4. Not reviewing candidates based on their merits.

How can these be prevented?

How To: Protect Yourself Against Unlawful Workplace Claims and Why is it important?

The EEOC has determined that there has been a significant increase in the volume of unlawful workplace claims since the early 2000s, with the biggest influx occurring when the economy plummeted in 2008. Some of the most common reasons employees file claims against their employers includes sexual and verbal harassment, racial, gender, age and disability discrimination, hazardous work conditions, and wage violations and worker's compensation. For this reason, it is very important, as a business owner or human resources manager, to ensure your company maintains proper procedures and documentation which demonstrates that they are compliant with Equal Employment laws and prevents them from being subject to unlawful workplace lawsuits (Gleeson, 2014).

The owner, who also acts as the human resources manager, of a small chain of restaurants in Chicago, Illinois discussed some of the biggest reasons employees file lawsuits against their employers and why you should protect your business against this from happening. According to the restaurant owner, "the most important thing to remember is that, as a business owner and employer of others, you have both a legal and moral responsibility to promote and maintain a fair work environment. I've never had a lawsuit brought against me for fostering an unlawful work environment, because I truly believe in the importance of preaching and practicing fair treatment of others in the workplace. Throughout my career, I have been asked by new business owners for my advice on 'how' to maintain an EEOC compliant workplace, but far fewer times have I been asked 'why' it is important to maintain an EEOC compliant workplace—and therein lies the problem."

The hiring process should be fair, thorough, and structured. It is important to know your local, state, and federal employment laws when structuring set criteria for interview questioning, especially if you delegate the interviewing to others who will represent your company. There are many questions you generally cannot and should not ask, such as age, race, religion, national origin, and

(Continued)

disability questions. During the interview process, it is not a good practice to ask about criminal convictions, marriage status, or anything that could suggest a biased viewpoint. It is always a good practice to require applicants to fill out a formal application, subject them to a background check, and even consider implementing a skills assessment or personality test that uncovers whether a person is "the best fit" for the job. This best practice for the hiring process is to make sure that your structured criteria is consistent, that all applicants are subject to the same set of criteria during the application process, and that you hire the most qualified person for the job—simple as that.

Your company should have clearly defined rules and regulations for behavior in the workplace and more, importantly, any action or incidence which brings these rules and regulations into question should be taken extremely seriously and should be investigated to the fullest extent. Many employers do not want to deal with potential violations and, as a result, they leave it to others acting on their behalf to resolve. This is when procedures are often not properly followed and a fair solution is not always implemented, which is a common reason lawsuits are filed against employers. For whatever reason, many employers fail to see the benefit of work environments where people feel safe. The most productive work environment is one where the employees want to be, and maintaining content employees should be a goal of all employers.

The termination process should also include a fair, thorough, and structured set of guidelines, and it is very important that, before terminating an employee, you make sure that other employees working in similar positions are also following the proper procedures or that their performance is "up to standard," so as to eliminate the claim that an employee feels they were wrongfully terminated because other employees were either doing or not doing the same thing and those employees are still employed at the company. Here again, consistency is key; at each job position, you should maintain the same standards of performance for all employees working at that position. Furthermore, you should ensure that all employees in your company who manage other employees are properly maintaining and documenting performance. When you terminate an employee, you need to provide a clear and actionable reason for the termination that is supported by documented citations for the occurrence of the actions that led to the termination. If you are going to terminate someone for not being compliant with your company's standards, then it is very important to ensure that you and others acting on your company's behalf are also adhering to these standards.

Internet Exercise

Visit the EEOC website (http://www.eeoc.gov/index.cfm). Pick 1 EEO law and discuss, in 1-page, what changes you would make to the law.

For example, do you think the Age Discrimination in Employment Act should start at the age of 40? Do you think Family Medical Leave Act provides sufficient coverage for workers having a child? Be creative and remember all laws are amendable if you follow the appropriate process.

References

Commerce Clearing House. (1991, November). Commerce Clearing House, "house and Senate Pass Civil Rights Compromise by Wide margin. *Ideas and Trends in Personnel,* p. 179.

Bloomberg BNA. (1995, December). No sitting for store greeter. *BNA Fair Employment Practices,* 150.

Bloomberg BNA. (1999a, February). Blind bartender not qualified for job, court says in dismissing Americans with disabilities act claim. *BNA Fair Employment Practices,* 17.

Bloomberg BNA. (1999b, February). EEOC's new nationwide mediation plan offers option of informal settlements. *BNA Fair Employment Practices,* 21.

Bloomberg BNA. (2008a, December). EEOC charges pace climbed to record high during fiscal 2008. *BNA Bulletin to Management,* 389.

Bloomberg BNA. (2008b, January). Ex-boyfriend harassed, but employer acted promptly. *BNA Bulletin to Management,* 14.

BLS. (2017). Retrieved October 15, 2017, from https://www.bls.gov/opub/reports/race-and-ethnicity/2016/home.htm

Gleeson, B. (2014). *6 big reasons employees sue, and how to protect yourself.* http://www.forbes.com/sites/brentgleeson/2014/06/27/6-big-reasons-employees-sue-and-how-to-protect-yourself/

Cornell Law School. (2012). Retrieved April 21, 2012, from http://www.law.cornell.edu/wex/Civil_rights

Dessler, G. (2011). *Human resource management* (12th ed.). Upper Saddle River, NJ: Pearson.

EEOC. (2011). Retrieved August 1, 2011, from http://www.eeoc.gov/laws/statutes/pregnancy.cfm

EEOC. (2013). Retrieved July 16, 2013, from http://www.eeoc.gov/laws/types/sexual_harassment.cfm

EEOC. (2015). Retrieved August 16, 2015, from http://www.eeoc.gov/eeoc/initiatives/e-race/bestpractices-employers.cfm

EEOC. (2017). Retrieved October 15, 2017, from https://www.eeoc.gov/eeoc/history/35th/milestones/early.html

Equal Employment Opportunity Commission (1978). *Uniform Guidelines on Employee Selection Procedures,* 29 Code of Federal Regulations, Part 1607, Sec. 6.A.

Garland, D. W. (1998). Sexual harassment: The risk one can control. *International Commercial Litigation, 29,* 35–38.

Gettman, H., & Gelfand, M. (2007). When the customer shouldn't be king: Antecedents and consequences of sexual harassment by clients and customers. *Journal of Applied Psychology, 92*(3), 757–770.

Gomez-Mejia, L. R., Balkin, D. B., & Cardy, R. L. (2010). *Managing human resources* (6th ed.). Upper Saddle River, NJ: Pearson.

Hall, F. S., & Hall, E. L. (1994). The ADA: Going beyond the law. *Academy of Management Executive, 8,* 17–26.

Iverson, K. M. (2001). *Managing human resources in the hospitality industry.* Upper Saddle River, NJ: Prentice Hall, p. 208.

Jerris, L. A. (1999). *Human resources management for hospitality.* Upper Saddle River, NJ: Prentice Hall.

Melton-Meaux, A. M. (2008, May/June). Maximizing employment practices liability insurance coverage. *Compensation & Benefits Review, 40*(3), 55–59.

© Pressmaster/Shutterstock.com

Chapter **4**

WORKFORCE PLANNING AND ORGANIZING

- ⟹ Human Resources Planning
- ⟹ Mission
- ⟹ Vision
- ⟹ Culture and Core Values
- ⟹ Core Values
- ⟹ Goals
- ⟹ Strategic Human Resources Leadership
- ⟹ Human Resource Core Functions
- ⟹ Operational Planning
- ⟹ Operational Goal Setting
- ⟹ Operational Strategies
- ⟹ Forecasting Employment Needs (Supply and Demand)
- ⟹ Forecasting Internal and External Candidates

- ⟹ Policies, Procedures, and Rules
- ⟹ Budgeting
- ⟹ Technology in HR
- ⟹ Job Analysis
- ⟹ The Uses of Job Analysis (Gomez-Mejia, Balkin, & Cardy, 2010)
- ⟹ Job Descriptions
- ⟹ Key Points
- ⟹ Key Terms
- ⟹ Discussion Questions
- ⟹ Ethical Dilemma
- ⟹ Case Study
- ⟹ Internet Exercises
- ⟹ References

Human Resources Planning

Things don't just happen by themselves—well, at least mostly not the way we'd like them to. Remember when you attended an interview and were on time only to wait for 45 minutes until the interviewer was available? This delay was likely because the interviewer did not plan their time correctly. This is an example of the simple, but important, concept of planning. There are, as we will see in this chapter and throughout the text, more complex forms of *human resources planning*.

After reading and studying this chapter, you will be able to:

1. Provide an overview on the importance of mission, vision, culture, and core values.
2. Discuss operational planning, goal setting, and strategies.

3. Provide an overview of the role of forecasting in human resources.
4. Define and explain the role of job analysis, job descriptions, and job specification.

Human resources planning cannot start without a clear company mission, culture, values, and goals (which should be specific and measurable). These may already be defined or, in the case of a new company or one that is struggling, may need to be developed from scratch. To do this, executives, including the human resources vice president or director, determine what the *organization is and where it wants to go*. In turn, the group must determine the organization's mission, vision, culture and core values, and goals.

Human resources planning cannot start without a clear company mission, culture, values, and goals (which should be specific and measurable)

© wavebreakmedia/Shutterstock.com

Learning Objective 1: Provide an overview on the importance of mission, vision, culture, and core values

Mission

> **Mission:** This defines the business activity, who the company is and what it does. It gives identity and direction to the organization (Schulze, 2006).

A **mission** defines the business activity, that is, what it does. It gives identity and direction to the organization (Schulze, 2006). A company's mission should be simply stated and easy to communicate to employees and external stakeholders. In the hotel industry, for Marriott International, for example, the mission is: "We are committed to being the best lodging and foodservice company in the world, by treating employees in ways that create extraordinary guest service and shareholder value." Shifting to the food and beverage side of the hospitality industry, Max's, a popular restaurant in Asia and California, has the mission: to be the most admired restaurant of choice where people celebrate and cherish great food and excellent service, every day, all the time.

In many cases, a mission will outline the type of business the firm is in and discusses the competitive landscape in which it operates. These short-written statements can also be used to answer questions such as

- What do we do?
- What is our purpose?
- Where should we put our current focus?
- How do we want to be perceived by guests?

A mission statement is important and often takes input from various stakeholders to create. With that being said, a mission is something that should on occasion be revisited and enhanced as a hospitality organization changes and innovates.

A easy to understand and communicate mission, vision, culture and core values, and goals are critical components to success

© Rawpixel.com/Shutterstock.com

Vision

A corporate **vision** lays the foundation for the direction of the company and answers the question of "What is our preferred future?" It is a guiding concept for what the organization is trying to become. Ritz-Carlton had the vision of winning the prized

> **Vision:** A statement focused on what the company aspires to be.

Malcolm Baldrige National Quality award. The vision was shared with all the "ladies and gentlemen," as they refer to their employees, and translated into actions that led not only to being the first hospitality company to win this award, but also the first service company to win and then, to cap it all, to win twice. Another vision is to be one of the 'Best Places to Work' by being recognized in the top 100 companies or top 500 companies.

Horst Schulze, the founder of Ritz-Carlton, said that the awards belonged to the thousands of employees who played a part in the company's success. Mr. Schulze tells an amusing story of when he first talked with the chairman of the Baldrige committee. Mr. Schulze said that at Ritz-Carlton they have the finest quality of rooms because they are inspected and inspected. So much so that, when the housekeeper has made up the room the floor housekeeper inspects the room, and then the assistant housekeeper inspects the room followed by the head housekeeper or assistant manager. Oh really, said the chairman, I wonder why the room was not perfect first time? Mr. Schulze said that on the way home he thought about it and realized that the chairman had a good point (Schulze, 2006).

Culture and Core Values

> **Culture:** This is the company's moral and social values, beliefs, and behaviors. It governs the way employees and owners think, act, and feel about the company.

Culture is the company's moral and social values, beliefs, and behaviors. It is how all employees interact with each other, guests, suppliers and the community. It is the way things are done. The leaders in an organization play an important role in establishing the culture. Cultural statements become

A culture is often implied, not explicitly defined, in hospitality organizations and as the work force changes, as does the culture of a company

The Walt Disney Company commits to providing a rewarding, inclusive, and supportive work environment

operationalized when management articulate and publish the values of the company, which provides patterns for how employees should behave. Culture, philosophy, innovation, mission, and continuous improvement are all, or should be, intertwined and in harmony.

At Marriott International, the culture and core values are expressed this way: "We believe our strength is rooted in our core values: putting people first, pursuing excellence, embracing change, acting with integrity and serving our world. These values are our legacy and our future. As we pursue our vision of making Marriott the #1 hospitality company in the world, we never lose sight of our founding principles and our proud heritage. Our business is always evolving . . . but we'll always stay true to who we are." (Marriott, 2013a).

According to the official website of Disney Company, since its founding in 1923, the Walt Disney Company has been committed to producing unparalleled entertainment experiences based on its exceptional creative content and unique storytelling. Walt Disney World Resort in Orlando, Florida is the largest single-site employer in the United States. It is operated every day of the week and staffed by a workforce of more than 55,000 "cast members." This city can handle hundreds of thousands of people in a crowded day and the cast members serve and entertain millions of "guests" every year.

The Disney Company's service ethic is reflected in what the following founder's statement, "My business is making people, especially children, happy." It is simple but it is the basis for its mission as a business. It represents what the company stands for and why it exists. In other words, the core purpose of Walt Disney is to make people happy. In 1955, their service theme was, "We create happiness."

We can learn the significance of having clearly defined core values from the Disney Company. According to Jim Collins and Jerry Porras, co-authors of the book, *Build To Last*, both the core purpose and core values constitute the core ideology of Disney Company. This core ideology drives the corporate culture of Walt Disney Company. The leaders would die, products would become obsolete, markets would change, new technologies could emerge, and management fads may come and go, but the core ideology in a great company endures as a source of guidance and inspiration.

Walt Disney once said, "You can dream, create, design and build the most wonderful place in the world but it requires people to make the dream a reality." This is why Walt Disney realized early on that the only way his parks would be successful is by implementing strategic training and organizational behavior methods; so that all of his employees would be able to create the environment, he was striving for. Walt Disney wanted his employees to be guest-responsive and this is why he implemented training for everyone in the company, which developed into the Disney Institute in 1986. The training that the employees receive can be easily seen by the superlative guest service they provide (Sparks, 2012).

These are just some of the ways The Walt Disney Company commits to providing a rewarding, inclusive, and supportive work environment.

Culture governs the way employees and owners think, act and feel about the company. A culture is often implied, not explicitly defined, in hospitality organizations and as the work force changes, as does the culture of a company.

Core Values

Core values, the core foundational behaviors important and define the culture of an organization, tell a lot about a company. For example, at Darden, (Darden, 2013) "we believe building and maintaining a strong, people-focused culture is the single most important reason we've become the world's largest full-service restaurant operating company—a $8.0 billion enterprise. Our 40-plus years of success have come largely as a result of our employees, who create great dining experiences for our guests. That is why we work so hard to provide a nurturing and sustaining environment for our 180,000 employees."

Darden has a long history of strong corporate values and culture that help employees learn, thrive, and grow. In fact, they believe their vibrant culture gives the company a competitive advantage. Their *core values* have been forged over a 70-plus-year history, starting with their founder, Bill Darden, who

The Disney website has an interesting section on culture (Disney parks, 2018):

Diversity and inclusion fuel innovation, creativity, and growth, and keep us connected to our communities around the world. We seek to recruit a highly talented workforce that includes individuals representing a wide range of ages, experiences, backgrounds, and ethnic groups. We foster a welcoming and respectful work environment where all of our Cast Members feel they are a valued part of the team.

- Innovation
- We are committed to a tradition of innovation and technology.
- Quality
- We strive to set a high standard of excellence.
- We maintain high-quality standards across all product categories.
- Community
- We create positive and inclusive ideas about families.
- We provide entertainment experiences for all generations to share.
- Storytelling
- Timeless and engaging stories delight and inspire.
- Optimism
- At The Walt Disney Company, entertainment is about hope, aspiration, and positive outcomes.
- Decency
- We honor and respect the trust people place in us.
- Our fun is about laughing at our experiences and ourselves
  - These values live in everything we do. They create a unified mission that all our people believe in and work toward. And to recognize individual efforts, we have a variety of reward programs, including
- Quality of work
- Length of service
- Community volunteerism
- Employee of the month recognition

Core Values: The core foundational behaviors that define the culture of an organization.

opened his first restaurant in 1938. They look to these values as we endeavor to deliver on Darden's core purpose—to nourish and delight everyone we serve (Darden, 2013).

Another interesting statement comes from Marriott International "We believe our strength is rooted in our core values: putting people first, pursuing excellence, embracing change, acting with integrity, and serving our world. These values are our legacy and our future. As we pursue our vision of making Marriott the #1 hospitality company in the world, we never lose sight of our founding principles and our proud heritage. Our business is always evolving . . . but we'll always stay true to who we are" (Marriott, 2013b).

Goals

Organization goals, which should be clearly articulated by leadership, should address the shortcomings between the vision and the current state of the organization. There are long or strategic and short or tactical goals. Long/strategic involves selecting goals that the organization wants to achieve over a long period of time, perhaps 2–10 years or even beyond, while short/tactical involves planning for the immediate future up to 2 years.

While the mission, vision, and culture and values will probably remain the same for many years, goals may need to change due to factors such as a changing market or a company's performance (good or bad). Many companies make it a practice to formally review their goals on a regular, perhaps yearly, basis. These are some examples of what strategic and tactical goals might be for a hospitality business:

Strategic goals:

- Improve employee satisfaction
- Grow revenue
- Increase the number of new guests and keep our current guests
- Reduce costs

Tactical goals:

- Implement a program to conduct employee satisfaction surveys on a yearly basis
- Reinvigorate guest loyalty program

Goals are established for each key operating area. In the hospitality industry, this could include goals related to guest satisfaction

© Tiko Aramyan/Shutterstock.com

Goals are established for each key operating area. In the hospitality industry, this could include goals related to guest satisfaction. If a goal is 100% guest satisfaction; say the current score is 89%, so the planning element would be to plan strategies to reach the goal of 100% guest satisfaction.

At this point, some companies may choose to continue the planning process with these steps:

Formulating Plans for Action to Meet or Exceed the Goals

If the goal is to have a 100% score on the guest satisfaction survey then several specific actions need to be taken. The following are among the many actions: train and coach all employees in guest service techniques, install a Total Quality Management Program, recognize and reward outstanding employees, make constant improvements to the property, utilize the latest technology, and improve employees' emotional intelligence. Have "on-the-spot" recognition with gift cards and prizes, employee and leader/manager of the month, quarter and year with appropriate prizes, and encourage continuous education.

Implement the Plan

Implementing the plan means to translate the plan into action by acquiring the necessary resources to meet and exceed the goals. In the example of a goal of 100% guest satisfaction, talented employees are needed along with training programs and coaching. These and any other elements must be available and delivered promptly.

Evaluate Performance

Evaluating performance assesses how well the strategy did when implemented by indicating to what extent the goal was met or exceeded. In the case of guest satisfaction, an outside company generally does a quick survey on randomly selected departed guests.

Strategic Human Resources Leadership

Strategic human resources leadership is largely about ensuring that human resources is fully integrated with the mission, vision, and goals of the company. Human resource directors are also the business partners who work with departments as a team to focus either directly or indirectly on key fundamentals (Strigl, 2011):

> **Strategic Human Resources Leadership**: This is largely about ensuring that human resources management is fully integrated with the strategy and the strategic needs of the company.

A human resources strategy is the use of human resources to meet or exceed the company mission. Remember the Marriott mission? To be the best lodging and foodservice company in the world by treating employees in ways that creates extraordinary guest service and shareholder value. Clearly, here the human resource strategy is how the employees are treated. One very good example of how Marriott treats its associates was just after the 9/11 tragedy when hotel occupancies were down to 10%. Instead of laying people off, as with other companies, Marriott kept all their associates on by reducing their hours. This was an excellent strategy because when business

Human resource directors are also the business partners who work with departments as a team to focus either directly or indirectly on key fundamentals

© Monkey Business Images/Shutterstock.com

Here are some of the mistakes managers and companies commit (Dessler, 2011, p. 5).

- Hire the wrong person for the job—90-day probation.
- Experience high turnover.
- Have your people not doing their best.
- Waste time with useless interviews—have candidates assessed to meet certain criteria.
- Have your company taken to court because of your discriminatory actions—hire the best person for the job.
- Have your company cited under federal occupational safety laws for unsafe practices—the safety committee tracks accidents
- Have some employees think their salaries are unfair relative to others in the organization—wage watch to ensure wages are in line with the competition
- Allow a lack of training to undermine your department's effectiveness—training plans for all
- Commit any unfair labor practices—compliance review

Dessler (2011, p. 5)

picked up so did associate morale. Other companies, by contrast, laid-off lots of people.

Human resources leadership is important to all managers because they are all involved with human resources. You may have encountered a business where turnover was high and morale low due to ineffective management. Additionally, one has only to look at the court records to see which company is shelling out millions in court mandated judgment settlements—just ask Brinker International and almost any other hospitality company.

We can see the importance of human resources directors' involvement with strategic human resources.

The minimum preferred qualifications for a vice president or director's position are: a bachelor's degree preferably a master's degree in human resources management and certification form the society for human resources management and 3–5 years human resources management experience, bilingual English Spanish, and excellent interpersonal and organizational skills.

Human Resource Core Functions

The human resources contribution to meeting the vision and goals is critical. It includes these functions:

- *Talent recruitment and selection*: Human resource professionals perform a needs analysis to determine the needs of the various departments—imagine HR professionals at a theme park preparing for the summer high season or at a ski resort in the Rockies—or staffing a new restaurant opening. Job descriptions and job specifications are prepared, recruiting plans drawn up and interviewing questions prepared and line managers educated as to what questions they can and cannot ask and how to prepare for and conduct an interview.
- *Policies and procedures development*: Human resource professionals, in conjunction with department heads, set the policies and procedures used to guide the company. Properly installed policies and procedures are more likely to ensure employees do things the company way instead of any old way. Policies and procedures also provide continuity and consistency—so when one supervisor leaves and a new one starts they will follow the company policy in the same way, which will result in a consistent managerial transition.

- *Employee training and development*: Giving employees opportunities to develop and be promoted not only prepares the company for future development but also improves morale. If training is required to help employees prepare for the next level, then it is provided. Cross-training is also helpful in maintaining employment as employees can me moved to areas where the needs are. Job shadowing programs are also helpful.

- *Compensation and benefits*: HR professionals help shape payroll policy—an example being, to pay in the top 10% for each position—or to be the market leader in paying the most for each position, based on 'wage watch' salary surveys. Bonuses are also ways of encouraging outstanding performance. They are also good for the company in that they are paid once not permanently. Benefits which are very important to employees are not just the medical insurance, sick leave pay, and vacations but also child care, flexible hours, and family leave. Complementary rooms and a 401K program are also very beneficial.

  It is important for hospitality companies to realize that they are not only in competition with other hospitality companies but also with other service industry sectors like retail. Due to the high and increasing costs of providing employee benefits, human resource professionals must find ways of reducing costs by teaming up with others in their trade associations or group purchasing benefits like healthcare.

- *Managing employee performance*: The human resources department is largely responsible for working with the departments and employees to set performance standards. By working with employees on setting the standards there is more likely to be a buy-in to achieving or exceeding the performance standards. Performance appraisal provides feedback on the department and individual performance. Formal evaluations are done yearly and midterm reviews assess how well an associate is doing in meeting the annual goals. Based on the feedback information praise and recognition or coaching and counseling are given to help associates ready for the next promotion.

- *Employee relations*: All relations or activities related to employees are employee relations. Among the many elements of employee relations are: employee communications, newsletters/TV monitors in the cafeteria and break areas, employee meals, employee recognition and award celebrations, and counseling and assistance may take place. Human resources assist department managers in setting up the evaluation process programs, suggestion programs, and the communication of company news, web pages, social media, and all relations relating to employees.

- *Labor relations*: Labor relations deal with all aspects of a labor contract when a union represents the employees of a company. Union representatives and management agree upon a contract and any grievances and disputes are handled by the labor relations manager or the HR director. The main focus of labor relations is to ensure compliance to the labor contract. Know the contract and always have it to refer to.

Learning Objective 2: Discuss operation planning, goal setting, and strategies

Operational Planning

Planning establishes the basis for the other functions. In fact, without planning, how could managers know how or what to organize, decide on, communicate, motivate, or control? Planning involved two main parts: goals and strategies.

We have seen earlier in this chapter that strategic planning takes place at the management level; now we look at operational, managerial, midlevel, and supervisory levels and see that most hospitality

© Rawpixel.com/Shutterstock.com

From a human resources perspective, operational goal setting would include assisting senior management with sales and marketing goal setting and attaining of goals

managers including human resource directors have a shorter planning horizon. *Operational plans* are generally created for periods of up to 1 year and fit in with the strategic plan. Most hospitality managers plan for periods from hourly, daily, weekly, and up to 90 days.

Operational plans provide managers with a step-by-step approach to accomplish goals. The overall purpose of planning is to have the entire organization moving harmoniously toward the goals. There are six steps in operational planning:

1. *Setting goals:* The first step in planning is identifying expected outcomes, that is, the goals. The goals should be specific, measurable, easy to track, and achievable and should reflect the vision, culture, values, and mission of the organization.

2. *Determining alternatives:* This involves developing strategic and operational courses of action that are available to a manager to reach a goal. Input may be requested from all levels of the organization. Group work is normally better than individual input. For example, Hyatt general managers hold Hyatt talk sessions with employees to get their input on topics of interest.

3. *Evaluating alternatives:* This calls for making a list of advantages and disadvantages of each alternative. Among the factors to be considered are resources and effects on the organization.

4. *Selecting the best solution:* The evaluation of the various alternatives should result in determining one course of action that is better than the others. It may, however, involve combining two or more alternatives.

5. *Implementing the plan:* Once the best solution is chosen, the HR director needs to decide the following:

   - Who will do what?
   - By when—date to be completed.
   - What are the resources required?
   - What is the benefit?
   - What is the cost?
   - What are the reporting procedures?
   - What is the authority granted to achieve goals?

6. *Controlling and evaluating results*: Once the plan is implemented, it is necessary to monitor progress toward goal accomplishment.

These six steps form the basis of planning and are used extensively in the hospitality and all other industries. A key part of planning is goal setting.

Operational Goal Setting

From a human resources perspective, operational goal setting would include assisting senior management with sales and marketing goal setting and attaining of goals. The HR director and department would also be involved in setting goals for each of the key result areas not only of the whole operation but also for the HR department's key result areas.

Given that all employees are involved with guest satisfaction, human resources plans, and organizes training for all levels of employees to meet and exceed guest expectations. As mentioned earlier in the chapter, an example would be setting a goal of 100% employee satisfaction; similarly, 100% conformance to all legal compliance issues is a goal that an HR director might set. There are also HR audits to ensure full compliance.

Operational Strategies

The **operational strategies** are the "how to" meet or exceed the operational goals. A strategy for getting 100% employee satisfaction begins with a survey to find out how employees currently feel about their job and the workplace culture and the leaders they work with. Any areas of weakness can quickly be determined and plans for rectifying the situation can be made. For example, if a survey reveals that satisfaction is low in one

Introducing HR Director Christine Ramos, The Ritz-Carlton Denver

I began my career in the hospitality industry working in Rooms Operations, and held roles as Director of Housekeeping and Front Office Manager. Next, I worked for Destination Hotels and Resorts, which is the fifth largest domestic hospitality management company in the United States. While employed with Destination Hotels and Resorts, I held roles as Director of Human Resources at both the Vail Cascade Resort and Spa and the Inverness Hotel and Conference Center in Englewood, CO.

I joined The Ritz-Carlton Hotel Company in 2008 as the Director of Human Resources at the renowned 5-diamond Ritz-Carlton Kapalua and The Ritz-Carlton Club and Residences, Kapalua Bay. My role there included direct responsibility for all functions within the human resources department for this 400+ room resort, which employs approximately 700 ladies and gentlemen, including both bargaining and nonbargaining units. In 2011, I relocated to The Ritz-Carlton Denver, where I currently work as the Director of Human Resources. Collectively, I have over 20 years of human resources experience as an HR Generalist in both bargaining and nonbargaining units. Additionally, I have served on several task force opportunities creating and implementing solid human resources processes. Unequivocally, my operations experience provided the foundation for a successful career in human resources.

HR planning and implementation is a priority for success in most industries, but especially in hospitality. It is important for the HR professional to be able to look beyond the day-to-day operation and focus on a more strategic and long-term approach to the business. Therefore, the HR professional must be able to act and think differently. These are not just words, rather behaviors that drive the business to meet its goals surrounding the people, product, and place. The new HR professional must be able to identify and articulate both the value and the costs associated with proposed actions. Thus, understanding the metrics and the analytics of the business is a necessity.

From a planning perspective, let's look at a key HR business discipline, *talent acquisition*. Being strategic in this area means identifying and assessing the talent needed to fulfill the business objectives. This includes being able to account for the talent gaps within the succession pool. HR planning in this area requires knowledge of the key competencies needed for the position, the values associated with those competencies, and where to recruit for the talent. Further planning would include a solid human capital plan within the organization that would consist of a talent review matrix, a succession plan that forecasts open positions, the high potential internal leaders/employees, and job readiness

(Continued)

for future assignments. This type of planning is much more complex than simply posting a job on one of the many career sites and hoping for the best.

HR planning is extremely important in all of the HR disciplines including forecasting, budgeting, learning and development, organizational policies and rules, etc. The HR professional will need to learn how to move from being transactional to transformational in leading their organization.

department, an investigation can often quickly ascertain the problem. It might be employee dissatisfaction with pay, conditions, leadership style, or some other factors which would come to light in the survey. The problem can then be addressed by human resources and the management.

Learning Objective 3: Provide an overview of the role of forecasting in human resources

Forecasting Employment Needs (Supply and Demand)

Forecasting human resources relies on the labor supply and demand in the particular market where the hospitality operation is located. The supply looks at the labor supply of available employees who possess the required skills that an employer might need. Labor demand is the number of full-time equivalent (FTEs') employees a company needs. HR planning is the process an organization uses to ensure that it has the right amount and the right kinds of people to deliver a particular level of output in the future (Gomez-Mejia, Balkin, & Cardy, 2012). Failure to plan can result in a labor shortage or too many employees.

When beginning the recruiting and selection process, which will be discussed in later chapters, it's best to start by first determining staffing needs. Many jobs in the hospitality industry require long hours, physical labor, and constant care and attention to guests. It will alleviate future problems and challenges in the hiring process if you accurately relay the details of the position, while still making it an attractive and important job. People not only look for jobs that they feel they are capable and qualified, but also those that motivate and encourage movement upwards in a company, offer benefits, and truly care about their employees. A key factor in forecasting staffing needs is determined by your operations. How many front desk agents do you need to operate efficiently? How many housekeepers must you put on a shift to guarantee rooms will be made ready on time? Does there need to be more than one Night Auditor? The answer lies within what it takes to make everyday operations at your business run to exceed the expectations of your guests.

People not only look for jobs that they feel they are capable and qualified but also those that motivate and encourage movement upwards in a company, offer benefits, and truly care about their employees

© tatianasun/Shutterstock.com

Determining what exactly, that is, will help you during the recruiting and selection process. If you are able to analyze your day-to-day operations, you can meet the needs of both your employees and your company. If during an interview, a candidate expresses his or her interest in working 40 hours per week, but explains that he or she cannot work 4 days out of a 7-day week because of a second job, it is your duty as a manager to determine whether this is in the best interest of your employee and your company. Do we have shifts that need to be covered on those 3 days? Can we ensure this person receives 40 hours of work each week? If the answer is yes to both, then you are fulfilling your staffing needs all while, potentially, keeping the company and employee happy.

Forecasting Internal and External Candidates

As we know the human resources function varies considerably depending on the size and type of company and its operations. Darden Restaurants for example, need a sophisticated system to accurately forecast the needs for each of their restaurant concepts. The needs for a much smaller independent restaurant or small chain are less complicated but forecasting human resources is still important. For the larger companies forecasting would estimate the number of stores or hotel openings and the number of management and hourly positions required at each.

Policies, Procedures, and Rules

Policies, procedures, and rules are needed in the workplace to guide associates in their actions and decisions. Policies, procedures, and rules development are all important functions performed by human resources. Effective policies and procedures have the following characteristics (Jerris, 1999, pp. 7–8):

- They need to be applied consistently and fairly.
- They reflect the values, culture, and philosophy of the company so as to minimize the chance of individuals interpreting policies according to their own interests and values.
- They set guidelines for managers to follow as they make human resource decisions. They are comprehensive enough to cover most situations that arise in the normal course of business, but are not so "nitpicky" that they put unnecessary constraints on management's judgment.
- Policies are written in response to the individual companies or operation's needs and requirements. They take into consideration its size and location. Whether it is centralized or decentralized, whether union or nonunion, and if it is affected by regional influences such as community customs and state laws.
- Policies are developed with input from line management and have the support of top management. Involving line managers helps make policies more understandable, increasing the likelihood that managers will accept them. Support of senior management means that policies will be enforced.
- Policies are introduced at the appropriate time. For example, policies that affect salaried workers, such as improved benefits or flex-time options, should not be introduced while the operation is in the midst of laying off hourly employees.
- Introduction of policies.

Budgeting

From an HR perspective, budgeting begins with planning months in advance of a new fiscal year; this is because it usually takes a few attempts before senior management and the corporate office signs off on it. The HR director works with department heads to formulate a budget for the whole operation, including the HR department. The HR budget often relies on the sales forecast from marketing and is expressed as a percentage of the total sales.

Budgeting begins with planning months in advance of a new fiscal year

When planning and organizing a human resources director will calculate the number of FTE employees that will be required, based on the number of rooms and the amount of sales revenues that will be achieved. With chain hotels, corporate will send a list of employees needed for each department. However, the human resources manager will still need to review the corporate list and negotiate any unusual situations—like for instance, having 200 residences as part of the complex—they will also want services and will also eat in the restaurants and drink in the bars.

Technology in HR

Human resources planning also involves orchestrating an HR system that gives employees the information they need. For example, one prominent hotel had a supervisory position available and four current associates were upset when someone from another hotel in the chain got the position, because they did not know about it. However, HR had posted the position on the website, on noticeboards, and in the newsletter. What the HR director learned from this was that Millennials like to be asked or approached personally. Now adjustments have been made to the company HR system so that associates can update their profiles and skills so they can be individually notified when suitable positions become available (M. Lucido, personal communication, July 13, 2013).

Learning Objective 4: Define and explain the role of job analysis, job descriptions, and job specifications

Job Analysis

> **Job Analysis:** The process to identify job duties and responsibilities and assess how each job contributes to the organization's goals.

A **job analysis** is the process to identify job duties and responsibilities and assess how each job contributes to the organizations' goals. It is the job and not the person doing the job that should be analyzed. The purpose of job analysis is to establish and document the job relatedness of employment procedures such as training, selection, compensation, and performance appraisal .

Hospitality work includes a series of tasks, which when combined, make up a job. The job is analyzed by a human resources specialist, and normally the person doing the job and their supervisor or manager. The steps involves in job analysis are

Determine which jobs will be analyzed. Determine how the job analysis information will be used; is it to provide information for recruiting and selection, for employee job descriptions or performance evaluations, or all of the above?

1. Collect the following information:

   ■ Analyze the job duties and units of work. A unit of work is one of several work sequences that combine to make up a job. A **task** is a procedural step in a unit of work. | **Task**: Is a procedural step in a unit of work. |

   ■ Write the performance standards for the job. (units and tasks).

   ■ Develop standard procedures.

   ■ Train the associates.

   ■ Test the training results.

   ■ Performance standards by which the jobholder will be evaluated, such as quality, quantity, or time taken for each aspect of the job.

   ■ Overall working conditions. These include physical working environment (such as indoors or outdoors, work space), work schedule, the kinds of people with whom the employer interacts (guests, other employees), the people whom the employee reports to and/or receives direction from.

   ■ Human requirements. These would include job-related knowledge or skills (such as education, training, and work experience) and personal attributes such as aptitudes, physical characteristics, personality, interests.

2. Review information with the jobholder and verify that it is complete, factually correct, and easily understood. By doing so you ensure that personal biases have not clouded the analysis process.

3. Determine what information you want to include in the job description/job specification.

4. Develop the job description/job specification.

Job analysis is done by asking people doing the job (individuals and groups) to explain what it entails, supervisors can add their perspective. Questionnaires may also be used to gauge the degree of difficulty of a particular task and the frequency of it. Another method of obtaining the necessary information is by observation, but employees may not like being "watched."

Job analysis can also help with recruitment due to a more precisely worded announcement a more suitable qualified applicant is likely to apply

© docstockmedia/Shutterstock.com

The Uses of Job Analysis (Gomez-Mejia, Balkin, & Cardy, 2010)

Job analysis is helpful for companies in complying with government regulations and as a defense against law suits. Job analysis provides the documentation for such a defense. For instance: The owner of a quick service restaurant who pays an assistant manager a weekly salary (without any overtime pay) may be able to defend herself from charges of an overtime pay violation with a job analysis proving that the assistant manager job is exempt from the overtime provisions of the Fair Labor Standards Act. The owner can prove this by showing that most of the job duties and responsibilities entail supervising and directing others rather than preparing food and providing service to guests (Gomez-Mejia, Balkin, & Cardy, 2010).

Recruitment: Job analysis can also help with recruitment due to a more precisely worded announcement a more suitable qualified applicant is likely to apply. This will reduce the amount of time spent on nonqualified applicants because the job duties are explained in detail.

Selection: Job analysis can help with selection by helping determine whether an applicant for a specific job should be required to take a personality test or some other kind of test. For example, personality test measures extroversion (the degree to which someone is talkative, sociable, active, aggressive, or excitable) may be justified for selecting a salesperson (such a job is likely to emphasize guest contact, which includes making "cold calls" on potential new accounts.)

Performance appraisal: The performance standards used to judge employee performance for purposes of promotion, rewards, discipline, or layoff should be job related. Under federal law, a company is required to defend its appraisal system against lawsuits and prove the job relatedness of the performance criteria used in the appraisal.

Compensation: Job analysis information can be used to compare the relative worth of each job's contribution to the company's overall performance. Normally, jobs that require greater skills are paid at higher rates. The job analysis helps determine the levels of skills required for each job.

Training and career development: Job analysis is an important input for determining training needs. By comparing the knowledge, skills, and abilities that employees bring to the job with those that are identified by job analysis, managers can identify their employees' skill gaps. Training programs can then be put in place to improve job performance.

Job Descriptions

Job Description: This details the job duties and responsibilities, how the job is to be done, and what the working conditions are.

Job Specification: This lists the knowledge, abilities, and skills needed to do the job.

Job descriptions are important because how can we operate a successful hospitality business if employees are not sure of what their job entails or how to do all the tasks that make up their job. Once the job analysis is complete then a job description can be written that details the job duties and responsibilities, how the job is to be done, and what the working conditions are. This information is then used to write a job specification, which lists the knowledge, abilities, and skills needed to do the job (**Figure 4.1**). Job descriptions include:

- Examples of front desk agent skills
- High school diploma/GED required
- 2+ years' front desk experience in the hospitality industry preferred
- 1+ years' customer service experience required
- Excellent written and verbal communication skills
- Familiarity with ResortSuite software a plus

https://www.indeed.com/hire/job-description/front-desk-agent

Figure 4.1 Sample Job Specifications for a Front Desk Agent

Job position/title: The job position or title identifies whether the job is classified as exempt under the Fair Labor Standards Act. Under this act administrative and professional positions are exempt from the act's overtime and minimum wage provisions. Other information at the top of the description is: the division and department (food and beverage, room service sales person), the location of the position, who the position reports to, and the pay range or scale step and date.

Relationships: Identifies the job holder's relationships within and outside the organization. For a restaurant general manager, it would look like this:

Reports to: Area manager/director.

Supervises: Managers and assistant managers.

Job summary: A summary of the essential aspects of the job.

Job duties and responsibilities: A detailed list of all the duties and responsibilities associated with the job. The job duties are used from the job analysis and from the government's Standard Occupational Classification (SOC) (www.bls.gov/soc/socguide.htm), which classifies all workers into one of 23 major groups of jobs and these have 96 minor groups of jobs, with 821 detailed occupations.

All job descriptions must be Americans with Disabilities Act (ADA) compliant. Under the ADA, the individual must have the requisite skills, educational background, and experience to perform the job's essential functions either with or without reasonable accommodation. If the disabled individual can't perform the job as currently structured, the employer is required to make a "reasonable accommodation," unless doing so would present an "undue hardship." (Dessler, 2011, p. 135).

Virtually all ADA legal actions will revolve around the question, "What are the essential functions of the job?" That's where a good job description can help convince a court that the functions are essential to the job (Dessler, 2011). Job descriptions have serious legal implications. The author once managed a luxury resort on a Caribbean island where in the first week after arriving, a hurricane drenched the resort with rain and a plumber (one of the few nasty employees) refused to "rod a drain" that had become blocked (due to a lack of maintenance). Now the union contract called for a verbal warning, which was given, followed by a written warning, followed by dismissal. During the grievance process the resort was able to show the job description which included "rodding a drain." Case dismissed!

Position authority: Details the extent of the authority the position carries.

Performance standards: Detail the expected standards and outcomes of the work. The performance standards help the employee and manager as both realize the job expectations. A restaurant server will know that the need to serve four tables; greet guests within 1 minute of their being seated by the hostess. Suggestively, "sell" beverage and menu items, take orders with 100% accuracy, post all charges with 100% accuracy, provide service that delights guests, work cooperatively with other employees, and so on.

Working conditions: Outline the general conditions under which the job will be done. For example the job of doorman at New York hotel requires a person to stand for long hours and be outside in hot and cold weather. By contrast, someone working in a hotel laundry has to deal with noise, chemicals, and heat.

Job specifications: Also referred to as "job requirements," job specifications detail the kind of employee characteristics and qualities are required to perform the job successfully. Job specifications should list minimum qualifications required for the job. An example being for a marketing director requiring a bachelor's degree would be acceptable but to expect a bachelor's degree for a front desk clerk would not.

When considering work experience qualifications, it is absolutely essential that they do not discriminate against minorities or persons with disabilities. This means that 5 years previous experience is not necessary for a theme park cashier position as it would discriminate against minorities and persons with a disability.

Organizing is defined as giving each subordinate a specific task, establishing departments, delegating authority to subordinates, establishing channels of authority and communication, and coordinating the work of others. Organization is naturally allied to vision, mission, and goals of an enterprise. Once decisions on strategies of how to accomplish the mission have been made, senior management organize the necessary resources to fulfill the mission.

> **Organizing**: This is defined as giving each subordinate a specific task, establishing departments, delegating authority to subordinates, establishing channels of authority and communication, and coordinating the work of others.

The purpose of organizing is to get a job done efficiently and effectively by completing the following:

- Divide work to be done into specific jobs and departments.
- Assign tasks and responsibilities associated with individual jobs.
- Coordinate diverse organizational tasks.
- Group jobs into teams.
- Establish relationships among individuals, teams, and departments.
- Install formal lines of authority.
- Ensure organizational resources are available.

Organization is the arrangement of activities so that they maximize goal accomplishment. No one person can do all the things necessary for a hospitality organization to be successful. Just imagine one person trying to do all the different tasks that make a hotel stay memorable.

At the corporate level, human resource vice presidents and other senior executives determine the organizational structure of the company. Let's consider a large international hotel company with divisions on all continents. Initially, as a company expands into a continental market by gradually establishing a presence an HR vice president will be very involved with planning and organizing the expansion. In Europe, for example, a company may expand into London, England first because of similar language and customs. An experienced HR vice president who knows the British market and labor laws will be engaged to oversee the individual property HR directors. Once a cluster of properties is being established, then it is time to begin operations in Paris, Berlin, and Rome followed by other cities. Prior to the beginning of operations in a country, it is necessary to determine each properties' departments and the number of employees required.

An organizational structure is like a skeleton in that it supports the various departments in an organization. It provides the total framework by which job tasks are divided, grouped, and coordinated. In today's leaner and meaner hospitality business environment, organizations are flatter—which means they have fewer levels of managers. They are also structured to better fulfill the needs of the guests. The general manager used to be at the top of the organization chart and the frontline associates at the bottom—the guests never appeared on the chart! Now we have guests at the top of the inverted pyramid and top management at the bottom of the chart.

Key Points

- Human resources planning begins with the mission, vision, culture, core values, and goals (which should be smart, specific, and measurable). These are the drivers of the company.
- A corporate vision lays the foundation for the direction of the company and answers the question of "What is our preferred future?"

- A mission defines the business activity, who the company is, and what it does. It gives identity and direction to the organization (Schulze, 2006).
- Culture—what governs the way employees and owners think, act, and feel about the company and core values—the values a company holds important, tell a lot about a company.
- Strategic human resources leadership is largely about ensuring that human resources is fully integrated with the strategy and the strategic needs of the company.
- Planning establishes the basis for the other functions.
- Operational plans provide managers with a step-by-step approach to accomplish goals.
- Forecasting human resources relies on the labor supply and demand in a particular market.
- Policies, procedures, and rules are needed in the workplace to guide associates in their actions and decisions.
- Budgeting begins with planning months in advance of fiscal year.
- A job analysis is the process to identify job duties and responsibilities and assess how each job contributes to an organization's goals.
- A job description is brief statement outlining duties and responsibilities and how the job is to be done.
- Job specifications are a summary of knowledge, abilities, and skills needed to do a job successfully.

Key Terms

Core values	Job specification	Strategic human resources
Culture	Mission	leadership
Goals	Operational strategies	Task
Job analysis	Organizing	Vision
Job description		

Discussion Questions

1. Explain why vision, mission, and goals are important.
2. What makes an organizational culture appealing? What are you looking for in a culture?
3. Give three examples of operational goal setting.
4. Why are job analysis, job descriptions, and job specifications important?

Ethical Dilemma

The author recently received a call from a local upscale hotel chain accountant asking if he knew of any good accounting positions available, as her job was being outsourced to India. Is it ethical for a major hotel company to outsource this and other similar positions?

Case Study

A high-end restaurant that has gone through many changes in its long existence offers two examples of planning. The first is changing the menu and the second relates to an operational planned decision to reduce the number of tables a server handles.

Changing the menu at a popular restaurant can be a difficult planning operation so the restaurant's management brought up the topic at the employee meeting and asked for suggestions from everyone. Everyone felt that they were a part of making the decision and were happy to help. The servers not only made their own suggestions but also asked guests for their input for what they would like to see on the menu. A couple of weeks later there were lots of suggestions for management to consider. Many were items that had previously been specials. After looking over the sales and finding that these items had, in fact, sold well. Additionally, the items suggested to be taken off the menu had the highest amount of 'comps.'

At a tasting for all employees they all tasted 10 different items and voted on which items to add and which to delete. The vote was unanimous as to which items should be added and deleted. The menu was updated the next week and the changes were a great success.

A few weeks later, during high season, the restaurant was extremely busy with an hour's wait and a big crowd waiting. The kitchen was backed up, the bar was taking 6–8 minutes for the wait staff to serve their table's drinks, and the bussers were taking too long to reset tables. In walks the company CEO and sees the state of the restaurant. He immediately decides to reduce the server's tables to three and informs the managers. The manager shares this with the servers at the pre-shift huddle the next day. Naturally, the servers are extremely upset because they felt that they were not responsible for the kitchen, bar, or bussers being backed up. They quickly figured that they would be losing about 25% of their income.

Questions:
1. What the management has done is right and wrong?
2. What would you suggest to handle these situations?

Internet Exercise

Go to the website of HR People and Strategy at http://www.hrps.org/?page=KnowledgePillars and see what points they have for Building a Strategic HR Function and HR Strategy and Planning.

References

Darden (2013). Retrieved April 23, 2013, from http://www.darden.com/careers/culture.asp
Dessler, G. (2011). *Human resources management* (12th ed.). Upper Saddle River, NJ: Pearson.
Disney parks. (2018). Retrieved January 30, 2018, from https://aboutdisneyparks.com/citizenship/workplace
Gomez-Mejia, L. R., Balkin, D. B., & Cardy, R. L. (2010). *Managing human resources* (6th ed., pp. 63–64). Upper Saddle River, NJ: Pearson.
Gomez-Mejia, L. R., Balkin, D. B., & Cardy, R. L. (2012). *Managing human resources* (7th ed., p. 166). Upper Saddle River, NJ: Pearson.
Jerris, L. A. (1999). *Human resources management for hospitality*. Upper Saddle River, NJ: Prentice Hall.

Marriott. (2013a). Retrieved April 15, 2013, from http://www.marriott.com/culture-and-values/core-values.mi
Marriott. (2013b). Retrieved April 23, 2013, from http://www.marriott.com/culture-and-values/core-values.mi
Schulze, H. (2006, March). *Service excellence.* Presentation to the Linda Novey White Lecture Series, University of South Florida, Sarasota.
Sparks, W. (2012). *The magic of Disney's organizational behavior concepts.* Retrieved April 14, 2012, from http://voices.yahoo.com/the-magic-disneys-organizational-behavior-concepts-550698.html
Strigl, D. (2011, October). Results drive happiness. *Human Resources Magazine,* 113.

© Look Studio/Shutterstock.com

RECRUITING

Introduction

You need to fill a vacant front desk position in your organization so you've placed an advertisement on your company website and the appropriate social media feeds. The advertisement explains the essential duties of the position and what those responsibilities entail. After receiving numerous applications and narrowing down to the few that seem the best suited for the position, you conduct interviews and fill the position with an enthusiastic and experienced agent. Only days later the new employee calls in "sick." After reiterating your company policy, including the 30-day probationary period in which no "sick days" were allowed, he still chooses not to come into work. You are left with no choice but to let your new hire go. So, you're back to square one and now frustrated and concerned that this empty position will begin to negatively impact the operation. Why is it this hard to find a qualified employee who follows through and becomes a productive employee?

You cannot control the actions and behavior of any person, and thus, finding a stellar employee is often limited to the presentation that a person can make. However, you must strive to have the best interests of your company and employees in mind when considering a potential new employee, and understand and communicate the ideal qualifications for any given position. In this chapter, we will delve into the process of recruiting employees in the hospitality industry.

After studying this chapter, you should be able to:

1. Provide an overview of the hiring process, and more specifically the function of recruiting.
2. Explain the strengths, weakness, and methods of internal recruiting.
3. Highlight the benefits and methods using in external recruitment.
4. Describe the components of an effective recruiting strategy.

Learning Objective 1: Provide an overview of the hiring process, and more specifically the function of recruiting

The Hiring Process

Potential employees are now looking for a more comprehensive package when applying for employment

The hiring process has many components that work together to ensure that an organization finds the right person to fill a position based the specifications of the job. The hiring process includes recruiting and selection. The hiring process includes assessing the open position, evaluating the talent and abilities of a future employee, and ensuring that person's personality and work ethic will blend with that of your company's vision, mission statement, culture, and goals. Recruitment will be discussed in this chapter, with selection being the focus of Chapter 6. **Recruitment** is the steps taken to find qualified individuals for a given job in your organization and convince them to formally apply for that job. Some have equated recruitment to the job of someone in sales and marketing in the way that recruiting is "selling" a product, in this case employment, to someone.

> **Recruitment**: steps taken to find qualified individuals for a given job in your organization and convince them to formally apply for that job.

As discussed earlier in this book, turnover in the hospitality industry is an inevitable (and costly) challenge. For example, many hospitality companies are gravitating toward promoting a holistic "package" of benefits when recruiting a potential applicant: compensation, benefits, work–life, performance and recognition, and development and career opportunities. Potential employees are now looking for a more comprehensive package when applying for employment and these key factors promote attracting the right employees and retaining them as well as rewarding them through employee engagement.

Internal vs. External Recruiting

Effective human resource recruiting can occur within (internally) and outside (externally) of an organization. As you will see below, there are pros and cons to each method in terms of cost, the size of a potential candidate pool, and an overall impact on culture within an organization. Thus, when determining the recruiting strategy for a particular open position, organizations must determine if they should recruit internally, externally, or both. It's important for those responsible for recruiting to understand that a strategy to recruit applicants may work well for one organization and not another. Additionally, what works well for a certain position may not work well for another.

Learning Objective 2: Explain the strengths, weakness, and methods of internal recruiting

Internal Recruiting

When recruiting for an open position within an organization, this is referred to as *internal recruiting*. Internal recruiting has proved to not only have a positive effect on employee morale, but has shown success in offering a position to someone who has already been established in the company. This potential to move vertically or horizontally in an organization is a desirable attribute of working in the hospitality industry since it provides experience and job security.

Promotion is moving someone to a higher position with more responsibility and typically more pay on the basis of their credibility proven work-ethic. Internal promotions are often preferred over external recruiting due to the knowledge, trust, and reliability an employee has already created for themselves within an organization. This is beneficial for the company, the employee and yourself, as you save time that would normally be consumed by screening, interviewing, testing, and reference checks. Having clearly defined performance appraisal systems provides critical insight into employees deserving promotions and seeking career growth with the company.

Interviewing a promotion candidate for the position is still the recommended practice even if we have confidence that an employee can fulfill the position. Sometimes, employees may accept a promotion without realizing the duties and responsibilities, and it can lead to a demotion or you have to start back at square one. Setting standards for promotion also helps you to make the right decision when promoting.

This could include meeting a certain score on an application evaluation or test, an additional interview, or even a time frame of being in the company. These standards will not only assist you in the correct selection, but help others understand why they may or may not have been promoted for that particular position.

When word spreads that a company values hard work and truly appreciates the efforts of their employees through the use of internal promotions, morale is raised and your turnover can be reduced. If there is no obvious person to promote to the vacant position, a next step can be to consider recruiting from within an organization. A common practice of informing employees of such available jobs is called job posting. Typically, a human resource representative will post a list of available jobs within the company in locations where employees will see the posting.

Internal promotions are often preferred over external recruiting due to the knowledge, trust, and reliability an employee has already created for themselves within an organization

© Prostock-studio/Shutterstock.com

This could be a break room, next to the time clock, or even in the hallway before employees exit the building, and on-line, including on the company intranet (website only accessible to current employees) and external job websites either operated by the company or a third party. We will discuss external websites as a recruiting tool later in the chapter.

Another way to spread the "internal" word is employee referral programs. These programs are commonly used by employers to draw in candidates who have a similar understanding and personality traits of those already employed in the company. This program can, again, benefit you as the manager not only in saving the recruiting time but also make your employees feel at ease knowing there is potential for "familiar faces." Bringing in strangers to a work environment can often be disruptive or create problems to the culture of an organization, thus companies encourage employees to refer those candidates they already know and believe would be good for a job and fit well with other employees. However, in reality, this is not always a guarantee. Sometimes people know others and when they work with them, they behave quite differently. For this reason, it's important to treat referred applicants the same as nonreferred applicants in terms of selection criteria. Just because someone is a "friend" of a current employee, it doesn't mean they are the most qualified for the job and will be the best fit for the organization.

In addition to improving morale of the employees, there are other benefits to recruiting from within an organization. First, because the applicant already is employed by an organization, those involved in the hiring process can better assess qualifications. If the person has worked for the organization for a significant period of time, performance appraisals (written and observed) are available to gauge how well someone may fit into an open job. If the applicant is from an external source, performance data on how well they did in their previous role may not be available. While a letter of recommendation may be provided, they are traditionally positively biased and provide only limited information.

An additional advantage to internal recruiting is that traditionally lower when compared to those related to external recruiting. Further, marketing of the job across a variety of internal sources and the time needed to train new employees is reduced since they are already "within" the organization.

With these benefits of internal recruiting, there are also disadvantages to this strategy. By promoting and hiring from within an organization, there is a risk of stagnation of new ideas. Sometimes the arrival of "fresh" ideas from an external applicant into the culture of an organization can be a useful tool in meeting constantly evolving needs of the customer. Additionally, in some cases, promoting from within the organization only could give the perception that it's all about "who you know" and only "friends of the boss" will get promoted and given opportunities to fill open positions.

Learning Objective 3: Highlight the benefits and methods using in external recruitment

External Recruiting

Although hiring from within the company may often be the cheapest and quickest source for qualified applicants, it is one of the ways to fill a position. **External recruiting** is seeking out employees from outside of the company who have no current involvement in the operation. Finding applicants can come through advertising, employment agencies, direct recruiting, and external sources.

> **External Recruiting**: is seeking out employees from outside of the company that have no current involvement in the operation.

In certain situations, you as a manager may have to make the decision whether to promote from within or find a qualified applicant using external sources. Take for example, if the position for Food and Beverage Director has just been made available at your hotel. Your first instinct is to spread the word around and create a job posting to see who would be qualified for the promotion versus fulfilling this position externally. You have four employees who express interest in the job and interview all four to find they are familiar and comfortable with their jobs, are reliable, and have strong work ethics. However, after realizing none of the current employees have the experience or knowledge required to operate as a Food and Beverage Director, you are forced to place an advertisement on the company website and/or a job website in hopes of finding someone to quickly fill the spot. Online and internal sources are always excellent means of finding talented employees, but external talent can also be the location for some of the most talented in all of the hospitality industry.

External staffing includes advertising, employment agencies, direct recruiting, and other organizations and external source

© Olivier Le Moal/Shutterstock.com

If a manager excludes a candidate because they have worked for the competition or for a company which has different values, they would be eliminating a large group of talented candidates. Many applicants, whether online or in person, will more than likely have experience in the hotel and restaurant industry; by recognizing the talent and guest service skills they may already have due to their knowledge of the industry or particular profession, you will broaden your spectrum for a group of talented employees.

> **Distribution Channel**: This is the source of reaching any given network of people, organization, or business.

The benefits of external staffing lie in the distribution channel. A distribution channel is the source of reaching any given network of people, organization or business. By using recruiting firms or job websites, you not only are able to narrow down specific criteria for a given position, but you are also reaching a much larger spectrum of applicants. The issue with hiring a Food and Beverage Director internally is that although benefits of internal staffing can be great, a higher up position needs a knowledgeable and confident person to take on a role; often times found throughout the country. Thus, sending a message through a larger distribution channel allows more options and most likely, highly qualified people to apply for the position.

Recruitment Through Advertising

The format and medium for advertisements varies, in some cases dramatically, from job to job and company to company

© Ken Wolter/Shutterstock.com

Just like selling a product or service to customers, advertisements are a great way to recruit potential applicants. The format and medium for advertisements varies, in some cases dramatically, from job to job and company to company. An advertisement for a job is tool that, in a matter of second, can convey a lot about an open job and the organization in which that job is housed.

Variations exist in what a recruiting advertisement can and should include based on where the advertisement is going to be placed. As with the determination to recruit internally or externally, this is not one best universal way to advertise. A hospitality organization should choose advertisement strategies based on several factors such as financial resources available, relevant labor market (where the advertisement will be placed), type, and quantity of jobs.

When using a tangible advertisement (newspaper, magazine, flyer, billboard) to recruit for an open position in your organization, there is a limit to how much information can be included. As such, a best practice would be to ensure the following are included, at a minimum:

- Company/business name
- Available position(s)
- How to apply (website, email, in-person)

If more space is permitted, recruiters can certainly incorporate more information such as the companies' values, mission, ideal qualifications of candidates, or other eye-catching images.

Isabelle Shaindlin: Lettuce Entertain You Restaurants

Your career can literally be anything you want, as long as you are two things: hungry and realistic.

I found myself in the exciting and always-changing world of recruiting 9 months after graduating college. Recruiting is exciting and fast-paced, and if you're good at multitasking it's even more fun. Recruiting brings me joy—I get to meet a lot of excited people who really want to work for my company. A huge piece of my job is simply networking and meeting new people. I am constantly on social media networks, browsing through people in my network to just keep up and stay familiar with what those people are up to. I like to get familiar with people, and it's always my goal to remember people's names and one fact about them. However, networking is on both the recruiter and job seeker. For example, I got my position at Lettuce Entertain You Restaurants in Human Resources because I networked and found my opportunity. Employers want you to reach out and make them aware of your interest. I would not have had the opportunity to apply for my position if I wasn't hungry enough to reach out to old contacts to find myself a position and company I loved.

Lettuce Entertain You is a national restaurant company that currently owns, operates, and manages 120+ locations. We have 60+ unique brands which make the hiring process so different from other companies; there is a restaurant for everyone. I am the only Internship Coordinator here at Lettuce, which means I handle all of our college recruiting endeavors, along with local events where I constantly meet individuals ready to star their career in restaurant management. I interview a lot of people and the ones who do the best are all one thing: realistic. At Lettuce, we look across the board for people who are motivated to work with a team, energetic, warm, passionate about hospitality, and loyal. We believe if you have the personality and drive, we can teach you some (not all) of the technical skills.

To make it easy on the future recruiters you work with, be realistic. Understand what your role at the current point in your career would be. Although we want to know you are aiming high and have big dreams, keeping yourself grounded and focused on your next role really hits home.

Contributed by Izzy Shaindilin. © Kendall Hunt Publishing Company

Employment Agencies

An **employment agency** is often used to assist an organization in their external recruiting efforts. An employment agency is a company that specializes in recruitment and provides assistance to another organization and their recruiting efforts for either a set or variable fee depending on situations. In most circumstances, the fee

> **Employment Agencies:** These are the external firms who fulfill a job opening for your company for a set fee.

is usually not collected until the agency successfully fills the position based on the requirements provided. Fees are generally 10% of the salary of the position filled or a one-time placement fee (T. Boyd, personal communication, July 2, 2011).

Some entry-level positions in the hospitality industry are filled through employment agencies. A recent trend has been the use of temporary staffing agencies for jobs in the hotel and restaurant industry. For example, a country club has a large wedding and may need additional servers for dinner or a hotel may need three more room attendants to operate efficiently for their 3-month busy season. Regardless of the need, employment agencies can save you time and the struggle of reaching out to find a qualified employee.

There are also groups and agencies that do not charge fees for assistance, but rather monitor, screen, and will provide you as a manager with a potential employee. Job service centers are the centers that assist unemployed or laid-off workers in finding a new job. These are usually organized through government agencies or nonprofit employment services. Job service centers can be an excellent and free source to find someone in search of a job; however, if it is a period of high unemployment, it may be less time efficient to try to browse through the numerous resumes than to use an alternative external recruiting source.

Direct Recruiting

Direct recruiting is normally the practice of larger organizations

© rki-foto/Shutterstock.com

Direct recruiting refers to when a company employee (a recruiter) is sent to seek out candidates for jobs, internships, and careers. Direct recruiting is normally the practice of larger organizations. Often, these large companies will send their recruiters to colleges with programs in hospitality management and take part in job fairs or interviews in hopes of gaining employees for their company with a knowledge of and experience in the industry (Moreland, 2010).

Another direct recruiting source is when there is a closing of another business in the hospitality industry. It's unfortunate when a hotel or restaurant cannot survive, but it gives the recruiter of your company an opportunity to interview employees who are obviously in need of work and who also have knowledge of the business. This form of recruiting is the best way for a company to gain employees who already have a "taste" of the hospitality industry; whether it be a recent college grad from culinary school or a server who just got laid off from the town's best steakhouse-direct recruiting is walking through an open door to find the candidate that will have some sort of advantage over general applicants you may find online or outside of the industry.

Advantages of direct recruiting include exposure for your company. If your company attends a job fair where 2,500 local high school students are looking for summer jobs with their parents, you could not only secure yourself one or two part-time employees for the summer, but advertise your company to 2,500 students and their parents. If a parent sees that Company A is willing to give their high-school-age son a work opportunity, they may be more likely to book a Company A next time they travel, or at least remember them and speak highly when in conversation with others. Certain companies will also partake in internal job fairs; showing current employees what it will take to be a manager in their department. It not only prepares employees for the next level, but shows that a company is willing and eager to promote within.

Outsourcing

Outsourcing: The use of noncompany labor by an organization.

Especially during tough economic times, hospitality companies may have to resort to drastic measures just to stay open. One such measure is outsourcing labor. Companies hire people to work on a temporary basis, and generally for less money per hour and with no benefits, vacation or sick days compared to regular employees. In hotels, they can be used in many departments: housekeeping, the restaurant, stewarding, laundry, or room service. The jobs don't go offshore to other countries, as they did with many accounting positions in hotels, these jobs go to little-seen labor agencies that provide hotel chains with large pools of bottom-rung workers (The Huffingto Post, 2013).

This practice, however, can have devastating impacts on the former employees. An example of this practice and how it affects employees is 57-year-old William Selm, who had been a bellman for 14 years at the Westin Indianapolis when his position was farmed out in 2008. Although he used to make $8.40 per hour plus tips, after the switch Selm lost all his seniority and soon wound up at another hotel making $3.50 per hour (The Huffingto Post, 2013).

Often, outsourced employees are hired through companies such as Hospitality Staffing Solutions (HSS) who operate in more than 35 cities in America. As might be expected, both the practice of outsourcing and HSS have received much criticism. The most noticeable of which was when Hyatt carried out a mass layoff of 100 housekeepers in Boston at three of its hotels, replacing them with workers from HSS. The wages for housekeepers then dropped from $15 per hour with benefits (add about 40% for benefits) to around $8 per hour without benefits. To make matters worse, Hyatt staffers claimed they had unwittingly trained their replacements thinking they were just supplemental help. At the time, Hyatt attributed the move to "challenging economic conditions." (The Huffingto Post, 2013).

Whether we like it or not, outsourcing looks as if it is here to stay. Operators argue that they need to cut costs in order to survive. Critics question that and add that it is morally and ethically wrong to outsource jobs in this way. As with many complex questions of this nature—the answer lies somewhere in between the two positions.

Especially during tough economic times, hospitality companies have to resort to drastic measures just to stay open

© wavebreakmedia/Shutterstock.com

Online Recruiting

Often, the most difficult part in the recruitment process is the availability of a person to fill that position. So where do you start? Online job posting sites, craigslist and viral sources of advertising jobs has drastically increased in recent years. While the classified section of a newspaper may have been the "go to" in the past, today, most recruiting is done online. Job websites, whether they are managed by a third-party (HCareers.com, Indeed.com, HospitalityOnline.com) or an individual company website (Hyatt.jobs, Disneycareers.com) have also made it easier for companies to post jobs and for

The benefits of electronic recruiting extend far beyond the employers to the people who are seeking employment as well

© jannoon028/Shutterstock.com

job seekers to search and apply for a position on their website. Hospitality career websites are, for the most part, easy to use and accessible on personal computers and mobile devices.

An *online job board* is a website that functions as a directory of job listings and employment positions available posted by a variety of employers seeking potential candidates for hire. Employers can only post job listings on the online job board if their company is a member. Some of the most popular online job boards include Monster.com, Careerbuilder.com, Craigslist.com, indeed.com, and Hotjobs.com. Corporate recruiting sites partner with different companies who hire them search for potential candidates. Some corporate recruiters function as outside businesses that offer their services to client companies, while others are part of a corporate recruitment department within a company. Similarly, recruitment application service providers offer their services to client companies by establishing recruitment websites, which may cause them to appear to be the website of the company itself. Studies have shown that companies with more established web presence, an easy to navigate recruitment site, and an eye-catching appearance or design are more attractive to potential candidates. It is critical for companies to continuously develop and maintain an innovative website that seeks to grab and hold the attention of job seekers, as well as various outlets that constantly direct them to the site (see **Figure 5.1**).

The benefits of electronic recruiting extend far beyond the employers to the people who are seeking employment as well. Now, it is much easier to get your application into the hands of employers with a few easy steps and the click of the mouse. This allows for the ability to apply for a multitude of jobs without ever leaving the house. This does present a drawback in the fact that a potential candidate will only be furthered along in the hiring process if their resume is sufficient. This leaves no room for first impressions until the actual interview takes place. When the application process was more personal, an applicant had the chance to offer their first impression before they even applied for a job. At the same time, the employer had the chance to evaluate the employee and make determinations about their character before taking the time to schedule an interview, which makes it easier to identify the better candidates from the outset.

Much of the ease of use in job websites is based on several factors. First, available opportunities are searchable by keyword (i.e., housekeeping, front desk, and server). This helps immensely when a potential employee wants to search for a specific job or area of a hospitality organization. In many cases, someone may not know the specific duties a job within an organization requires, but they know generally what they are looking for. For example, someone may know they want to work in a kitchen or the front desk of a hotel.

> **Applicant**: Once a person has formally applied for a position online, in person, or through other means, they become an applicant.

Second, many recruiting websites have the ability to allow the potential employees to apply for a job. Once the person applies for the job, they officially become an **applicant**. Job applicants vary in terms of requirements based on the needs of the organization and position, and it's important to ensure that all aspects of the application follow guidelines outlined by the law (i.e., asking appropriate questions). If a potential applicant can't apply for the job through the actual website, it's a best practice to include specific information on how to apply for the position. This could be, for example, by email, in person, or even via fax. It is up to the organization how they choose to manage the application process, although some methods are easier to manage than others.

https://jobs.hilton.com

Figure 5.1   Hilton Jobs Website

https://twitter.com/LettuceJobs

Figure 5.2   Lettuce Entertain You Jobs Social Media Post

Third, an online job website, particularly those designed and maintained by the actual organization doing the hiring, has total control over the content on the website. This means that, in addition to providing information about the job itself, the organization can provide other helpful company-specific information. For example, it's common for companies to provide information on their culture, mission, benefits, and diversity statement on their HR websites.

A third party or company website is not the only way that firms can recruit potential applicants. Today, companies are taking to social media to promote their job opportunities. From Facebook to Instagram and Twitter, organizations are capitalizing on trends to reach a large number of potential applicants. In some cases, a company may create a dedicated social media feed for careers in their organization (Figure 5.2).

Social media plays a leading role in recruiting top talent with professional sites such as LinkedIn. Candidates can join social networks to engage in dialogues with human resources staff who can get to know those seeking job positions even before they apply for one. For example, you placed an ad online for a room attendant position. A currently unemployed candidate, Eric, has worked as a valet part time and is interested in possibly getting hired full time at a hotel as a room attendant. When Eric logs into his account at a third-party website, he can search in the "hospitality industry" and use the key word of "room attendant" to find any employers seeking such an employee. Three positions happen to be open for three different hotels in the area, one of which is your own. Eric decides to apply to all the three, but when he tries to submit his resume to your hotel, he is asked to take a situational test to help determine his placement and measure his knowledge and skills of the job. Not willing to put in the effort for a test, Eric chooses not to continue applying to your hotel.

As a manager, this example is precisely why these websites can help narrow down the type of applicant you are looking for. Someone who is not willing to attempt to take a short test to submit a resume is probably lacking the work ethic you are looking for, and thus, has helped eliminate candidates who would not be right for the position.

Application Forms

An application form is a document asking questions that will help managers gain factual information regarding a prospective employee. Application forms are typically the most logical and legal way of gaining information from an applicant. When someone fills out an application, they are willfully providing you with presumably truthful information because they know background checks, reference checks, and other information can be verified and will have a deciding factor in the selection process. It is also the most legal way because application forms ask for standard information and do not leave room for someone to consciously or unconsciously discriminate by asking for different information from different applicants.

An application form can not only provide facts such as names, birth date, previous employers, and lengths of time employed, but can also provide characteristic and work ethic traits by the way a person fills out the form. Did they proof read their work? Is the handwriting legible? Were they able to follow instructions? Answering these simple questions can assist you in narrowing down your choices and making sure your selection is one based on your staffing needs, as well as facts.

By requesting each applicant fill out an application form, you can help avoid lawsuits and accusations of discrimination during recruiting and selection

© Brian A Jackson/Shutterstock.com

Requiring a formal application from each prospective employee can keep you out of legal trouble. Take, for example, a situation where a room service supervisor position has opened up and you have had several inquiries to your email address. Instead of asking each of the potential applicants to fill out your company's application form, you hold open interviews on Wednesday from 9 to 11 a.m. and invite all prospects to attend and bring a resume. You review resumes, conduct small interviews with each prospect, and quickly make a decision to hire a 22-year-old female who has had previous experience in the hospitality industry. Everything you have done seems legal and you are sure you did not discriminate; however, there happened to be a 35-year-old pregnant female who also showed up the interview and has inquired as to why she did not receive the position. It was not because she was pregnant, or because she was older, but because she was not qualified. But because you neglected to have applicants fill out application forms, you have no proof of your knowledge and you may appear to have discriminated during the hiring process. By requesting each applicant fill out an application form, you can help avoid lawsuits and accusations of discrimination during recruiting and selection.

Social media outlets have increased the number of applicants for available positions to the point where some hospitality corporations are using online recruiting systems. When Burger King rolled out an online-only hiring system in April 2010, featuring an applicant tracking system (ATS) from Kronos Inc., line and HR managers were quick to embrace it. Now, when candidates stop into a restaurant to apply for jobs ranging from hourly team member to management positions, they're handed cards that provide detailed instructions for applying at bkcareers.com. Burger King is among the first quick-service restaurant chains to abandon paper for an electronic-only hiring system in all of its corporate-owned U.S. locations. Candidates can apply from their personal computers and cell phones or from computers in libraries or coffee shops. Human resources staff experimented with placing hand-held devices in restaurants during a pilot test but found most applicants preferred to complete applications in more-private settings. The online application process includes a 100-question behavioral assessment tool developed by Kronos' industrial–organizational psychologists. The assessment tool is designed to gauge the proficiency of candidates for restaurant jobs in two key competencies: customer service and reliability.

Technology in HR Electronic Recruiting

The current trend in human resources departments is the implementation of a more web-based approach to recruiting, selecting, and hiring potential candidates for employment, which has significantly impacted both the amount and quality of applicants in the workplace, as well as the range of awareness with which people are finding out about job openings. Recruiting electronically is extremely beneficial to employers, because it allows them to reach applicants locally, nationally, and even globally in a convenient and affordable manner (Johnson & Gueutal, 2011).

Introducing: HR Director Katrina Wyand-Yurish, MS, SPHR Roy Rogers Restaurants

As the Director of Human Resources for the Roy Rogers Restaurant franchise and one of the largest hotelier companies headquartered in Maryland, my role encompasses experience in all HR functions. I am a generalist and a business partner who builds HR teams that add value to the entire organization. This chapter focuses on employee recruiting and selection of talent, the backbone of every organization.

Talent management always raises the question of whether to *build or buy*. The term *build* refers to the process of promoting and coaching an existing employee into a role.

To *buy*, refers to the process of seeking employees from outside the company. Organizations need to strategically determine the pros and cons of each strategy and set goals for internal development of employees. The ability to recognize internal talent through promotions or career advancement and external talent by way of recruiting is talent management which is central to a solid human capital strategic plan.

We hear the phrase, "People are truly your biggest asset," but what needs to be added is, "*The* **right** *people are truly your biggest asset*." Hire right, be selective, because your company's success counts on it. The ability through effective recruiting and selection to choose the best talent is not easy. Yet nothing is more important than hiring the right candidate. Careful selection as discussed in this chapter will yield the most engaged and skilled talent. Use the measurement and performance characteristics and reference checks to gain a comprehensive picture of the candidate. I view employment testing, aligned interviewing questions to performance characteristics, and reference checks to be valuable tools. Use of one recruiting tool alone will not always provide the best analysis of a candidate. I encourage you to consider all recruiting and selection methodologies and tools when making your hiring decisions.

Additionally, when recruiting, you must have the ability to place your personal biases aside. Human nature guides us instinctively to want to hire people that are like us. But skilled recruiters use the tools mentioned above and discussed in more detail in this chapter to fight against any discrimination biases. Look for cultural fit too. The culture of your organization impacts the type of hire and your retention. Is your organization quick in decision making, do you empower employees, what forms of recognition are available? The culture you as a leader create can make a lasting impression and impact on your workforce.

Human resources through forecasting and other human resources metrics, such as turnover data and return on investment calculations, lead the strategic effort thereby adding value to the profession. I wish you much success in your HR leadership journey.

Contributed by Katrina Wyand-Yurish. © Kendall Hunt Publishing Company

Learning Objective 4: Describe the components of an effective recruiting strategy

Effective Recruiting

There are many ways to recruit internally and externally but *effective* recruiting ultimately lies in the actions of the hiring manager. Were you able to attract experienced applicants? Did you overlook anyone because you were on a time crunch? Did you clearly communicate with the employment agency as to what

In order to evaluate effective recruiting, it's imperative you as a manager understand its importance

© Pixsooz/Shutterstock.com

you're looking for? The answers may come in the form of trial and error. Over time, you will be able to see what recruiting sources worked best, and which ones caused problems in the work place or an employee who was not right for your company. It comes from many factors—how strong the application is, how well the recruiting strategy works to scout top talent, and how well the recruiter probed in interview to uncover the candidates' experience and career attitude.

In order to be effective when recruiting, you must also analyze the time and money put in to each recruiting source you used. Say for instance you used an employment agency that requires flat fee of $250 to hire two new servers for your country club. Six months later you decide you do not want to pay the staffing fee required by the agency, and hire two more servers through an online job advertisement. You spend 3 days sorting through resumes, emails, and set up six interviews for Thursday. Each interview takes half an hour and, even after you narrow it down to two servers, you still must lay out pros and cons for each as they both have qualities you are looking for and previous serving experience. After a day of pondering, you hire one server after they fill out an application form and you screen and complete a reference check, and get them started training that week. All of the servers hired turned out to be stellar severs, but which form of recruiting was more effective? You spent $250 and 0 hours hiring servers through an agency, and spent $0 and 10 hours of your time hiring servers on your own. Choosing to spend $250 over a full 10 hours is the more effective recruiting choice in this scenario.

A tip is to learn as much as possible about any company you interview with and always have a question ready when the interviewer asks "Do you have any questions?" That is the time to ask about career development opportunities.

Ever wonder what hospitality recruiters are looking for when they are interviewing graduating hospitality seniors? A study by Linchi Kwok, Charlie Adams, and Margaret Price (Kwok, Adams, & Price, 2011), surveyed 22 selected hospitality recruiters from five industry segments to determine the influential factors in recruiters' hiring decisions. The most influential factors were:

- Leadership
- Relevant job experience
- Person and organization fit
- Person and job fit
- Personality

The Importance of Effective Recruiting

In order to evaluate effective recruiting, it's imperative you as a manager understand its importance. Determining which sources provide you the hardest working and most efficient employees are the ones you will want to use again and again. The reasoning is not because just to avoid people quitting or having to fire someone who is not doing well at their job tasks, but because your company as a whole can excel and better themselves if you select employees on the basis of your company's goals and values.

It is also important to determine the relationship between human resource practices and firm performance. This can be done by establishing scales of hospitality culture and climate in order to assess a candidate's fit to the organization (Dawson & Abbott, 2011). Ideally, candidate who score higher are more likely to be more hospitality service orientated and could foster the "spirit of hospitality" through the organization and thus, on to the guest. Hiring the right people will also lead to increased organizational commitment, consequently reducing turnover levels. This in turn will lead to higher service levels, increased guest satisfaction, and loyalty (Dawson & Abbott, 2011).

A night auditor may be doing their job well and meeting all their job tasks, but maybe there's a person that would go above and behind their assigned duties to make your hotel a better place. Do they get along with other employees? Are they willing to take on additional responsibilities if asked? Could they impress a hotel guest by conversing in passing in the hallway? All of these questions lead to the importance of effective recruiting. Ensuring you communicate the job description, the work ethic and goals your company seeks and personality traits you are looking for in an employee will lead you to your most effective source of recruiting.

One human resource director suggests that there is a lot to learn for new employees so when interviewing prospective employees, it makes sense to evaluate not only the skills and knowledge that they bring to the table, but their willingness and ability to acquire new skills and to assimilate new information (Bayless, 2011).

One of the most determining factors of recruiting a qualified candidate is understanding where to find that person. There is a group of talented people that will most likely fit what a manager is looking for, but where will you find that "talent"? The answer can be found in three different locations; online talent, internal talent, and external talent. Jim Sullivan, a restaurant writer and consultant says (Sullivan, 2011) "It's important to know what talent looks like and to teach hiring skills to all managers." Gregory Flynn and Joe Fugere of Apple American Group, a 269-unit franchisee of Applebee's have achieved a double digit sales growth per store by hiring people who have a natural talent to sell (Liddle, 2011). They find out who is likely to be a good sales person by inviting 20–30 candidates to a group interview to see who the outgoing people amongst strangers are, because that is just like being a restaurant server.

Legalize

Immigration and Customs Enforcement (ICE) questioned the validity of 450 Chipotle employees in Minnesota and required Chipotle to prove the employees' validity to work in the U.S. The employees were later dismissed. The ICE investigation was later expanded to include Chipotle restaurants in Virginia and Washington where another 40 employees were dismissed (Ruggless & Frumkin, 2011). Chipotle has since changed its hiring practices for verifying documentation. The company now uses the electronic E-Verify system to check worker eligibility and has shifted to an electronic I-9 form to eliminate errors (Ruggless & Frumkin, 2011). Pei Wei Asian Diner restaurants received visits from investigators who found that 121 of the company's 800 employees in Maricopa County Arizona appeared to have false documents, including false social security numbers (Jennings, 2011).

In another case, Minneapolis-based Nash Finch denies hiring gender bias. However, the U.S. Department of Labor's Office of Federal Contract Compliance Programs (OFCCP) filed an administrative complaint against the company challenging the hiring of order selectors. The OFCCP's claims arise not from any complaint of discrimination from anyone seeking a job with Nash Finch but as the result of OFPPC's investigation into hiring practices at the company. In view of other cases against Nash Finch they and OFCCP have agreed to lay their cases before an administrative tribunal to avoid the tremendous cost of potential litigation. Still, there will be thousands of dollars spent defending the complaint (Anonymous, 2010).

Key Points

In this chapter, you should feel comfortable and understand the steps necessary in the employee recruiting and selection process. We have discussed:

- The hiring process from start to finish.
- Forecast staffing needs and how to relay that message when hiring.
- Understanding a day in the life of an Area Recruiting Manager and how it helps him or her successful specifically with their company.
- The important techniques of recruiting and where to begin.
- Identify the key points in recognizing performance characteristics and the usefulness of references, testing, and measuring talent.
- Evaluate the standard methods for screening, interviewing, and selecting the best person for the job.
- The ability to follow the steps necessary for hiring new personnel by ensuring you take part in all proper steps of the hiring process to reduce and eliminate negligent hiring.

Key Terms

Applicant	Employment agencies	Outsourcing
Distribution channel	External recruiting	Recruitment

Discussion Questions

1. What are the strengths and weaknesses of internal and external recruiting?
2. Do you believe it's better to hire an external candidate with a more impressive resume or an internal candidate who's worked with your company for a year and has excelled, to fill a job position? Discuss and support your answer.
3. Which of the following questions are appropriate to ask applicants?
   a. What rate of pay are you looking for?
   b. Are you a healthy person?
   c. Do you have reasonable transportation?
   d. Do you have any kids?
   e. Are you married?
   f. In this job you will have to answer phones, do you know how to answer phones?
   g. Are you an American Citizen?
   h. You look like you may speak Spanish, can you?
   i. How did you find this job opening?
   j. Are you disabled?
   k. Do you own a home?
   l. Are you pregnant?

Ethical Dilemma

You have been applying to various hotels in your area and receive a call from the Breeze by the Bay hotel for an interview. You impress the manager and he extends a job offer in writing for you to start next Monday at the rate of $10.50 an hour. You gladly accept and are prepared to start work, when you receive yet another call from a different local hotel, The Knickerbocker, who had once turned down your application and resume, but they are offering 12.50 per hour. You're anxious to attend an interview but you just accepted a job offer from The Breeze by the Bay who seemed eager and appreciative to have you accept the offer. What do you do?

References

Anonymous. (2010, November/December). Nash Finch denies hiring gender bias. *Food Logistics*, 10, from https://www.foodlogistics.com/home/news/10269887/nash-finch-denies-gender-bias-in-hiring

Bayless, M. (2011, May). Hire people who like to learn. *Gourmet Retailer*, *32*(4), 24–25

Dawson, M., & Abbott, J. (2011, October–December). Hospitality culture and climate: A proposed model for retaining employees and creating competitive advantage. *International Journal of hospitality and Tourism Administration*, *12*(4), 289–304.

Jennings, L. (2011, March 21). Employers under fire. *Nation's Restaurant News*, 11–14.

Johnson, R. D., & Gueutal, H. G. (2011). Transforming HR through technology: The use of e-HR and HRIS in organizations. *SHRM Foundation's Effective Practice Guidelines Series*, 8–11.

Kwok, L., Adams, C., & Price, M. (2011, October–December). Factors influencing hospitality recruiters' hiring decisions in college recruiting. *Journal of Human Resources in Hospitality and Tourism*, *10*(4), 372–399.

Liddle, A. J. (2011, January 10). Operators roll out fresh hiring, talent retention ideas in 2011. *Nation's Restaurant News*, 34.

Moreland, Y. (2010). *Area employment manager Hyatt hotels*. Presentation to University of south Florida HR class, November 12, 2010.

Ruggless, R., & Frumkin, P. (2011, May 16). ICE expands Chipotle hiring practices probe. *Nation's Restaurant News*.

Sullivan, J. (2011, February 7). Seven strategies for success. *Nation's Restaurant News*, 30.

The Huffingto Post. (2013). *As hotels outsource jobs, workers lose hold on living wage*. Retrieved January 10, 2013, from http://www.huffingtonpost.com/2011/08/24/-hotel-labor-living-wage-outsourcing-indianapolis_n_934667.html

© Werner Heiber/Shutterstock.com

SELECTION

Introduction

A bar manager decides to interview two applicants for a bartender position that has recently become available. The bar manager will have the ultimate decision of which applicant to hire after the interviews have been conducted. As each interview begins, the manager has a list of questions he wants to ask each person and thinks to himself "how hard could it be to interview someone?" He conducts the first interview and gets answers to all his "necessary questions." As he begins the second interview, he realizes the second candidate is answering the questions completely different than the first candidate. What does this mean? How should he interpret each answer? Who is the most qualified?

Continuing the Hiring Process

In chapter 5, recruitment was discussed as a function of Human Resources (HR) that promoted available job opportunities in an organization, both internally and externally, with a goal of developing a pool of qualified applicants. Now, as the hiring process continues, we move on to the function of selection. The terms "recruitment" and "selection" are often used interchangeable; but, in reality, they are different functions and each require their own set of strategies to be successful. In many organizations, recruitment and selection may be undertaken by different managers—recruiters recruiting and hiring mangers doing the selection of the best applicant(s) to extend job offers to.

After studying this chapter, you should be able to:

1. Provide an overview of the employee selection process.
2. Identify the different types of interviews used in the hospitality industry.
3. List effective interview strategies with a specific focus on appropriate questions.
4. Describe different types of employment tests used in the hospitality industry.
5. Explain the concepts legal concerns associated with the selection process.
6. Describe the importance of the reference check and job offer process.

Learning Objective 1: Provide an overview of the employee selection process

> **Selection**: The process of identifying the best candidate who has applied for the job based on a pool of applicants.

Selection: The process of identifying the best candidate who has applied for the job. This involves knowing what characteristics are necessary to complete the job tasks and responsibilities and finding a way to accurately determine how well each candidate matches those characteristics. Impressions made in in-person interviews, conversations held on the phone, and even written tests can help measure match of an applicant to the opening. Selection also involves conducting background and reference checks, and, if you have found a qualified candidate, extending a job offer.

Why Careful Selection Is Important

In understanding the process and tasks necessary to hire a new employee, you may find yourself asking, "Why should I take so much time and effort to find an employee when there are plenty of people willing to work in the hospitality industry?"

In the hospitality industry, the guest is more than important, the guest *is* the business. Opening a door, offering directions to the best steakhouse in town or giving a recommendation for a fantastic bottle of red wine are small, seemingly optional efforts that are in reality what the hospitality industry is all about. Making sure you take the time to select the right employee for your company is crucial in many levels. Most jobs in restaurants and hotels involve face-to-face interaction, problem solving, and kindness. Guests go out to eat, go on vacation, or check into a hotel with the expectations to be taken care of. An employee may have qualifications, but a resume alone cannot project someone's kindness, ability to problem solve, or ease of interacting with guests on any given level. Thus, taking the time to carefully recruit, screen, evaluate, and select a new employee will have a positive and successful outcome for you and your company.

Selection and the Organization Fit

Resumes, interviews, and testing can reveal information you need to know about the capabilities of a candidate to perform a job; extracting information throughout the hiring process that will reveal a person's "fit" within your company is what defines a good employee from a great employee. In addition to looking at a candidate's professional qualifications (previous work experience, education), you may also look at how well they will work with existing employees and the culture of the organization. **Organization fit** is the qualities in an organization that define moral, teamwork, and personality.

> **Organization Fit:** The qualities in an organization that define moral, teamwork, and personality.

One of the best ways to hire and keep top talent is to create a company culture where the best employees want to work, a culture in which people are treated with respect and dignity at all times. Hospitality organizations such as Marriott, Hilton, Disney, Carnival Cruise Lines, Darden Restaurants, and Wyndham Hotel Group each have their own organization fit and concept of what characteristics in people will contribute most to their company. Staying flexible is also important. If any employee you hire proves to be a good fit for your company but not for the specific position filled, try moving them to another position that capitalizes on their strengths and experience. Employees who are a good fit organizationally can be hard to find.

Organization fit does not just include personality traits, but diversity as well. Marriot International's CEO Bill Marriott's annual letter to associates was distributed in 28 languages to its diverse workforce. In the United States, the majority of Marriott's associates are nonwhite Maintaining a diverse group of employees in the United States as well as internationally defines an important part of the selection and organization fit of Marriott Hotels.

Evaluating Candidates

Recruiting, screening, and making a job offer often seem like a step-by-step process that will flow so long you follow the guidelines. Unfortunately, those steps are not possible without effectively evaluating each and every candidate applying for a job. **Evaluating** means using what information has been provided, and the knowledge you have and analyzing what each piece of information means for each candidate.

> **Evaluating:** The information and the knowledge you have and analyzing what each piece of information means for each candidate.

Evaluating candidates is candidate-specific. Take for instance Jill and Jessica. Both applied for a supervisor position to oversee the front desk. Jill has had 4 years in the industry as a front desk agent at a 50-room lower-end hotel but has never received education or training in the field of hospitality management. Jessica has no previous experience working in the industry, but just graduated with her bachelor's degree

In order to evaluate your candidate, you must be able to identify what it is you need out of the position and, in turn, which questions need to be asked for each candidate in order to accomplish an evaluation

© jesterpop/Shutterstock.com

in hospitality and hotel management and a minor in business management. You see both are qualified, but on different terms; thus, you must evaluate each candidate based on the terms provided. Obviously, Jill will have a better grasp on how to run a front desk due to her previous experience, but Jessica has an extensive education in the hospitality field and professional training in business. Who is the better candidate?

In order to evaluate your candidate, you must be able to identify what it is you need for the position and, in turn, which questions need to be asked for each candidate in order to accomplish an evaluation. Because Jill has experience, you may focus your attention on situational questions. How would you do if your rooms were over-booked and had a party of five checking in? What would you do if someone was stuck inside an elevator? How would you handle an upset guest who was given a room next to the ice machine? Because Jessica has the benefit of education but the lack of work experience, her questions may be more structured. Why do you feel this is the job for you? What do you believe makes a good supervisor a great supervisor? How would you effectively manage your staff? While the specifics of a question may vary slightly candidate to candidate based on a situational experience, the general nature of a question should remain the same to ensure candidates can be compared fairly. As will be discussed later, this is what is called a semistructured interview.

Other ways of evaluating candidates include information given on applications or resumes. Age may give help you eliminate a candidate, that is, a 19-year-old applying for a bartender position in a state where you must be 21. Military status can help you identify the training, experience, and work ethic a military personal may have. Work history can show you how long an applicant stayed at a job, what fields of the industry, if any, they've worked in, and if they ever received any promotions or raises. Evaluating candidates' qualifications is not only necessary, but an indicator of previous work ethic, education, and indicators of an employee who may excel in your company.

The Screening Process

Screening Process: An initial review an applicant's application, resume, and any references or sources pertaining to their previous employment.

The **screening process** includes an initial review of an applicant's application, resume, and any references or sources pertaining to their previous employment. Every company's policy may differ; the screening process typically will include reference checks, background checks, and drug tests, but other screening techniques may further help you choose the best candidate for the position.

Using tips and standard practices to screen an applicant before the interview may greatly reduce your candidate pool. After applications and resumes have been reviewed, and a selection of candidates have been chosen for the next step, the best way to continue to screen is by conducting a brief interview with the candidate. This interview may be done over the phone or even in person. The ultimate goal is to continue to screen while also getting to know the candidate and their abilities for the job. This is often done in the early stage, so depending on your company's policy; the screening interview may be conducted by a HR manager or the department manager.

An initial screening interview should not only review the applicants' previous work history, but interest in the job, how they found the job, what education or training have they received, availability to work, and also questions that you must ask that formed based on your initial screening. Questions that could have formed on your first screening of the applicant through their resume or application could include

- You answered "yes" to being convicted of a misdemeanor. Can you elaborate on this?
- I see you have a year break in work history, could you explain?
- You mentioned in your application you were terminated from your last job. Could you tell me why?

It is best to look for immediate indicators when reviewing an application or resume. The following are recommendations to look for that may help you in the screening process:

- Did the applicant follow directions when filling out the application?
- Did the application and/or resume have correct punctuation and grammar?
- Did the applicant ever have long periods of rest or breaks in their work history?
- If applicable, is the applicant's schooling or college degree relevant to the job position?
- What skills does the applicant possess that will assist them in the job?
- Did the applicant provide contact information for previous employers and references?

Questions during the screening interview will provide clarification and also help you as the interviewer to get to know some of the personality traits of the candidate and develop a rating (see **figure 6.1**). Using screening techniques can accurately reduce and refine your applicant pool and assist in the final selection.

Company Name:			
Position:			
Rate each candidate on the below skills on a scale of 1–10 with 1 being the lowest and 10 being the highest.			
Job Skills	**Candidate 1**	**Candidate 2**	**Candidate 3**
Verbal communication			
Job experience			
Service skill			
Education			
Reliability			
Professionalism			
Friendliness			
Team experience			
Career goals			
Work ethic			
Understanding of company			
Total score			

Figure 6.1 Sample Applicant Screening Form

Learning Objective 2: Identify the different types of interviews used in the hospitality industry

Interviewing for Selection

> **Interview**: A formal procedure designed to solicit information from a candidates oral responses to oral questions.

A more in-depth interview is a formal procedure designed to solicit information from a candidate's oral responses to oral questions (Dessler, 2009). The concept seems simple and concise, but in actuality, the end result may be more difficult to achieve than you would expect. A selection interview aims to forecast the future job performance of a candidate based on the responses to questions posed by an interviewer.

Interviews are one of the most informative, yet challenging, steps of the hiring process. These challenges arise for different reasons in different scenarios and amongst different people. The challenge lies in your confidence to evaluate a person based on a line of questioning. How do you know the responses to the questions you asked truly showed the person's capabilities of doing the job? Did the candidate answer truthfully, and how would I even know if they were lying? Was the interviewee too nervous to show their personality and ability to interact with people? Each individual interviewer and even companies have their own strategies and procedures when interviewing someone to fill a position. An interview doesn't need to be difficult, and the content of this chapter should provide some insight into how to enhance your interview skills.

Interviews are one of the most informative, yet challenging, steps of the hiring process

© jesterpop/Shutterstock.com

Effective Interviews

As a best practice to ensure they are getting the most qualified candidate, most hospitality organizations use interviews in employment decision-making. But, how effective is their interviewing process? By structuring an interview and making sure that the characteristics to be evaluated are clearly identified and that all interviewers ask the same question of all candidates, that the interviewers are trained, and that interviewee performance is evaluated using well-developed rating scales leads to a more effective interview (SIOP, 2013). The following steps will help create an effective interview (SIOP, 2013):

1. Identify the candidate characteristics that should be assessed during the interview: Questions to consider include: Is this a knowledge, skill, or characteristic that is important to success on the job or some outcome of interest (e.g., low turnover)? Is the interview the best way to assess this important knowledge, skill, or ability? How much overlap would there be between the interview and other tests

used in the decision-making process? Interview questions should only relate specifically to the job the applicant is interviewing for.

2. *Develop interview questions*: Questions need to be created that relate to the knowledge, skills, and abilities and used with all candidates for a particular position.

3. *Plan likely "probes" and follow-up questions*: If interviewers are not allowed to ask follow-up or probing questions, often key information is not elicited. Thus, the interview should not only be designed to give interviewers the freedom to ask follow-up questions but also to guide them in the types of follow-up questions that would be most appropriate for the given interview structure. A list of possible probes can accompany the list of interview questions, and/or training in effective probing be provided to interviewers.

4. *Evaluate responses using anchored scales*: A systematic evaluation of individual's responses to interview questions is helpful for several reasons. It allows for a comparison across candidates who are often interviewed by different individuals or even by the same individual over a wide time span. It requires the interviewer to evaluate the candidate on the job-relevant characteristics identified as important, not any idiosyncratic set of criteria. Standardization in rating scales provides documentation that all candidates will be evaluated on the same basis.

5. *Train interviewers*: Despite the beliefs of many individuals that they are good judges of others, interviewer training has been demonstrated to be effective in improving the judgments of interviewers, in ensuring that all candidates are treated similarly, and in calibrating interviewers with one another.

6. *Understanding legal parameters*: Using business-related job requirements as the foundation for creating interview questions usually means the interviewer will be in compliance with the law. In deciding which questions to ask in an interview, understanding the legal requirements for selection will help the interviewer avoid asking inappropriate questions. For example, as discussed in chapter 3, in the United States, laws such as Title VII of the Civil Rights Act (1964), the Americans with Disabilities Act of 1990, and the Age Discrimination in Employment Act of 1967 outline several areas of concern with regard to employment discrimination. These characteristics include race, color, gender, religion, national origin, age (over 40), and disabilities. Generally, questions directly about these characteristics will be problematic, but questions that ask about a job requirement may relate to a characteristic and be acceptable. For example, one cannot ask "Are you a member of a religion that holds services on Saturday?" but one can ask "This job requires work on the weekends. Can you work Saturdays and Sundays?"

7. *Use the interview to provide a realistic job preview*: Interviews are not just opportunities to learn more about candidates; they are also opportunities for HR professionals and managers to help candidates learn more about the job. When candidates have a realistic understanding of their job, their expectations are more likely to be met. When a job

The processes most employers use to find and select the best talent possible for an open position include the following (SHRM, 2012):

- Posting open positions on career sites and social media outlets to solicit resumes and employment applications.

- Prescreening to eliminate candidates who do not meet the basic requirements of the position.

- Use of a preliminary assessment to screen out those who lack the desired level of skills and competencies for the job.

- In-depth assessment through interviews and job simulations to select candidates with the highest potential for job success.

- Verification of the candidate's stated employment record and qualifications.

fails to live up to an individual's expectations, he or she is more likely to be dissatisfied and ultimately leave the position.

8. *Use the interview as a selling opportunity*: To increase the chance of hiring a good candidate, use the interview experience to sell the job and the company. Prior to the interview, talk to employees in the company and find out what they like best about the organization. Then, when talking with candidates about what they are looking for in a work experience, relay how the job and the organization can meet their needs. To make the most of this selling opportunity, think about the interview experience from the candidate's perspective. A candidate's experience in the interview process affects his/her opinions about the organization. Being treated professionally and talking with a well-prepared interviewer creates a positive impression and experience.

Types of Interviews

Every organization interviews differently based on existing policy, procedures, and norms

© Production Perig/Shutterstock.com

> **Structured Interviews**: A structured form of interview used to compare one job candidate to another. This is usually practiced when a company wants to analyze and compare candidates based on identical factors.

Every organization interview's differently based on existing policy, procedures, and norms. This is ok. Additionally, based on an individual job, different jobs may warrant different types of interviews. That is also ok. There are four primary types of interviews: structured, unstructured, semistructured, and patterned. Whatever method you choose, just remember that you should be consistent. For example, if you use a structured interview for a front desk candidate, you should also use a structured interview for other front desk candidates.

Structured Interviews: These are a structured form of interviews used to compare one job candidate to another. This is usually practiced when a company wants to analyze and compare candidates based on identical factors. While interviewing, if the employer follows a set list of questions for each candidate, the focus of the interview is going to be on the capabilities for the position that the candidate would fill and not necessarily their personality or ability to adapt to situations. This makes the selection process easier for the employer due in part to the fact that the line of questioning and the answers the candidate gives cannot be misinterpreted for anything else other than the answer that would be correct for that particular position. For instance, if you are interviewing candidates for a management position; you as the interviewer will select and ask questions based on the requirements for management. By engaging in structured interviews, an employer is able to gain the abilities and qualifications of a candidate rather than focus on their personality traits or other characteristics left to interpretation.

> **Unstructured Interviews**: Interviews in which questions could be altered based on the responses of the candidate being interviewed.

Unstructured Interviews: Structured interviews seem the most logical to select a candidate, however, unstructured interviews can often reveal the most information about an individual. *Unstructured interviews* are interviews in which questions could be altered based on the responses of the candidate being interviewed. This does not mean the employer conducting the interview shall begin unprepared and questionless; it more so allows for an experienced interviewer to stray from their typical "structured" questions to find out the true personality and characteristics of a candidate. This type of interview is not only often seen as casual or informal, but can also make the interviewee feel more at ease, as the questions are not formatted or intimidating. The only down fall with unstructured interviews is they may not be reliable. If a male HR director is interviewing a male, recent college graduate, and through unstructured questions finds they both played basketball at the same university only 10 years apart, the interview could be skewed. Not because they both have common ground, but because a positive factor in the interview that does not pertain to the job at hand could alter the decision of the director. It is vital that any employer choosing to use unstructured interviews understands the possibility that answers to questions may not be as reliable as other forms of interviewing.

Structured interviews seem the most logical to select a candidate, however, unstructured interviews can often reveal the most information about an individual

© Anton Gvozdikov/Shutterstock.com

Structured and nonstructured interviewers each have pros and cons. In structured interviews, all interviewers generally ask all applicants the same questions. Partly because of this, these interviews tend to be more reliable and valid (Dessler, 2013). Structured interviews can also help less talented interviewers conduct better interviews. However, structured interviews don't always provide enough opportunity to pursue points of interest as they develop (Dessler, 2013). In reality, it is not structured versus unstructured but a matter of the degree most interviews are somewhere between structured and nonstructured known as a semistructured interview.

Semistructured interviews: These are the combination of structured questions and unstructured questions that are usually practiced at the discretion of the employer. An interviewer may start out by asking unstructured and casual question and interact with the candidate to make them feel at ease, while slowing working in structured questions that will ultimately decide whether the candidate is worthy of the job. These interviews can also be used in reverse; an interviewer may begin asking structured questions from the start to first determine their qualifications and then, after determining their status, may continue with unstructured questions that will reveal the personality and traits of the candidate. Semistructured interviews can be the most beneficial type of interview for both parties.

> **Semistructured Interviews:** The combination of structured questions and unstructured questions that are usually practiced at the discretion of the employer.

Patterned Interviews: A patterned interview is similar to that of a structured interview. A *patterned interview* is a series of questions prepared in advance that follow a definitive pattern. This may take place in a pattern of sequence,

> **Patterned Interview:** A series of questions prepared in advance that follow a definitive pattern.

steps for a given position or even emotion. This type of interview may help to first, eliminate and screen any candidates not capable of the job requirements, and secondly to assess if a job offer should be made to the interviewee based on their answers. These questions may be already laid out for each job position, or may be questions that are general to any position within a company.

Learning Objective 3: List effective interview strategies with a specific focus on appropriate questions

Interview Questions

Questions asked in interviews are some of the most crucial indicators regarding a candidate's knowledge for a job. Over the years, interview questions have developed into more than just "why do you think you'd be good for this job?" or "what's your best quality?" You can gain quality information from a question and not only get a question answered that pertains to the job, but analyze the character of that person based on the way they answer.

The Society for HR Management offers a lot of excellent practical advice including the following regarding interview questions: The guiding principle behind any question asked of an applicant (whether in an interview or on the employer's application form) should be: Can the employer demonstrate a job-related necessity for asking the question? The Equal Employment Opportunity Commission (EEOC) examines the intent behind the question, as well as how the information is used, to determine whether any discrimination has occurred. Therefore, employers should ask applicants only *job-related questions*. Before asking the question, the interviewer should determine whether this information is necessary to judge the applicant's qualifications, level of skills, and overall competence for the position (SHRM, 2013b). When a question is focused on the job, it is called valid. *Validity* in interview question design protect an interviewer from potential discrimination cases that may arise if an interviewee feels they were evaluated based on something unrelated to the job (marital status, sexual orientation).

Examples of common interview questions are displayed in **Figure 6.2**.

> **Here are some prepared questions that could be asked of all candidates in a telephone interview (SHRM, 2013a).**
>
> Is the salary range we have set for this position within your acceptable range?
> Why are you currently searching for a new position?
> What are the top three duties in the job you now have or in your most recent job?
> What are some typical decisions that you make and how do you make them?
> Give me some examples.
> What do you think you would do for this organization that someone else wouldn't?
> Where do you see yourself in 5 years?
> Describe for me your ideal company.

Here are some general interview questions (SHRM, 2013a).

Could you share with us a recent accomplishment of which you are most proud?

What would you have liked to do more of in your last position? What held you back?

Tell us a bit about your work background, and then give us a description of how you think it relates to our current opening.

What are your qualifications in your area of expertise, that is, what skills do you have that make you the best candidate for this position? Include any special training you have had (on-the-job, college, continuing education, seminars, reading) and related work experience.

Why have you applied for this position?

What skill set do you think you would bring to this position?

Tell me about your present or last job. Why did you choose it? Why did you/do you want to leave?

What was your primary contribution/achievement or biggest challenge?

What are your short-term and long-term goals?

In what areas would you like to develop further? What are your plans to do that?

What are some positive aspects of your last employment/employer? What are some negative aspects?

What do you think about SOPs (Standard Operating Procedures)?

What are your career path interests?

What do you know about our company?

Why should we hire YOU?

If the position required it, would you be willing to travel?

If the position required it, would you be willing to relocate?

If you were offered this position, when would you be available to start?

After learning about this opportunity, what made you take the next step and apply for the job?

If you are the successful applicant, how would you expect to be different after a year in this position?

Now that you have learned about our company and the position you are applying for, what hesitation or reluctance would you have in accepting this job if we offer it to you?

Tell me anything else you would like us to know about you that will aid us in making our decision.

What questions would you like to ask me?

Here are some hospitality industry-specific questions (SHRM, 2013a):

How would you define guest satisfaction?

Describe a time when someone failed to provide satisfactory service to you. How could that person improve his or her performance in that particular situation?

Give an example of one thing that is important in building repeat-customer business.

What types of behaviors do you find most annoying or frustrating in a guest? How do you handle those behaviors?

What specific process do you go through when a guest is dissatisfied?

Describe a time when you had to deal with a difficult guest-relations problem.

Tell me about a time when you needed to work as part of a team to satisfy a guest.

"Yes" is the word guests like to hear. However, if you had to say "no," how would you do it?

How well do you communicate with others? What communication techniques do you use?

How do you think our guests would describe you and your work?

Figure 6.2 Interview questions

Interviews not only lead you to information that cannot be gained from an application or resume, but also give you the opportunity to assess the reliability, friendliness, and appearance of a prospective new employee

© indukas/Shutterstock.com

Hotels, restaurants, convention centers, and other types of companies in the hospitality industry often require specific skills. Do you know how to pour wine properly? Can you carry 60 pounds of luggage? Do you know how to speak to hotel guests in passing? Your job as a manger during an interview is to make sure that you retrieve all remaining information pertinent to a job through questioning.

Interview questions do not need to be intimidating or even difficult to answer, but should give you as a manager a solid indication of the abilities a person has to perform a job.

Questions You Can't Ask

One of the most important tasks of an interview is understanding what you as the interviewer may or may not ask an interviewee. In earlier years, when job discrimination was neither of concern nor illegal, companies got away with asking extremely personal and sensitive questions to someone interviewing for a job. In fact, formal interviews weren't so "formal" until the United States, state and local governments passed many laws to regulate discrimination in hiring. Not only do these laws protect particular groups or classes of people, but determine what you cannot ask a candidate in an interview. As discussed in earlier chapters, these laws are called Equal Employment Opportunity (EEO) laws.

> Questions you cannot ask:
> How old are you?
> Where were you born?
> Are you married?
> Do you have a car?
> What is your sexual orientation?
> Do you have children?

Figure 6.3   Interview questions that may lead to discrimination charges

Any use of discriminatory questions (see **Figure 6.3**) during an interview can put you and your company into a legal jeopardy. The EEOC strictly enforces all laws and ensure complaints of discrimination are handled efficiently and thoroughly.

Importance of Interviews

You've been sifting through online resumes for a Director of Sales position for three full days, have found your top three candidates, and based on brief phone interviews and their completed application forms, only one of the three is really qualified for the position. So, is it okay to just skip the in-person interview? Your mind is already set so why bother with the waste of time? The answer is no, you should never turn away an in-person interview based on a mindset.

Interviews not only lead you to information that cannot be gained from an application or resume, but also give you the opportunity to assess the reliability, friendliness, and appearance of a prospective new employee. If you were to extend a job offer to that candidate who you thought would be perfect for the Director of Sales position, but the day he showed up for orientation was dressed in slacks that were not tailored, white sports socks, worn dress shoes, a shirt with no tie, an unshaven face, and a haircut that was less than professional, you would be to blame. You couldn't retract your job offer because you choose not to interview the candidate, all you would be left to do is explain your company's dress code and expectations and hope the new director would abide.

A clean appearance in the hospitality industry is vital to the success of any company. A valet attendant, a room service staff member, and a restaurant hostess are all seen by guests at some point in time. Suits and ties may not be necessary, but clean uniforms, appropriate hair styles, and a cared-for look are impressions gained guests and customers no matter the staff's position. One of the only ways to gage someone's level of care in their appearance in a professional setting is an in-person interview.

Phone interviews and aptitude tests online have been increasingly popular forms of narrowing down candidates. Do not be mistaken; both forms are excellent tools in the narrowing process, but neither should be used alone to determine the selection for a job opening. Phone interviews can help you gain answers to important questions, learn the ability for a candidate to respond promptly to a question or situation and also give you a feel for their personality. It's no doubt a helpful tool, but doesn't always allow you to gain the true personality of a person.

With all of the amazing tools and technologies in today's world, the in-person interview has been one of the tools that has withheld the test of time. It not only gives a company a clarified look at a potential employee, but gives a potential employee a look into the company and the goals and expectations your organization will have.

Introducing HR Director Staci Simpson at the St. Louis Union Station Hotel-A Doubletree by Hilton

Hi, I am Staci Simpson, Director of Human Resources at the St. Louis Union Station Hotel-A Doubletree by Hilton. I am one of those weird stories, in that I have stayed at the same hotel property for 23 years. The not-so-weird thing is that within those 23 years, I have worked for three different large name hotel companies.

I started out just like you, a student, hoping to get a "hotel manager" job when I graduated. Well, when I did interview for a manager position, I quickly decided I needed to learn from the ground up before taking on a leader role. I began my hotel career as a front desk agent. It didn't take long, and as always in the hotel business, it is all about timing . . . when someone above you leaves, you had better hope you have had enough training to step into that role. My hotel path took me from the front desk to Accounting before taking me to my ultimate home in HR. Not a lot of people that study hospitality management think about a career in HR. But I soon learned that no matter what position you become as a leader, you will always be "part HR manager".

All leaders soon learn that the large part of their job is HR related, and that is especially evident when they need to hire someone. Hotel turnover usually runs between 40% and 60% per year, and if you have 25 associates in your department, that means you will be hiring 10 or more associates per year. Hiring these people is not a one-person job, HR depends on the leaders of each department to know the proper policies and procedures on interviewing. You may be saying,

(Continued)

"Isn't it HR job to do all the hiring?" Well, yes and no. We assist with the process. The process looks like so:

1. Job requisition is created by the department head.
2. HR posts the job.
3. Applicants apply.
4. HR inputs the application information on affirmative action log.
5. HR reviews the application and screens for:
   - basic skills needed for the position,
   - reliability/stability in past jobs,
   - compatibility/customer service, and
   - availability.

During the HR screening process, we look over the applications and/or resume to see if they fit the qualifications from the requisition. If they meet the qualifications on paper we then call them to come in and meet with the HR manager. This is a way for us to see if they show up on time, how they present themselves, and most of all have a positive attitude and a SMILE! If either of these very important things are lacking, they will not make it to the next interview. If they DO have these characteristics they will be forwarded on to the department manager to ask more detailed questions about the specific position they applied.

This is the time that we depend on the department managers to "become the HR Manager" by asking the right interview questions. If the manager or supervisor asks the wrong questions, they end up sitting in front of a judge regarding an unfair hiring practice or discrimination. All we ask managers or supervisors to do is stick to pertinent questions regarding the position and what skills would be needed to do that job. It is normal to want to make the candidate feel comfortable by asking something personal, but the interview is not about making someone feel comfortable, it is about if the person can do the job. The interview also shows the manager or supervisor if the person will work with the others in the department.

Interviewing may scare some managers because they may feel that they will ask the wrong questions and end up in trouble. If that is the case, you may try what we did at our hotel. The HR department held a HR standard operating procedures training for managers and supervisors. This class trained on employee coaching and counseling, how to correctly evaluate an employee, and most importantly, how to correctly interview a candidate. Many managers really appreciated the suggestions and some even preferred to use a set of standard questions that they can tweak to meet their department needs. This helps them to keep each of their interviews someone conforming. These standard questions also made them feel more at ease during the interview then when they became more comfortable, they would find their own style and questions.

It does not matter the size of the establishment, interviewing is one of the most important skills that any manager or supervisor can possess. Practice does make it easier, but each person needs to find the questions and techniques that work best for them and their position that is open. This means that it may take a few 'bad hires" before finding the right interviewing techniques, but it will be worth it to match the right person for the right position.

Contributed by Staci Simpson. © Kendall Hunt Publishing Company

Interviewing Tips

A manager in the hospitality field may be responsible for interviewing candidates for jobs they will oversee. It is sometimes more effective for the manager to interview a candidate because the level of knowledge and skills needed for the job will be better asked by an individual actually working in that department.

If a HR director of a large company is responsible for hiring two banquet servers for their convention center events, is it more effective for the more experienced "interviewer" to conduct the interview, or the manager who will actually be responsible for managing the employee? Managers better understand the job duties and more commonly understand what types of personalities and attitudes will or will not work with the rest of the company. Even though the HR director may be more knowledgeable in conducting an interview, a manager should have input and hopefully the final say in the hiring of a candidate.

HR Technology: Computerizing Interviews

Technology has revolutionized how organizations hire people, from simplifying the posting of available positions, to building large candidate pools online, to electronic scanning of resumes, to automated screening, testing, and applicant management. The interview, meanwhile, has remained much the same people sitting across a desk or conference table talking to one another.

As previously mentioned, the modernization and technology capabilities during the hiring process have become outstanding tools for any HR manager. Online testing, online applications, and online interviews have allowed time saving and efficient hiring tools. One of the latest and most innovative technologies for HR departments is the ability to conduct online interviews.

Say you are a HR director for large resort hotel in Colorado, and your resort is almost constantly hiring for new positions, and always looking to diversify your employee selection. You need to hire three new front desk agents. You've selected resumes, conducted phone interviews, completed reference checks, and all you have left to do is an in-person interview. The problem lies; the applicants are in different states and one even lives in Puerto Rico. You do not have the time or funds to fly each person into your resort simply for an in-person interview, so you're left with two options. You can bypass the in-person interview and hire each agent based on the information you already have, or take part in an online interview. Knowing that you take pride in meeting a potential employee face-to-face before extending a job offer, you opt for the online interview. The ability to web chat and see someone's face not only assures you're selecting a presentable employee, but gives you an opportunity to meet the person face-to-face before they pick up and move their lives from one state to another for a job.

Online interviews can work well for both parties. The employer saves time and money and it gives employees that are not local a better chance at a job, as well as a sense of relief when it comes to the "final" interview. Websites such as Skype or greenjobinterview.com and interviews.liveinterviewsonline.com give any manager the ability to sign up for online interviewing sessions. By utilizing secure, browser-based technology and support services, organizations and candidates interact face-to-face while minimizing costs, maximizing time, and reducing environmental impact because no travel is required.

Learning Objective 4: Describe different types of employment tests used in the hospitality industry

Employment Testing

Some companies will even make certain testing mandatory and an applicant must pass with a certain percentage or grade to be eligible for the job offer

© fizkes/Shutterstock.com

In order to further understand a candidate's abilities for a job, many employers gain additional useful information from testing. Some companies will even make certain testing mandatory and an applicant must pass with a certain percentage or grade to be eligible for the job offer. As mentioned before, it is important to pay close attention to questions or actions that could be against the law. If a multiple choice or fill in the blank paper test has verbiage that implies discrimination against a protected class, you and your company could be held liable. To avoid such legal incidents, ensure any type of testing you choose is based only on job-related tasks.

There has been an increase in employment testing due in part to post 9–11 security concerns as well as concerns about workplace violence, safety, and liability. In addition, the large-scale adoption of online job applications has motivated employers to seek efficient ways to screen large numbers of online applicants in a nonsubjective way. As a result of increased testing, the number of discrimination charges raising issues of employment testing, and exclusions based on criminal background checks, credit reports, and other selection procedures, is on the increase (EEOC, 2013).

There are legal trends that strongly support the use of preemployment testing. Employers have been forced to defend an ever increasing number of negligent hiring lawsuits that seek redress for crimes committed by their own employees. Those crimes range from rape of a customer by a pizza delivery driver and the rape of a Carnival crew member by another to assaults, homicides, and theft against coworkers and customers alike (Saterfiel and Associates, 2013). The lawsuits contend that the employer negligently placed an applicant with dangerous propensities, which should have been easily discovered by reasonably diligent investigation, into an employment situation where it was foreseeable that the subject employee posed a threat of injury to others (Saterfiel and Associates, 2013). At lease, preemployment testing provides employers with some defense with evidence of a reasonable and prudent investigation of the applicant's fitness (Saterfiel and Associates, 2013).

There are many different types of tests and selection procedures, including cognitive tests, personality tests, medical examinations, credit checks, and criminal background checks. The use of these tests can be a very effective means of determining which applicants are the most qualified for a particular job (EEOC, 2013). However, intentional uses of tests to discriminate based on race, color, religion, age, marital status, national origin, or disability are forbidden by law. Use of tests and other selection procedures can also violate the federal antidiscrimination laws if they disproportionately exclude people in a particular group by race, sex, or another covered basis, unless the employer can justify the test or procedure under the law (EEOC, 2013).

Types of Employment Tests

Examples of employment tests, many of which can be administered online, include the following (EEOC, 2013):

- Cognitive tests assess reasoning, memory, perceptual speed and accuracy, and skills in arithmetic and reading comprehension, as well as knowledge of a particular function or job.
- Physical ability tests measure the physical ability to perform a particular task or the strength of muscle groups as well as strength and stamina in general.
- Sample job tasks (e.g., performance tests, simulations, work samples, and realistic job previews) assess performance and aptitude on particular tasks.
- Medical inquiries and physical examinations, including psychological tests, assess physical or mental health.
- Personality tests and integrity tests assess the degree to which a person has certain traits or dispositions (e.g., dependability, cooperativeness, and safety) or aim to predict the likelihood that a person will engage in certain conduct (e.g., theft and absenteeism).
- Criminal background checks provide information on arrest and conviction history.
- Credit checks provide information on credit and financial history.
- English proficiency tests determine English fluency.

Drug and alcohol screening and physical medical tests are also common practices contingent upon job offers. As long as a company makes it clear that a job offer will be given based on the ability to pass a medical test, it would be considered appropriate. No matter what the type of testing may be, it's always best to have your questions or concerns answered by your or your company's attorney when in doubt of the repercussions a test may have.

Employment testing may include situational testing, job replica tests, problem analysis, task direction tests, and various medical tests. Remember, the test must be relevant to the job.

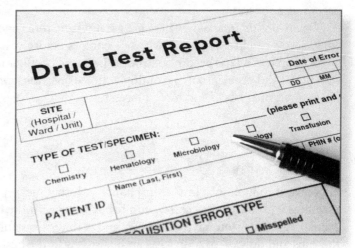

Drug and alcohol screening and physical medical tests are also common practices contingent upon job offers

© one photo/Shutterstock.com

Carla Delgado has just applied for the Events Coordinator position at one of Disney World's resort hotels. As a manager, you typically use situational testing and problem analysis to determine candidate's qualifications, but want to have different tests prepared in case you should need some additional options. Take for example:

Situational testing: In situational testing, the applicant would take on a role of the manager or of a service employee and acts out a situation as given to them. For the test, you would have Carla act out the position of the Events Coordinator and you would act as a bride who has just booked her wedding at the hotel's largest ball room. The bride would be complaining to Carla that she wants five more tables added to the ballroom and she was told it could not happen. Carla would need to find a solution in this situation to resolve the issue at hand.

It is important that any employer shares all the "ups and downs" of a job to a candidate

© fizkes/Shutterstock.com

Job replica tests: Replica tests are narrowed to the specific job tasks and duties of the job opening. In this example, you may have Carla draw out a sample event, arrange a flower display or place table settings for an event.

Problem analysis: The applicant will analyze information that has various possible solutions to a problem as it relates to that particular job. An applicant would choose what they think is the best course of action for that problem and explain why. In this example, you would give Carla a problem such as an event room being double booked, and give her three different possible solutions. She would have to choose which she thought was the best suited and explain why.

Task direction tests: The applicant would be given a task that needs prompt attention, organization, and delegating. For our example, Carla could be given a Bat mitzvah party for 125 people that needed to be coordinated for next Saturday. She would have to prove she could take proper direction to ensure the party was a success.

Behavior and interview: These are great testing tools once you have an applicant in front of you, but what if you need to narrow down your choices before you have someone sitting face-to-face? Online application testing has become one of the best tools to filter underqualified applicants. Having a series of situational and problem solving multiple choice questions for a particular job will undoubtedly help your job as a recruiter easier and more successful.

Truth in Hiring

Let's face it: not all jobs in the hospitality industry mean pressed pants and blazers, conference room meetings with bagels and coffee, and happy hour with the boss. Many jobs in the hotel and restaurant industry are labor intensive, strenuous, and at times stressful. It is important that any employer shares all the "ups and downs" of a job to a candidate. It is in the best interest of the employer and the candidate; the truth in hiring can indirectly help or hurt your company.

> **Truth in hiring**: This is revealing the details of a job and its requirements; whether they are positive or negative.

Truth in hiring is revealing the details of a job and its requirements; whether they are positive or negative. Overtime hours, physical labors, pay rates, uniforms, benefits, and other job-related issues are all relevant when hiring a new employee.

If you hire Tim for the dishwasher position, but neglect to inform him that he often has to stay past closing time and that he is only tipped out by the servers if they make over a certain percentage on any given night, you could not only quickly loose an employee, but lose guests and respect for your restaurant. It is the fourth night in of Tim's job and it's the fourth night he has worked 2 hours after closing. He was not aware he would be working overtime, or that he would be stuck in the kitchen by himself 2 hours after closing. On Tim's fifth day of employment, a bus boy unloads his dishes and dirty water splashes in Tim's face. With rush hour approaching and a backload of dishes to be washed, Tim throws his apron in the water, storms into the dining room where customers are eating, yells "I quit this filthy no-good place!" to his manager behind the bar and storms out. Not only are you left with no dishwasher, you have just made a poor impression in front of guests and the rest of the staff. These impressions made would fall on you due in part to the fact that you were not truthful when you hired Tim.

For any dishwasher, obviously busier nights will mean overtime hours, food and water may often splash on your clothes and the overall job of a

In today's litigious society, it is critical to avoid lawsuits and EEO scrutiny by planning and organizing all interviews and training all interviewers

© fizkes/Shutterstock.com

dishwasher is not that of glorious. If you would have respectfully informed Tim of the both the good and bad that come with the job, you would not have guests wondering what kind of operation is being ran. Guests and staff talk to family, friends, and coworkers a regular basis; rumors will most likely spread from guests, employees, and even Tim himself in this situation. The best, most safe practice is keeping all information open and honest with all employees during the hiring process to avoid such situations.

Learning Objective 5: Explain the concepts legal concerns associated with the selection process

Legal Concerns with Interviewing

There are two main areas of major legal concern with interviewing. Saying or doing the wrong thing during an interview and employing someone as a result of a flawed interview and selection process. In today's litigious society, it is critical to avoid lawsuits and EEO scrutiny by planning and organizing all interviews and training all interviewers. Asking the same questions of all candidates and having a diverse representation on the interview team will help diminish the chances of problems.

The second major legal concern is negligent hiring. **Negligent hiring** is a claim made by an injured party against an employer based on the theory that the employer knew or should have known about the employee's background which, if known, indicates a dangerous or untrustworthy character. Preemployment background checks, employee drug testing, and employment physical exams are some

Negligent Hiring: A claim made by an injured party against an employer based on the theory that the employer knew or should have known about the employee's background which, if known, indicates a dangerous or untrustworthy character.

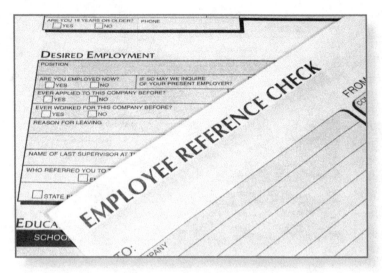

Reference checks can help narrow down your selection if two candidates are equally qualified and can also help to avoid legalities in relation to negligent hiring

© Ryan R Fox/Shutterstock.com

of the ways negligent hiring claims can be avoided (US LEGAL, 2013). Your employer could be sued for negligent hiring, so it is best to use practices such as multilevel criminal record searches and any other available in depth criminal searches before extending a job offer.

As an employee of your company, you have a duty to act appropriately and in the best interests of your company and coworkers. Checking backgrounds for records, lengthy gaps in employment, or frequent change of addresses could be signs to further investigate an applicant's character. It's also a good practice to follow any initial "bad" or "off" instincts you or your fellow employees should have with a new hire. Looking for strange behaviors or warning signs from a new hire is imperative to ensuring the safeguard of yourself, your company, and your team.

Learning Objective 6: Describe the importance of the reference check and job offer process

Reference Checks

Reference Check: A way to verify information provided by an applicant.

Throughout this chapter we have mentioned reference checks, but what is a reference check and why is it so important? A reference check is a way to verify information provided by an applicant. Reference checks can help narrow down your selection if two candidates are equally qualified and can also help to avoid legalities in relation to negligent hiring. Specific job-related questions should be asked during a reference check, and can be done so by phone, faxing, or emailing a form to a previous employer to help verify information for an applicant.

Reference checks are typically sent to the applicant's previous employee supervisor. In recent years, it has become somewhat difficult to complete a reference check through a supervisor alone. Many corporations have installed policies which prohibit direct supervisors to provide information beyond start and end dates and job title of a previous employee. These particular companies require that additional requests including salary, how they worked among others, why they are no longer employed with the company, and additional job-related questions be answered by HR personnel at the corporate level. This can make your job as a manager difficult and time consuming, but keep in mind that reference checks are often times the most reliable source for an applicant's past work experience and performance.

Telephone Reference Check Form

All sections should be completed to be considered a valid reference. Indicate N/A if the question is not applicable.

DO NOT CONDUCT A CHECK WITHOUT A COMPLETED APPLICATION FORM

Applicant Name:_____

Date of Reference Check:_____

Person Checking Reference:_____

Reference Name:_____

Reference Organization:_____

Relationship to Applicant: Supervisor Peer Other (Specify)_____

Dates of Employment: From _____To_____

Salary:_____

Position(s) Held:

Reason for Separation:　☐ Voluntary　☐ Involuntary

Give Explanation:

_____

_____

Additional Questions:

Were there any disciplinary actions? Please explain:

Were there any performance issues? Please explain:

What are the candidate's strong points?

What are the candidate's weak points?

If given the opportunity, would you reemploy this individual?　☐ Yes　☐ No

Any additional comments?

Some tips from HR professionals are (USC Division of Human Resources Employment Office, 2013): Have you got a release form signed by the applicant allowing for you to conduct reference checks?

1. You should state during the interview with a job applicant that references will be checked. Also, don't just rely on letters of reference or personal references provided by the job applicant.

2. A telephone reference check takes less time than a written reference check and usually more information is gained. Forms really uncover negative information. Employers hesitate to put into writing what they may say in conversation.

3. The hiring supervisor should be the one to make the call because she or he is most familiar with the information received by the applicant and the responsibilities of the job. Supervisors should be prepared with a written list of questions to ask.

4. To gain as much information as possible, let the person speak without interrupting. If the reference pauses in the conversation, it usually means she or he has other information and is hesitant to share this information. Get them to talk about everything that would be helpful, but only ask for information that will be used in your hiring decision.

5. Again, ask only job-related questions and document all answers. Avoid questions that can be answered "yes" or "no."

6. The most important question to get answered is whether the previous employer would rehire the applicant you are considering. If you get no other response, try to get this question answered.

7. Avoid questions that screen out minorities, women and persons with disabilities, or will bias the reference in terms of age, gender, or religion.

Final Selection

The final selection of a candidate could be easy or difficult based on your choice of interview formatting, the qualifications of the candidates, and other contributing factors. Before making the final selection, ensure you've checked with all necessary channels that are and have been involved in the hiring process. Whether it is an HR Director, HR recruiter, or even the president of the company, communicating your plans to all important personnel before selecting a candidate is a great system to follow.

Before you choose a candidate, you must also perform all necessary checks. Reference checks and background checks can often prohibit a candidate from working; do not make your selection or extend a job offer without completing your due diligence. If your company uses a hiring software system or employee tracking system, you will need to follow necessary procedure to enter all relevant application or candidate information into the system. Once you have a finalist in mind, they should be advised of all the job responsibilities, they are being seriously considered for the final position, start dates, rate of pay, salary or bonus information, and the steps it may take before they are able to work at the company. Relaying all details to a finalist will ensure they neither stray from the position nor you have an angry employee on your hands the first day of the job.

Making the Offer

You've found the ideal candidate, you've done your due diligence, and you are ready to make a job offer! Even though companies have different hiring policies, job offer should always be made in writing. A verbal job offer can often lead to misunderstandings and even legal battles, so it's best to always have hard copies of job offers on the record even if the employee respectfully declines. It is often the most rewarding to give a job offer in-person, but circumstances may force you do so over the phone, via email or fax. You should also ensure you include anything that was previously discussed throughout the hiring process, in the job offer and have it signed by the candidate—so you have a record. The following should typically appear in the offer letter:

- Department
- Position title
- Supervisor
- Location
- Rate of pay
- Schedule of shift including days off
- Training period and arrangements
- Start date and where to report
- Clothing and equipment needed [if applicable]

- Meal periods
- Parking
- Description of benefits
- Probationary period

Making the offer is typically the only official way to state that a job offer has been made. It is common practice to send a formal letter confirming the employment of the new employee after they have accepted the job offer. At this point, you may go through a step-by-step of the start process including start dates, orientation dates, when benefits will take place, any probationary period, uniforms, where to check-in and whom to report to, and what they can expect for training.

A verbal job offer can often lead to misunderstandings and even legal battles

© Andrei_R/Shutterstock.com

After your candidate accepts the job offer, it is appropriate to notify all other finalists or candidates waiting to hear back and inform them of the filling of the position. This not only provides a definitive answer for the candidate, but shows that you cared enough to stay in contact and that you would most certainly be interested in that candidate for any future positions that should open up. All documents including offer letters, confirmation letters of acceptance, and nonoffer letters to candidates should be maintained. Depending on your company's policy, you may also be required to keep applications and resumes attached to any other pertaining documents for a given period of time. This may seem unnecessary but it may help you quickly find someone to fill a position if you have their information on hand and readily available for review.

Onboarding

Onboarding refers to the pre- and posthire process of bringing a new employee into an organization. This is a time when organizations have the opportunity to make a great first impression or leave employees totally frustrated. Onboarding or socialization refers to the mechanism through which new employees acquire the necessary knowledge, skills, and behaviors to become effective organizational members and insiders.

An onboarding plan helps focus everyone's efforts on the new employee. Where do they park? Which entrance? Who will greet them? Which locker? How to get to their department? When and where are breaks to be taken? How long are breaks? What are the lunch

Onboarding is all about the pre- and posthire process that helps an employee become acclimated to their new working environment

© El Nariz_R/Shutterstock.com

arrangements? The list goes on. Then there is the question of getting the new employee on the payroll and all the paperwork completed. Of course, the new employee wants to know when they are getting paid and how they will be paid, plus, new employees. HR will need to go over the deductions and arrange for the new employee to receive benefits when they become eligible.

Technology in HR Electronic Recruiting and Selection

Once applications have been analyzed and prospective candidates identified, an organization can start the process of selecting and hiring the best possible candidate for a job position. HR departments are incorporating innovative technology more often to ensure this process is conducted in a quick and efficient manner, as well as to help select the right person for the job. Selection assessments are being conducted using a combination of web-based and hand-written tests in order to determine the range of knowledge and skills possessed by the candidate. These two methods for assessment and testing have been shown to produce similar, but somewhat differing results, as a candidate's knowledge of technology usage may reflect a variance in skills.

Ethical Dilemma

An HR director was interviewing Gregory for Marketing Director of the newest and most hip restaurant in town. As the director begins the interview with structured questions, it shortly comes out that Gregory and the director went to the same high school and even had a few of the same teachers. As the interview continues, the subject of the interview strays away from the job position and begins to focuses on the past, people they knew, and what a "small world it is." When the "interview" comes to a close, the HR director implies Gregory will be the one hired for the position. They shake hands and walk out of the office together. Forgetting he even had another interview, the HR director sees another candidate waiting for an interview but already has in his mind that Gregory is the ideal candidate. Is Gregory right for the position because of his skills and experience or because they went to the same high school? Was the director actually able to get enough information out of Gregory before making a personal connection to know he is the right choice? What could the director have done in this case to avoid letting the interview go astray?

Internet Exercise

To apply some of what you've learned in this chapter, log onto http://www.commoninterviewquestions. org/ and search for a career that would relate to the hospitality industry, that is, server, hotel manager, finance director, and so on. Read the "commonly asked question" and think about what other questions you would want to ask if you were interviewing a candidate for that position. Write down all the questions you feel would be necessary for an interview and then analyze what type of "interviewer" you are. Are your questions structured? Are they patterned? Are all of your questions legal? The questions you choose to ask may help you identify what type of interview personality you have and assist you in any future endeavors involving the interview process.

Key Points

In this chapter, you should feel comfortable and understand the steps necessary in the employee recruiting and selection process. We have discussed:

- The role of selection in the hiring process and how it differs from recruiting.
- The screening process as a tool to determine which candidates to formally interview.
- Different types of interview, including structured, unstructured, semistructured, and patterned.
- Effective interviewing strategies including what types of questions should and should not be asked to a candidate.
- Different types of employment tests used in the evaluation of hospitality job applicants.
- Identify the key points in recognizing performance characteristics and the usefulness of references, testing, and measuring talent.
- The role of truth in hiring as a best practicing in selecting the best applicant for a job.
- The ability to follow the steps necessary for hiring new personnel by ensuring you take part in all proper steps of the hiring process to reduce and eliminate negligent hiring.

Key Terms

Evaluating	Patterned interview	Semistructured interviews
Interview	Reference check	Structured interviews
Negligent hiring	Screening process	Truth in hiring
Organization fit	Selection	Unstructured interviews

References

CNNMoney. (2013). Retrieved January 23, 2013, from http://money.cnn.com/magazines/fortune/bestcompanies/2010/snapshots/82.html

Dessler, G. (2009). *Fundamentals of human resource management: Content, competencies, and applications* (p. 133). Upper Saddle River, NJ: Pearson.

Dessler, G. (2013). *Human resource management* (11th ed., p. 255). Upper Saddle River, NJ: Pearson.

EEOC. (2013). Retrieved January 10, 2013, from http://www.eeoc.gov/policy/docs/factemployment_procedures.html

Saterfiel and Associates. (2013). Legality *issues supporting the use of pre-employment testing.* Retrieved January 16, 2013 from, http://www.employment-testing.com/legality.htm

SHRM. (2012). *Screening and evaluating candidates.* Retrieved January 4, 2012 from http://www.shrm.org/TemplatesTools/Toolkits/Pages/ScreeningandEvaluatingCandidates.aspx

SHRM. (2013a). *Telephone pre-screen questions.* Retrieved January 4, 2013, from http://www.shrm.org/TemplatesTools/Samples/InterviewQuestions/Pages/TelephonePreScreen.aspx

SHRM. (2013b). *Screening and evaluating candidates.* Retrieved January 5, 2013, from http://www.shrm.org/TemplatesTools/Toolkits/Pages/ScreeningandEvaluatingCandidates.aspx

SIOP. (2013). *Employment testing.* Retrieved January 10, 2013, from http://www.siop.org/Workplace/employment%20testing/interviews.aspx

US LEGAL. (2013). Retrieved January 23, 2013, from http://definitions.uslegal.com/n/negligent-hiring/

USC Division of Human Resources Employment Office. (2013). *Conducting reference checks.* Retrieved January 9, 2013, from http://hr.sc.edu/employ/reference.html

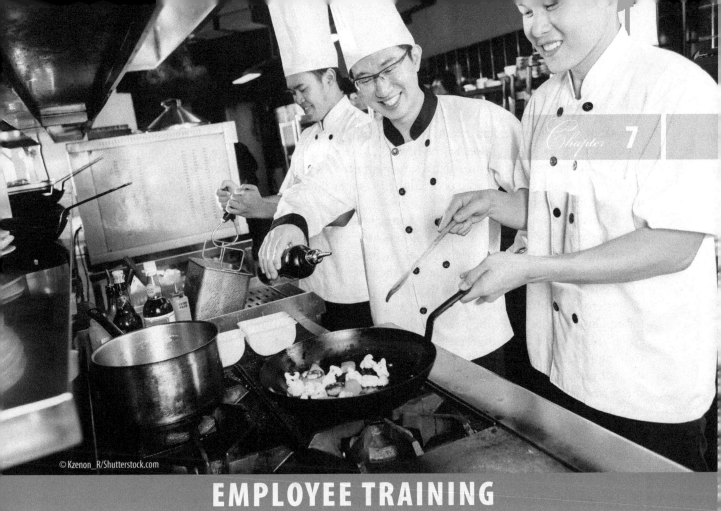

© Kzenon_R/Shutterstock.com

EMPLOYEE TRAINING

Introduction

Ever sat in a restaurant and observed a server handling the blade of a knife or the prongs of a fork as they lay the table or handling glasses by the rim? Or, have you ever seen a server struggling to open a bottle of wine? Or, remember the time when a server appeared at your table with your entrée not knowing who is having what and they say "who ordered this?" as they interrupt conversation holding a plate. All these indicate a need for training.

No matter if you work for a small or a large hospitality company, training is a very important aspect of a company's responsibility to the employee. Many times, untrained or poorly trained employees create an unpleasant experience for the guest. We have all experienced these many times during the course of our lives. Most people do not go back to the place they were not treated well or properly. Hospitality companies go out of business all the time and one of the reasons is a lack of proper training.

After the HR functions of recruiting and selection have identified and hired qualified candidates for employment, it's now time to begin the process of training. Training refers to process of providing employees with the knowledge, skills, and abilities needed to perform their current job. Often, the term training is used interchangeably with development. However, this book will separate those two terms distinctly by chapter—training in this chapter and development in Chapter 8. As opposed to focusing on the current job an employee fills, development focuses on knowledge, skills, and abilities an employee may need in the future. For example, what knowledge or skills might a housekeeper need to eventually fill the role of a housekeeping supervisor?

After reading and studying this chapter you should be able to:

- Describe the orientation process.
- Describe identification of training needs and goals.
- Describe the various training methods.
- Discuss process used to evaluate training programs.

Learning Objective 1: Describe the orientation process

Employee Orientation

Generally, there is a period of time between the acceptance of a job and the starting date. During this time, company information can be sent to the new hire. These days, companies mostly use the Internet and send the employee links to or copies of a company handbook, a departmental operations manual and other relevant information. A call or email from the persons' supervisor or manager is a good follow up and offers a time for questions to be answered.

> **Employee Orientation**: An introduction of a new employee to a company, their job, and the workplace.

Then, one of the first formal training opportunities that a newly hired employee goes through is the employee orientation. Orientation is the opportunity to introduce the new hire to general information on the company and its company vision, values, culture, mission, goals, policies, and procedures. (That's the onboarding part that has gained prominence in recent years).

The length of time that orientation takes varies amongst companies from a few hours to a few days, usually depending on the size and complexity of the company. Generally, an orientation features a welcome by the trainer or an HR representative. This may include an overview of the company's past, present, and future. Then, the companies' vision, values, mission, and goals are presented and discussed. Another good presentation at this early point in the process might be on what the company considers service excellence with lots of examples included.

Traditionally, an externally recruited employee will go through a new hire orientation although for internally recruited employees this may not be necessary. With that being said, it's up to the company and their respective policy to determine if all employees should attend an orientation when they start a new job, regardless if they were an internal or externally hired employee.

Examples of the goals of an employee orientation program are:

Orientation is an opportunity to introduce the new hire to the company vision, values, culture, mission, goals, policies and procedures

© Rawpixel.com/Shutterstock.com

- To familiarize a new employee with the company's vision, values, mission, and goals.
- To make the new employee feel welcome and a part of the team.
- To introduce the new employee to their job, supervisor/manager, and workplace.
- To impart information on a variety of topics including place of work, hours of work, breaks, dress code, etc.
- To explain expectations and performance standards.

Other examples could include, but are not limited to:

- History of the company
- Medical and dental benefits
- Company benefits
- When are employees paid
- Company culture
- Parking or how best to get to work such as light rail and bus system
- Company holiday and summer outings
- Sexual harassment
- Drug and alcohol-free workplace policy
- Workplace safety and health
- Employee hand book review
- If possible (because of location or size of company), an extra step is to have a senior manager or even owner of the company stop in during orientation to introduce themselves

As an example, Marriott's orientations last 8 hours and include introductions of the department leaders and a served lunch. At the end of the orientation, new employees are assigned a mentor, known as a "buddy." Members of the orientation class then attend a refresher course after the first and second month and the class attends a banquet to celebrate 90 days of employment. Marriott and other companies invest time and effort in new employees because they know that, in the hospitality industry, the first few weeks at a new job are critical as many people leave a new job during the first few months if they are going to leave at all.

With the continued innovation of HR functions and incorporation of technology into this process, some organizations are opting to conduct portions of their new hire orientation online using web-based training. This works particularly well for large-scale compliance training, for example, sexual harassment training, that all employees, regardless of their department or position, must complete. Putting parts of training online gives flexibility in terms of when the employee can take the training session. As a best practice, it's always good to ensure that employees are paid for the training if it's done online and firms should ensure they provide computers for training in situations where the employee might not have access to one.

Introducing Dr. Mary Jo Dolasinski: Assistant Professor, DePaul University School of Hospitality Leadership

I started my career in the hospitality industry over 20 years ago. Much of my career had been in leading the training initiatives for White Lodging Corporation, a large hotel management company, and had been focused on developing training and training programs for hourly employees and all levels of leaders. Recently, I made a move to teach for DePaul University's Hospitality Leadership program in Chicago, IL. My current focus is on providing leadership training and development for the next generation of hospitality leaders through my classes and my research.

While I have always believed that training is important, I think it may be even more important now than any time in our history. The hospitality industry has a changing landscape with new customer expectations, new technologies, and a diverse, growing workforce. These changes, along with new types of owners and different types of products are creating a very competitive environment. For any organization to thrive and experience long-term success, training is mission critical. For the company, training provides efficiency, quality, engaged employees and a better bottom line. For the employee, training is central to expanding their knowledge, strengthening their skills and preparing for future personal success.

Training is not new, but the ways in which we deliver training are changing. New employee expectations and the pervasive nature of technology have created a demand for training that is offered in shorter segments, with frequent feedback and the ability to leverage an anytime, anyplace, on any device design.

Technology and changing expectations will continue to shape how the hospitality industry will evolve but the one thing that will not change is the importance of developing employees through training. Every leader and line level employee will need training regardless of whether a part of a big brand or a small independent owner. Great training is the competitive edge that results in customers excellent service, creates a culture of engaged employees, and builds a business that sustains long-term financial success.

Contributed by Mary Jo Dolasinski. © Kendall Hunt Publishing Company

Training

Given the commitment to providing excellent service to their customers of hospitality companies, it is critical to have a staff that is capable of delivering world class service and that takes training. Training is different from orientation programs, which give general information about the company, its policies, and its procedures. Training teaches techniques for ensuring employees have the baseline skills to enhance job performance. Training helps ensure that all employees know how to best perform their job. How would you or I do as a housekeeper servicing 18 rooms without training? One time one of the authors arranged for a group of students to service some hotel rooms—it took 45 minutes to do just one room! Similarly, without training on the hotel's property management system, we would probably make a mess of checking in a guest.

The first step in training does not actually involve the new hire or current employee. The first step is to do a **needs analysis** that identifies the company, department, or individual job goals, including performance standards. Any areas needing improvement that is, where there is a difference between the needs and the current performance of the employee, can be identified and a training plan developed to make the necessary improvements.

Needs analysis can be used periodically to improve performance of an organization. In the hospitality industry, guests' comment surveys can identify the strengths and weaknesses of the operation from the guest's perspective. For example, if there are several comments in regards to slow service, then it is obvious that there is a training need. A service training program, with goals, is developed by HR and the training manager with the departments.

Given the commitment to excellent service by hospitality companies, it is critical to have a staff that is capable of delivering world class service and that takes training

© ESB Professional/Shutterstock.com

Now, here is an onboarding treat, new employees at Four Seasons Hotels and Resorts are asked to stay in the hotel where they are going to work one or two nights so they can experience first-hand the kind of service they will be become a part of (Jefferies, T., personal communication, August 28, 2013). This is also a good idea for managers to stay in the hotel for one night twice a year so they are sure they see what the guest sees.

Needs Analysis: An analysis of the training needs at the company, department, or individual job level.

Tasks: The steps necessary to do a unit of the job.

Knowledge: What a person need to know in order to do the job.

Skills and Abilities: Competence in performing a task.

Job Description: A list of the duties and responsibilities for a position.

Job Analysis and Training

In an ideal scenario, jobs are analyzed; this is called Job Analysis to find out the **tasks**, (the steps necessary to complete a unit of a job), **knowledge**, and **skills and abilities** needed to do the job and which is the best way to do the job. **Task analysis** breaks the job down into smaller tasks and records the knowledge, skills and ability necessary to do the job. Once all the tasks have been recorded, they are grouped in the best way to do the job.

The specific duties and skills are recorded and become the benchmark for the **job description** and possible training need. Job analysis is very important as it is the basis for other HR functions such as recruiting, selection, pay rates, performance standards and evaluations, and even legal aspects of employment. A job analysis may be done on a single type of job, perhaps when a new position is created. But it can also be part of a department or company-wide project to assess current roles in an organization. There are five steps in job analysis (Jerris, 1999, pp. 81–83):

1. Identify which jobs will be analyzed by selecting jobs that can be grouped such as servers, front desk associates, and housekeepers.

2. Decide how the information will be used.

3. Gather information such as

   ☐   The tasks that make up the job

   ☐   The behaviors involved planning, communicating, decision making, etc.

   ☐   Tools, machines, and other equipment used

   ☐   Services rendered such as food preparation and service.

   ☐   Products produced, knowledge used or applied.

   ☐   Performance standards that the job holder will be evaluated on. How many? In what time?

   ☐   Working conditions, is it hot, noisy, wet, indoors, or outdoors?

   ☐   Work schedule, is it shift and what are the hours?

   ☐   The knowledge or skills required for the job must be job related.

There is potential legal issue if a requirement for a position is not job related. For example, if we say a person needs a college degree to be a front desk agent then we must be able to prove that it is necessary.

Training helps ensure that all employees know how to best perform their job

© bernatets photo/Shutterstock.com

Job Descriptions and Training

In addition to job analysis, before training can begin adequate job descriptions must be developed. Job descriptions were briefly covered in Chapter 3 and they provide specific details about a job. Job descriptions are important because they include an overview of specific duties, requirements, and skills necessary for the job. Job descriptions relate to training in that all the tasks required in order to do the job are listed so training programs cover all aspects of the job.

Job descriptions are very important to let the employee know what they are going to be doing (see **Figure 7.1**). As an example, the list should include information on how much they will need to be able to lift. For example, a wait person will have to be able to lift at least 40 lbs. at one time several times during their shift. A banquet houseperson should know that they will be on their feet most of their shift moving tables and chairs.

Position

Banquet Houseperson

General Description

Set-up, breakdown of meeting space including the ballroom for breaks, breakfasts, luncheons, dinners as well as other functions such as meetings and events.

Job Requirements

Able to lift and carry 60 lbs. at a time.
Able to read and follow Banquet Event Orders
Know how to set-up the required types of tables being used
Move a minimum of 10 banquet chairs or tables on a dolly at a time
Vacuum and clean any area that is associated with the meeting and events area
Clean meeting spaces including sweeping floors, mopping, and discarding trash
Maintain a professional and friendly environment

General Work Hours

Be available to work up to 7 Days a Week on 1st shift (7:00 am–3:00 pm), 2nd shift (3:00 pm–11:00 pm), or 3rd shift (11:00 pm–7:00 am)

Equipment Used

Tables and chairs
Chair and table dollies
Basic food line equipment such as a coffee maker
Basic cleaning equipment

Figure 7.1 Example of a Job Description for a Banquet Houseperson (Greer & Plunkett, 2003)

Why is this type of information important to the employee? This will let the employee know exactly what is expected of them. Why would this information be helpful for the company? It will help avoid unwanted lawsuits from employees who say they didn't know what they would be required to do.

In addition, a job description helps in the selection process. If a person who is applying for the banquet houseperson cannot lift the required amount that person would automatically be disqualified for the position. This might help ward off lawsuits for discrimination if the person is physically challenged. The courts would clearly see that the requirements are laid out in writing.

All job descriptions should include a disclaimer at the end of the list. That disclaimer should read something like: "This list is not meant to be all inclusive. Employees will be asked to complete other tasks in their job function as needed."

No matter if a company has 20 employees or 10,000, job descriptions are extremely important to the employee and the employer.

Learning Objective 2: Describe identification of training needs and goals

Determining Training Needs

As we have seen, determining training needs begins with identifying the skills and knowledge employees need to know in order to do their jobs to the standards required. Then an evaluation of each employee's skill and knowledge must be made to determine shortcomings that must be solved by training. Training for new employees is likely to be very different then training an employee who has been working in their position for years.

> **Performance Analysis**: An analysis of performance to assess the degree to which goals are met.

When a possible training need is identified (likely from surveys) a **performance analysis** is done to quantify the gap between the desired performance standard and the current employee's performance. An example is when an attraction cashier does not balance the transactions and cash at the end of a shift three times out of ten. Performance analysis determines that this happens with one particular cashier.

When doing a performance analysis, it is important to assess why performance is below expectations. If a worker rates below standard in one or more areas, you have to diagnose the troble. Is the standard too high? If the reason for the performance gap is because the employee is not sure of what to do or how to do it; training can help. But, if the performance gap is due to an employee not wanting to do the job, then training will not help. In this case, it is better to investigate why an employee is not totally engaged or motivated. It could be the reward system.

New employees need to be shown everything in their new position, including details like where things are stored and how to use equipment. Both current and new employees should have a training needs assessment. Once the assessment is completed, the manager then needs to create a training checklist that can be used to ensure that employees learn everything they need to know for their job.

Difficulties in Training Practices

The best way of training would be for the manager to train each new employee themselves

Many managers fail to do a good job in training employees. They often simply have the new employee work with a veteran employee and the new employee then learns all the bad habits of the person that has been around for a long time. The best way of training would be for the manager to train each new employee themselves. That way the employee would know exactly what is expected of them in their position. However, this is rarely realistic. Many managers today are doing the job of two or three people and find it very difficult to find the time to spend with each new employee.

Another reason that managers fail to train well is when they believe it won't make much difference if they train employees adequate or not. Often mangers don't want to spend the time training because they believe the employee is not going to stay long enough in their jobs so they think "why bother training them when they are going to leave soon anyway." This of course is not a positive attitude for the manager to have, but because of high turnover rates in many areas of the country it feels that way to some managers.

Training Goals and Costs

When training a program, it is important to set specific goals for the training program. Senior management will want to know exactly what the training program will accomplish and how much it will cost.

Some examples of goals are

- To successfully register and room a guest within two minutes.
- To raise the guest satisfaction index from 88% to 94% by December 31 20xx.
- To increase employee satisfaction and engagement from 86% to 92% by December 31, 20xx.
- To successfully have all servers complete the National Restaurant Association's Serve Safe program.

Besides the goals being very clear, the goals also have to be realistic. To expect a new room attendant in a hotel to be able to clean 18 rooms and know everything about their job the first day is not realistic. A goal like this could easily turn an employee off to the point that they don't show up again. Expectations need to be clearly defined. That way the employee will know the expectations and the manager will be able to evaluate them according to the job description.

In addition, training costs must be factored in. How much will it cost to develop the training? Will it be done in house, or will a third party (vendor be used)? Will the training be done on-site using existing facilities or will be training need to be done off-site? Will you be paying the employee for the training (it's a best practice to do so)? Will training materials (books, equipment, etc.) will be required? All these factors are important to factor in when determining the total cost of training each employee to the standard set by an organization.

Introducing Calvin J Banks Jr. Director of Training at The Broadmoor Hotel

Training and Development at The Broadmoor Hotel
Calvin J. Banks Jr., Director of Training at The Broadmoor Hotel, is responsible for the overall direction, coordination, and evaluation of the training department to include staff and leadership development programs for the hotel and related businesses. Also included in his responsibilities are employee events and internal communication.

The Broadmoor is the longest-running consecutive winner of both the AAA Five-Diamond and Forbes Travel Guide Five-Star awards. Since first opening in 1918, The Broadmoor has offered guests a unique way to experience the beauty of the American West, and continues that tradition through our Forbes Travel Guide Five-Star day spa as well as our restaurants (including the only

(Continued)

Five-Star, Five-Diamond restaurant in Colorado, the Penrose Room), 54 holes of championship golf, six tennis courts, indoor/outdoor pools, distinctive retail shops, specialty tours, activities and programs for guests of all ages and interests. In addition, The Broadmoor welcomes meetings and events with 185,000 square feet of meeting space.

When an employee, either frontline or management, joins The Broadmoor he or she will attend a two-day hotel orientation (sometimes called onboarding). The purpose of the orientation is to introduce the new team member to the hotel's facilities, history, policies and procedures, but most importantly culture. The orientation includes a tour of the hotel as well as introductions to and presentations from several members of the Human Resources and hotel management to include the President and CEO. After hotel orientation each department is then responsible for conducting a departmental orientation, on-the-job-training, and safety training among other topics.

All new employees receive a training checklist to complete during position training. This checklist includes all standards to be learned, all policies and procedures to be understood, and safety practices. Once an employee becomes excellent at their current position and has completed all required training for their role, they have the opportunity to advance by continuing their education through introductory leadership courses.

As the director of training, Calvin has the opportunity to work with employees throughout their career. He and The Broadmoor Training Team deliver leadership training classes to new, current, and potential/future supervisors and managers. Topics he facilitates include but are not limited to Managing Generations, Training, Time Management, Running Effective Meetings, and Leadership. Employees also have the opportunity to become certified as trainers. As a certified trainer, this employee trains new team members on how to perform a specific position. For example, certified housekeeper trainers train new housekeepers on their tasks and duties. Certified server trainers train new servers on their tasks and duties. This process continues throughout the hotel in every department. Getting certified as a trainer is the first step in becoming a leader.

During a given year, a full-time employee receives on average an additional 65 hours of training during department pre-shift and line up meetings. Employees' skills are honed annually through class room retraining on the hotel's service standards. Additional training is also done in fun and innovative ways that may include role playing, game show, and quizzes for prizes, and class room training.

Training is the second most important responsibility in an organization next to hiring the right people. The Broadmoor hires first on attitude and second on experience. Think about your favorite restaurant or hotel. Why is it your favorite? Is it the building? Is it the food? The bed? The chandelier? More than like the answer is no, because it's the people and how the people make you feel when you are there. Training is the foundation of creating memorable experiences for guests, but you have to have a person with a heart to serve and a positive attitude.

Training is the difference in most successful organizations. Training provides an opportunity for everyone to get better for the good of guest, the employee, and the organization. A well-trained employee is confident in their role, provides excellent service to guests, and is loyal to the organization.

Contributed by Calvin Banks, Jr., © Kendall Hunt Publishing Company

A Training Proposal

As an HR professional, you will be required to be an advocate for training, and one of the best ways of doing that is to prepare a detailed, data-driven **training plan** for senior management's approval. This may be a proposal for company-wide training over a specific time-frame (such as a year) or for only certain departments.

> **Training Proposal:** A proposal for a training program.

The *first* step is to align the proposed training program with the organization's vision, values, mission, and goals.

The *second* step is to determine the training need from guest, associate and management feedback.

The *third* step is to set outcomes for the training.

The *fourth* step is to outline the costs of the training and estimate the benefits of the training.

The *fifth* step is to assess the training outcomes. Also important is the feedback from trainees—did they learn what they wanted to or were supposed to learn? More on the evaluation of training follows later in the chapter.

Legalize

Take the case of Beltre Morello, (Wexler, 2013) an immigrant from the Dominican Republic, who began working at a major hotel chain who in her lawsuit names a sous chef who she says walked up behind her and touched her undergarments, and another colleague who allegedly walked up behind her and put his hands in her pants. She contends that when she complained, her supervisor did nothing, but her coworkers became vindictive. They left scalding hot plates for her to pick up so she burned herself. They also threatened to beat her up and worse break her bones (Wexler, 2013). In this case, the company must be able to show that they provided training and had policies in place for a variety of issues including sexual harassment, hostile work environments, and workplace safety.

Keep in mind that educating your employees and having as adequate written policies as possible will help keep employees safe and prevent law suits from being filed. There is no way to guarantee staying out of law suits, but there are many ways to try to prevent them, including mandatory sexual harassment training for all employees on your company's zero tolerance policy for such behavior.

Learning Objective 3: Describe the various training methods

Training Methods

There are a variety of **training methods** available for HR professionals to select from. Among the more popular ones are given below.

> **Training Methods:** Available for HR professionals to select from.

On-the-job training (OJT) is one of the basic types of training where one person (the trainer) shows another person (the trainee) how to do the tasks that make up a job. OJT works well in situations where the trainee learns best by doing the tasks on the job. This by far is the most common method in the hospitality industry.

> **On-the-job Training (OJT):** Is one of the basic types of training where one person (the trainer) shows another person (the trainee) how to do the tasks that make up a job.

On the Job Training works well in situations where the trainee learns best by doing the tasks on the job

© Andrey Burmakin/Shutterstock.com

Job Instruction Training: Trainees are taught the basic skills needed to do the job.

An example: A new wait person is learning how to be a waiter at XYZ Restaurant. The manager pairs the new person with a person that has been a waitress there for over seven years. The new person learns the ropes from the more seasoned employee. The downfall that occurs with this type of training is that the new person picks up all the bad habits that the veteran has learned over the years. The best-case scenario is the manager trains each and every employee themselves. However, this is simply not realistic in many cases.

Job instruction training (JIT) is a popular form of training on the job where employees learn the basic skills needed to perform their job. All the tasks that make up the job are identified and taught one by one. The explain, tell, show, let the trainee do the task and finally give feedback works best along with such aids as DVD, the Internet, company Intranet, computer-assisted learning, simulations, and role-playing. For best results, be sure the trainee knows why they are doing what they are doing and explain where it fits in with a goal.

Internships

Many large hotel and restaurant employers will hire students to learn a specific job or jobs in a short period of time (usually three to four months). The student may work in two or three job functions. For example, the student might start working in the housekeeping department for a month and a half and then move to the front desk and learn how to be a front office agent. If the internship is paid, this can be an expensive venture for the company, but often times it works out that the student is then hired on full-time by the company. This is a win–win situation for both the company and the student.

Many large hotel and restaurant employers will hire student interns for short periods of time. This is a great chance to learn about the industry and gain valuable experience

© ALPA PROD/Shutterstock.com

Re-Training

Each manager needs to assess their employees' abilities and work performance and determine if re-training is necessary for that specific employee or the entire team (Gomez-Mejia, Balkin, & Cardy, 2010). For example, A housekeeping staff that has been working in their positions for over 10 years needs different training than employees that require all the basic training to start their job. Management needs to determine if there are any deficiencies in the employee's work. If not, there really is no need to re-train employees on what they are already doing well. However, employees often need refreshing on what is expected of them in their positions.

Programmed Learning

Programmed learning is a step-by-step method of learning that consists of three parts (Peltz, 2012).

> **Programmed Learning**: A step-by-step method of learning.

1. Presenting questions, facts, or problems to the learner.
2. Giving the learner a chance to respond.
3. Giving feedback on the accuracy of the answers.

Programmed learning can be done via a computer program that allows the trainee to answer prompts on the screen and gives immediate feedback on answers to the questions. Programmed learning allows the trainee to progress at their own pace. Some "off-the-shelf" programs help reduce the costs of developing a program. Most of these programs are computer based.

Many people learn more by taking their time when going through the material. When the employee has read some of the material, the program will ask the employee to answer a question or two to see if they understood the content. Employees feel comfortable that they are not rushing through the material and embarrassed in front of others if they need to re-review this information. More sophisticated software can bring the employee back to content that they didn't understand.

The cost of some of this type of software can make it difficult for small companies to absorb. Even larger companies have a difficult time finding the funds in their budgets (Blanchard & Thacker, 2010, pp. 263, 266–268). This type of training can be very productive for many of the employees, but not all. There are many issues, such as access to computers if the employee is supposed to complete training at home. There is also the issue of employees who do not speak English. In hotels especially, there can be many different languages spoken.

Role Playing or **Simulated Learning** can be a more interesting way for trainees to learn some aspects of a job and a way of retaining more information relating to the job. For example, a restaurant server or a front desk associate may find role playing how to respond to a difficult guest's demands helpful when handling a real-guest situation.

Role playing can be especially effective when working with new hires. New hires that have not worked in the hospitality industry before may not have the customer service experience to deal with many difficult situations that may arise. This is a great form of training for them. It is realistic, live, and they can receive instant feedback. This is also a very low-cost form of training (Greer & Plunkett, 2003).

A different, but similar model of training, is simulated learning. Most simulated learning takes place when an employee works on a computer or point-of-sales (POS) system that is in training mode. This allows the employee to explore and learn the program without actually working with actual real data in the system. This is used extensively in the restaurant industry.

There are very sophisticated programs that are available to managers for in-depth simulation learning, but the cost can be very high for this type of training (Blanchard & Thacker, 2010, pp. 229–230).

Seminars

A seminar is a lecture and a dialogue that allow participants to share experiences in a particular topic. A seminar is guided by an expert discussion leader, and there are usually 30 or fewer participants (Walker,

2013). Seminars are generally given to supervisors and management on specific topics such as leadership or motivation. Some companies have a series of seminars on selected topics of interest or necessity to supervisors and management. The Society of Human Resources Management (SHRM) offers seminars and certification programs for HR professionals.

Cross Training

Cross training benefits both the employee and employer. It benefits the employee by being trained to do another job so that they can get more hours or transfer to a better position and it benefits the employer by having employees who can perform more than one job. When an operation has a slow period or low demand it is a time that cross training can help an employee maintain hours by being able to cover an additional job instead of being laid-off. In addition, in busy times housekeepers can be cross trained to banquet servers or front desk agents to help out during the busy evening check-in period. Likewise, front desk agents can also be banquet servers or banquet cashiers. Bell staff can be cross trained to be front desk agents and so on.

Management Training Programs

Many large hotel and restaurant companies have a formal Management Training Program (MTP) for a select few employees. Each company names it something special, but in the end it is a training program set-up by the company to train employees who are interested in management positions in the future. These programs are usually filled by graduating students from hospitality programs throughout the country.

Management Training Programs are a great way for a recent college graduate to learn about a company, gain valuable experience, and eventually transition into an entry-level leadership position

© Phovoir/Shutterstock.com

Most MTP hires will work in a number of departments in a hotel over a 6–12 month time period. Restaurant companies will have the MTP hire work all the positions within a restaurant and maybe have them work in two or three different stores during their training time.

Once the employee finishes the formal training, most of the trainees will receive assistant manager positions within the company. Often times they are watched closely and will be able to move quickly up the corporate ladder if they have been successful in their positions.

Learning Objective 4: Discuss process used to evaluate training programs

Evaluating the Training Program

Evaluating the training program is a very important part of the training function as hopefully it validates the investment made by the company in training. There are five possible approaches or methods to evaluate the training program, but it should be noted that every organization may choose to approach their evaluation slightly differently. One or more of these methods can be used.

1. After the training has taken place, a survey is completed by the trainees to determine the extent to which they felt they met the goals of the training program.

2. Another way is to chart the employees performance prior to and after the training (hopefully there is an improvement after training!).

3. Yet another way of assessing the training is to test participants to see if they gained the necessary information.

4. Results from guest satisfaction surveys/indexes can provide data showing the effects of training.

5. A company can measure its employee turnover percentage and calculate the amounts involved for each position. For instance, if the employee turnover rate dropped from 64% to 39% one can assume that training had a positive impact on that drop in employee turnover and a dollar amount can be placed on it.

Topics Requiring Training

In addition to learning how to do their specific job, all employees in most hospitality companies require training on additional topics such as the following.

Sexual Harassment

Sexual harassment training is strongly advised in order to avoid or reduce lawsuits. If a harmonious workplace environment can be maintained, it will substantially reduce the risk of any form of harassment taking place with serious consequences. Just ask anyone who has had to defend a lawsuit; it can cost thousands of dollars even if you are not guilty. A recent high profile case against the head of the International Monetary Fund (IMF) Dominique Strauss-Khan was indicted, accused of sexually assaulting one of the hotel's housekeepers—he denied the charges and later settled the case. This and another high-profile case at the Pierre hotel that was not immediately reported, caused proposed laws requiring sexual harassment training to staff and management-and to protect employees who speak up from retaliation (Hollon, n.d.). Several hotels are now requiring housekeepers to wear panic buttons so they can immediately call security for help when needed.

Every company no matter how small or large should have a sexual harassment policy in place (usually can be found in the employee handbook) as well as regular training.

Serve Safe

Serve Safe is a series of training programs from the National Restaurant Association for the restaurant and hospitality industries. The main programs are (Servsafe, n.d.) Manager training Serve Safe, Employee Training Serve Safe, Responsible Alcohol Serve Safe Alcohol, and Serve Safe Allergens. Managers learn about foodborne illness, how to prevent it and how to train employees in food sanitation. There are online and classroom options in several languages. The employee food handler course covers the basics of preparing and serving food and

OSHA training is an example of a mandatory compliance training that all employees in a hospitality and tourism company should attend

© designer491/Shutterstock.com

successful trainees receive a food handler certificate from the National Restaurant Association. The Serve Safe Alcohol training program teaches the essentials of responsible alcohol service and helps protect operations form risks and liabilities relating to alcohol service.

Hazard Communication Standard

> **Hazard Communication Standard:** Known as the employee right to know, requires employers to inform employees about hazards through training, labels, alarms, color-coded systems, chemical information sheets.

The Occupational Safety and Health Administration (OSHA) developed a Hazard Communication Standard known as the Employee Right to Know Law. This law requires employers to inform employees about hazards through training, labels, alarms, color-coded systems, chemical information sheets and other methods. It also requires that employees are trained in a language and vocabulary they can understand and that accurate records of work-related injuries and illnesses (OSHA, n.d.). For a full description of OSHA's requirements go to: https://www.osha.gov/.

Key Points

- Deterring training needs begins with identifying the skills and knowledge employees need to know in order to do their jobs to the standards required as well as determining any deficiencies in their current performance.

- New employees need to be shown everything in their new position. Including where things are stored to how to use equipment. Managers also need to be very clear on their expectations for the new employee.

- Determining training needs begins with identifying the skills and knowledge employees need to know in order to do their jobs to the standards required as well as determining any deficiencies in their current performance.

- When completing a training program it is important to set the goals for the training program. Senior management will want to know exactly what the training program will accomplish and how much it will cost.

- As an HR director, you will be required to be an advocate for training, and one of the best ways of doing that is to prepare a detailed data driven **training proposal** for the executive committee's and the president's approval.

- **On-the-job-training (OJT)** is one of the basic types of training where one person (the trainer) shows another person (the trainee) how to do the tasks that make up a job.

- Sexual harassment training is strongly advisable in order to avoid or reduce lawsuits.

- Evaluating the training program is a very important part of the training function as hopefully it validates the investment made by the company in training.

Key Terms

Employee orientation	Job description	Needs analysis
Hazard Communication Standard	Job instruction training	On-the-job training
	Knowledge	Performance analysis

Programmed Learning   Task analysis   Training methods
Skills and abilities   Tasks   Training proposal

Discussion Questions

1. Is training important?
2. Is orientation worth the time and effort?
3. How are training needs identified?
4. Which training method is best for a front desk agent?
5. Which training method is best for a restaurant server?

Ethical Dilemma

You are a Training Director in a hotel chain of 15 hotels. You have created a new customer service training. The CEO of the company had reviewed it before it was rolled out and loved it. She even sent an email to all the managers and employees requiring everyone, including himself, would be taking the training.

A few days before the training, your boss calls you and tells you that he doesn't want to attend because he knows he can't learn anything new about customer service. He wants you to fudge the records and mark him as present for the training.

What do you do?
Do you tell anyone?
Can you lose your job because of this?

References

Blanchard, N., & Thacker, J. (2010). *Effective training: Systems, strategies, and practices*. Upper Saddle River, NJ: Prentice Hall.

Gomez-Mejia, L., Balkin, D., & Cardy, R. (2010). *Managing human resources* (pp. 246–267). Upper Saddle River, NJ: Prentice Hall.

Greer, C., & Plunkett, R. (2003). *Supervision: Diversity and teams in the workplace*. Upper Saddle River, NJ: Prentice Hall.

Hollon, J. (2013). *Sexual harassment bills proposed for hotels*. Retrieved August 28, 2013, from http://www.workforce.com/articles/print/sexual-harassment-bills-prop

Jerris, L. A. (1999). *Human resources management for hospitality* (pp. 81–83). Upper Saddle River, NJ: Prentice Hall.

OSHA. (n.d.). Retrieved August 28, 2013, from https://www.osha.gov/publications/osha3021.pdf

Peltz, J. (2012, December). Dominique Strauss-Kahn Settlement: Former IMF Chief, Naffissatou Diallo Setlle sexual assualt lawsuit. *Huffington Post Online*. Retrieved September 18, 2013, from http://www.huffingtonpost.com/2012/12/10/dominique-strauss-kahn-nyc-hotel-maid_n_2272391.html

Servsafe. (2013). Retrieved August 28, 2013, from http://www.servsafe.com/home

Walker, J. R. (2013). *Introduction to hospitality* (6th ed., p. 467). Upper Saddle River, NJ: Pearson.

Wexler, D. (2013). Worker sues Grand Hyatt for alleged sexual harassment. *NY Daily*. Retrieved August 28, 2013, from http://www.nydailynews.com/new-york/kitchen-worker-sues-grand-hyatt-claiming-sexual-harassment-article-1.1412285#ixzz2dCw4GZbw

© Dmitry Kalinovsky/Shutterstock.com

Chapter **8**

EMPLOYEE CAREER DEVELOPMENT

Introduction

Planning your career or the careers of your employees is not always easy. Things happen, but, if we are well prepared with a solid grounding in our chosen field and if we "pay our dues" career advancement will usually come either from within the company or with others. For the readers who are college students, it is beneficial to gain experience in several departments of a recognized company while going to school so that you are better prepared for employment and advancement on graduation. Many of the better-known and preferred companies offer structured management training programs, which give an excellent overview of the company and training in a variety of areas, making it easier for graduates to find their pathway to the top.

After reading and studying this chapter you should be able to:

1. Describe the employer's role in developing employees.
2. Discuss the employee role in employee development.
3. Identify barriers to career development.
4. Discuss the various motivation theories.

Learning Objective 1: Describe the employer's role in developing employees

Employers' Role

> **Turnover**: The number of employees that leave in a given time period.

> **Retention**: The number of employees retained in a given time period.

> **Career Development**: The professional development efforts undertaken to attain jobs later in a career.

The hospitality and tourism industry typically suffers from high employee **turnover** and low **retention** rates, at the lower levels of the operation and sometimes middle and upper management. Various factors such as location and economy can influence turnover rates. However, HR managers can decrease turnover by providing new employees with career development through training, mentoring, and other types of programs. **Career development** is essential at all levels of operation, because it provides the foundation for employees to be promoted from within and progress within a company. According to Maureen Lucido, area Director of Human Resources for Hyatt hotels, most companies promote from within as it's good for employee satisfaction and morale. (Lucido, M., personal communication, July 23, 2013). It is far cheaper to retain an employee over the long-term and promote them through the company than it is to seek out and hire new employees. As employees reach higher levels of management within a company, turnover generally becomes less frequent as employees start to settle into a steady career path within a company.

Mentoring can be a very useful step in career development. Many managers at higher levels of operation, including the executive committee, have taken on the role of a mentor to a lower-level employee or manager, as well as having been mentored themselves at some point in their career. Mentors assist in the overall education and training of other employees, with the goal of fostering their future development with a company. Managers at all levels of operation are encouraged to participate in mentoring for the overall benefit of a company and their employees. Lower-level employees want to be mentored, because it increases their chances of

> **Mentoring**: A more senior employee giving career development guidance to a junior employee.

success. A recent study in career development in the tourism industry determined that "the majority of junior employees entering the industry have aspirations of hierarchical career development and the role of leaders is to support and foster these career ambitions" (Ayres, 2006).

Depending on the property, HR or department heads may appoint trainers to work on the execution of training programs

© Kzenon/Shutterstock.com

Career Progression: Progressing in a chosen career.

Career progression is a direct result of an employee's personal skills, characteristics, experience, work ethic, and planned career path. A challenging and structured training program can increase the motivation, efficiency, and overall development of employees. Upper-level managers and directors should use their already attained skills to maintain positive working relationships with their employees, which have proven to be a necessary component in employee retention and progression within a company. Some of the pertinent skills required to achieve a successful career in the hospitality industry include technical, interpersonal, analytical, and self-management skills. While acquiring all of these skills is not a requirement to advance in a company, the ability to attain a steady balance of skills gives an employee a strong competitive advantage.

Recruitment, Training, and Progression

For **employee development** to be successful, it is important for HR managers to establish effective recruitment and selection strategies. It is more efficient to train a qualified candidate with ample industry experience than it is to train a candidate with no industry experience at all. Furthermore, the ability to recruit from within is even more beneficial to the development of the company's employees, resulting in the overall success of a company.

As discussed in Chapter 5, the two primary sources of recruitment are internal and external methods. In hotels and restaurants, internal recruitment can come from within the same establishment, or from a property under the same brand name. For example, a kitchen line employee at the Hyatt Regency Atlanta is recruited to be the kitchen supervisor at the Hyatt Regency Sarasota. The employee remains with the same company, but is transferred to a different property. Similarly, if that same kitchen line employee is promoted to the kitchen supervisor position at the Hyatt Regency Atlanta, they will remain at the same property. Both of these scenarios are examples of internal recruitment.

External recruitment refers to seeking out employees from outside the individual hotel, restaurant, or company in general. This can be accomplished via job fairs, websites, social media, newspapers, internships, apprenticeships, etc. Both internal and external recruiting are undergone in order to train and further develop employees to succeed within the company.

Training and development is the responsibility of operations supervisors/managers and department heads. Trainers who have been identified and certified are usually paid additional salary. However, HR professionals will be involved in the strategy but not the execution of the training and development. For example, in a hotel of 500 employees there may be just four HR professionals but there are 75 supervisors/managers. Depending on the property, department heads may appoint trainers to work on the execution of training programs.

Different hotel companies employ their own set of career training and development standard practices. The Four Seasons hotel group, one of the most well-known luxury hotel companies throughout the world, is committed to hiring employees who have the potential to be true leaders of the company. This is ensured by the Four Season's rigorous hiring process, which subjects applicants to be interviewed by four of the hotel's managers, including the applicant's direct manager, as well as the hotel's general manager.

The focus of these interviews is not primarily to determine the applicant's skill set and industry knowledge, as these are elements that can be taught on the job. Instead, the interview process seeks to assess the applicant's personal characteristics, and qualities inherent in the ability to provide extraordinary guest service. Finally, the interview process is structured in a way that allows managers to "assess a leader in a group situation similar to the one he would take up were he to be employed.

In a study conducted on the retention of hourly employees in the hospitality industry, it was concluded that the biggest factor resulting in employee retention was connected with intrinsic fulfillment and positive working conditions. Employees want to feel a sense of self-worth, and believe that their job is important to the overall success of the company. Employees are more likely to stay with a company when they are treated with respect and care.

Employees respond positively to additional benefits offered by hospitality companies

© Kzenon/Shutterstock.com

Studies have shown that employees respond positively to additional benefits provided by the company that are conditional upon employment. Some of the additional benefits offered include insurance and medical coverage, raises in pay, company 401 K contributions, bonuses, paid vacations, and tuition reimbursement. In addition, human resources can ensure that department managers are properly trained in coaching, praising, and disciplining employees in an appropriate manner. Handling employee relations has proven to be a necessary factor in creating an effective, efficient, and favorable work environment (Ricci, Peter, & Milman, 2002).

Learning Objective 2: Discuss the employee role in employee development

Employees' Role

Employee progression relies on the ability to create a working relationship that motivates and encourages employees to put forth their best effort in return for being provided with desirable benefits and working conditions. Employee performance is dependent upon all aspects of the job that effect what they do and how they feel about their job. If an employee truly cares about their job, they will do their best to excel, resulting in a dedicated and effective employee, which benefits the company overall.

A recent notion that has been fashioned is known as spirituality in the workplace. An informal definition of spirituality in the workplace can be summarized by an employee's awareness and feelings of purpose in what they achieve in their jobs; their engagement and sense of belonging, as part of a bigger picture in a company's overall philosophy, and reasons for existing. In hospitality, this can relate to outside factors as well, such as providing a unique experience, through extraordinary guest service, which results in overall guest satisfaction. An example is the Ritz Carlton mystique, which is more than just a guest database; it is a way to help ensure guests have a memorable experience. Ritz Carlton "ladies and gentlemen," as their employees are called, enter guest preferences into mystique so that all Ritz Carlton properties can be aware of individual guest's preferences (Michelli, 2008). Imagine, without your knowing it, someone observes that you like something, in the authors' case, Warsteiner beer and the next time you stay at one of the Ritz Carlton hotels you find this beer in your refrigerator.

Employee progression relies on the ability to create a working relationship that motivates and encourages employees

© Andrey_Popov/Shutterstock.com

Employee development can be evaluated on three levels of performance within an organization: **individual, group, and organizational**. Individual performance can relate to an employee's feelings about the quality and contribution of their own work as it relates to the

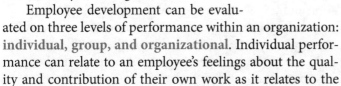

Individual, Group, and Organizational Goals: Goals for individuals, groups, and organizations.

overall success of the company. Employees who display success on this level raise the urge for further development and progression within the company, and are generally more passionate about their work because it is more meaningful to them personally.

Group performance refers to an employee's feelings about their role in the workplace, as it relates to themselves and other coworkers. Employees who display success on this level are generally more connected with their coworkers and involved in the workplace. They see themselves being a part of the workplace community as a whole.

Finally, organizational performance refers to an employee's feelings toward the company's principal philosophies, rules and regulations, and overall purpose for existence. Employees who display success on this level are more adept to encouraging standard procedures and practices, and their values usually run parallel with the companies. They are dedicated because they believe in what the company stands for. The combination of success at all three levels of performance is usually indicative of an employee who yearns to work their way to the top of an organization. These are the people who are committed to becoming directors, general managers, presidents, and CEOs of companies (Crawford, Hubbard, Lonis-Shumate, & O'Neill, 2008).

Danielle Muffat, SPHR | Director of Human Resources Waldorf Astoria Chicago

"Nobody cares how much you know, until they know how much you care"

—Theodore Roosevelt

I was at a BBQ recently and a guest commented "It's been my experience you people are neither resourceful nor human" when he overheard I was a Director of Human Resources. It was a remark made in jest, but it left me thinking about my personal leadership legacy. Regardless of the discipline

(Continued)

you choose to pursue in hospitality, if you show team members you care about them, you will reap the rewards. Team members who know their leaders care are much more willing to go above and beyond fostering a culture where excellence is the norm, not the exception.

How do you show you care? It's really pretty easy. Get to know your team on a personal level (that doesn't mean take them out drinking), show an interest in what is important to them. Do they have children? What is their favorite sport or hobby? When they return from a vacation or just a day off, ask them how their time away was and listen. My first couple management positions were in Front Office and Reservations. There were a lot of checklists, action items, phones to answer; I took great pride in being extremely efficient. I was a task master, I was a manager, but not yet a leader. One of my most valuable lessons came early in my HR career. My immediate supervisor, a notoriously bad driver, inevitably one day had a mild fender bender, thankfully no one was injured. Several months later, she was coaching me on relationship building and gently explaining if you take time to build rapport, people will naturally do their best for you. The example she gave? I was the only person in the office who had failed ask about her wellbeing following the accident. That was truly an "aha moment!"

To sum up some best practices in three words—"Communicate and Celebrate". Communicate. Have a suggestion box in a prominent location and follow-up on suggestions personally. Conduct an annual Team Member Engagement Survey that measures engagement and job satisfaction and allows for written comments. The reality of hospitality in today's economy is there will be some transition and uncertainty. This could be a change in the management contract, sale of the hotel, renovations, or closure of a restaurant for financial reasons. Tough business decisions will be made that may include layoffs or decisions to forego annual pay increases. You must deliver tough messages with transparency, grace and compassion. Celebrate. Our executive team signs and sends out personalized birthday cards every month. It seems like such a minor thing, but it feels wonderful when an employee says "I got my birthday card! That was so nice you took the time". We send monogrammed baby blankets congratulating new parents. We host special lunches and dinners when the hotel wins awards and accolades. Once a month we get together and recognize all birthdays, anniversaries, engagements, new babies, we call it "Life Celebrations". This monthly event always features treats, raffles and music. We have many ways to recognize team members, but we also have a formal Employee of the Quarter and Manager of the Quarter program. If you show people you care, they will be much more willing to listen and demonstrate their pride and loyalty through both the successful and challenging times.

Contributed by Danielle Muffat. © Kendall Hunt Publishing Company.

Learning Objective 3: Identify barriers to career development

Barriers to Career Progression

A career in the hospitality and tourism industry is very demanding and time-consuming. Success moving up the ladder of an organization requires dedication, long hours, including holidays', and a flexible schedule. These factors, along with many others, can result in various barriers to career development. In a recent study, a number of managers at different levels of organizations throughout the industry reported either having personally encountered an obstacle to career development, or being aware of different barriers that have encountered fellow employees and coworkers. Among the various barriers to career development in hospitality and tourism companies include but are not limited to (Whitelaw, Barron, Buultjens, Cairncross, & Davidson, 2009)

- Age
- Degree of education
- Gender
- Background
- Willingness to relocate
- Lack of mentorship experience
- Lack of competition in the market—If there is only one hotel in a town, which makes it hard to move up; but if there are several hotels, then more opportunities are afforded for career advancement.

Self-Reliance

Today, a college diploma does not automatically secure a job with a decent starting salary and opportunities for upward mobility through the company. According to Maureen Lucido, area human resources director with Hyatt Hotels: "A degree does not trump others without one." (Lucido, M., personal communication, July 23, 2013). However, a degree with great interpersonal skills and the right experience will.

There is a heavy increase in competition for job positions, which has become more intense and requires more experience than a college degree can provide. Now, it is necessary for individuals to adapt to the idea of career self-reliance in order to make oneself a more attractive prospect for a job position. The idea of career self-reliance essentially refers to an individual's ability to adapt to a constantly changing work environment by teaching oneself to survive, much like a business. A person must manage and market themselves in a way that creates demand for them as an employee. Ultimately, **self-reliance** means that we are in charge of our own destiny and we determine our fate. Remember the old expression: It's your attitude that determines your altitude.

Self-reliance in the hospitality industry includes going above and beyond in performing the basic job functions, as well as taking on tasks that are outside the realms of the assigned job functions

© wavebreakmedia/Shutterstock.com

Career self-reliance places much emphasis on the idea that continuous learning is important in the workplace. In hospitality, many companies foster this idea by providing employees with annual training programs and seminars to keep them fresh and up-to-date on major trends in the industry, as well as improving skills relating to their individual job functions. The hotel industry is unique in that there are many occasions when employees in different departments must cooperate with one another in order to ensure overall satisfaction for a guest or group of guests that are staying in the hotel.

Self-reliance in the hospitality industry includes going above and beyond in performing the basic job functions, as well as taking on tasks that are outside the realms of the assigned job functions. For example, a front desk manager is walking through the hotel lobby and a guest asks for a towel to be brought up to the room. The manager calls housekeeping to take a towel up to the room, but no one answers. A self-reliant manager would assure the guest that a towel would be brought up to his or her room, and then personally take the towel up to the guest's room, or have one of their employees take the towel up, and follow-up to make sure the guest was satisfied.

Self-reliance means that we are in charge of our own destiny and we determine our fate. The problem is that not all employees know that or think that way. They expect to be spoon-fed by their managers to advance their careers. Those are the ones that end up quitting or being terminated (Owen, M., personal communication, February 23, 2013).

HR Technology

The HR department is responsible for maintaining all information that is relevant to a person's employment with the company. The HR department is also responsible for maintaining records of a company's rules, regulations, and training programs, as well as benefit packages for employees. With this amount of information, it is important for a company to have an information system that is capable of maintaining large amounts of data. HR directors are finding it increasingly necessary to adapt to more advanced forms of software and information technology to assist in providing the necessary features to accommodate all of HR's functions and requests (Heathfield, 2012).

As technology is constantly changing, so are the technological demands of companies. With the high costs of new information technology, it is necessary to select software that is able to adapt with the ever-changing needs of organizations. HR departments have access to a variety of options for software and information technology systems. It is extremely important to evaluate the costs and benefits of all options available before making a decision. Choosing an HR information technology system should be viewed as a long-term investment that will continue to develop with the company's needs. Some additional questions HR managers must take into consideration are as follows:

- With the variety of functions performed by the HR department, will the information technology software provide the ability to integrate with different systems throughout the hotel?
- What types of maintenance are required and how frequently can the hotel expect to service or update the system?
- What security measures are built into the software and how can you protect date from being stolen or lost?
- Will the software provide employees with the ability to select and update benefits plans as well as make changes to their personal data?
- What types of reporting capabilities are provided by the software?
- Will the technology provide Human Resources with the authority to determine what degree of access employees are allowed within the system?
- Does the software provide features that allow the HR department to better communicate with employees? (Brooks, Art., n.d.).

The increase in more advanced HR information technologies has led to more technology-driven methods of training and development in the hospitality industry. HR directors are implementing more efficient "high-definition video, mobile networks, social networking sites, and ultra-sophisticated Human Resource Information Systems" into orientation and training programs. HR departments throughout the world are utilizing more technology-based tools as a platform for collecting information on guests and employees. For example, Mark Gasta, Sr. Vice President Human Resources for Vail shares claims that his employees at Vail Resorts in Colorado are utilizing new technologies such as mobile devices and iPads to administer employee and guest engagement surveys throughout their hotels (Rosen, 2011). At Hyatt hotels, associates can access Hyatt Connect to update their information and benefits. In addition, interviews can be done via Skype.

Electronic Learning

Employee training and development is more frequently being delivered via web-based applications and company portals, which has successfully cultivated a more effective learning environment for employees. Many organizations are using a blended learning approach, which incorporates instructor-led training, combined with computer and web-based training, as well as podcasts and mobile training methods to provide a much wider range of learning techniques. Using a combination of training methods, both personal and technologically-driven, significantly increases an organization's ability to deliver the necessary learning tools for employees to develop their knowledge and skills, which they can then apply while on the job. Many companies are having Webinars on specific topics and conduct online training through their intranet.

In addition, the implementation of electronic training can benefit an organization in the following ways:

- **Decreasing training expenses:** Organizations are able to cut back on the additional labor required for instructor-led training sessions by providing employees with self-administered training that they can complete on their own time. This also decreases travel expenses and time away from work to participate in external training sessions.

- **Increasing training effectiveness:** Electronic learning allows employees to allocate themselves as much time as needed to fully comprehend the training material. This helps to guarantee a higher rate of understanding and application of the knowledge and skills developed.

- **Tracking and managing results:** Many computer and web-based training methods include an assessment and certification of course completion at the end of the training course to determine how well an employee grasped the materials. Managers and employees can track which training courses have been completed, or still need to be completed per company policy or regulatory requirement (Johnson, & Gueutal, 2011).

The incorporation of different forms of technological equipment and devices allows employers or managers to monitor the behavior and production of their employees. In the past few years, the number of companies using electronic monitoring of their employees has increased by 43% (Schumacher, 2011). Electronic monitoring or "e-monitoring" consists of video, computer, and web-based technology used to monitor and control the actions of employees that are unrelated to their work, as well as to increase overall productivity and decrease the misuse of company assets. Employee monitoring has resulted in both positive and negative effects on employee performance. To a certain extent, monitoring will increase the speed and productivity of employees, keeping

(Continued)

them from trailing off task for extended periods of time. However, monitoring is not beneficial for all circumstances; as it may cause a decrease in self-confidence and an increase in complacency, dissatisfaction, and strained relations between employee and employer.

Employers are finding it necessary to use advanced methods to evaluate employee performance on the job. Employers have the ability to keep a running record of all employee information through advanced technology, which allows managers and employees the ability to collect and store data on individual job performance. This also provides an increased ease of accessibility when attempting to retrieve data for use during employee appraisals and other purposes. This form of technology makes it easier for managers to maintain focus on the overall progression of an employee's performance throughout the year, instead of pinpointing recent events or actions that are not directly related to the job.

Learning Objective 4: Discuss the various motivation theories

Motivation

> **Motivation**: The process by which someone is engaged, energized, and driven to reach a goal.

Ask someone the definition of motivation and you are likely to get several different answers, which is why it is not easy to define motivation. Motivation is such a complex topic because we are all motivated by different things and to different extents. We come from diverse backgrounds, tend to be motivated by different things at different life-stages, and have different experiences and abilities. Management experts have tried to not only define motivation but to explain it also. Thus, people are known as motivated are driven by reasons that are intertwined with their personalities, needs, and wants, making motivation a psychosociological factor. In other words, motivation comes from within (Linda, 1999). Motivation is the why we do things.

HR professionals and line managers working together can dramatically influence the workplace culture and climate thus helping motivate employees to enjoy their work and do a good

We come from diverse backgrounds, tend to be motivated by different things at different life-stages, and have different experiences and abilities

© Monkey Business Images/Shutterstock.com

job. For example, at Hyatt, new hires fill out a questionnaire indicating their likes and what motivates them (Lucido, M., personal communication, July 23, 2013). Management and human behavior scholars suggest theories that give indications about motivation. Among the better-known theories that have application to the hospitality industry and personal development are The Hawthorne Studies, Maslow's Hierarchy of Human Needs, Herzberg's Motivator-Hygiene Theory, McGregor's Theory X and Theory Y, McClelland's Acquired-Needs Theory, Equity Theory, Reinforcement Theory, Participative Management, TQM, and Leadership.

The Hawthorne Studies

One of the most interesting studies of organizational behavior took place years ago beginning in 1924 but its findings and relevance still resonate today. The Hawthorne Studies were conducted at the Western Electric Company works in Cicero, Illinois. The studies were initially designed by Western Electric industrial engineers as a scientific management experiment. They wanted to examine the effect of various lighting levels on worker productivity. The study examined two groups: one a control group and the other an experimental group. The experimental group was exposed to various lighting intensities and the control group worked under a constant intensity. If you were the industrial engineers for this experiment, what would you have expected to happen? It's logical to think that individual output in the experimental group would be directly related to the intensity of the light. However, they found that as the level of light was increased in the experimental group, output for both groups increased. Then, much to the surprise of the engineers, as the light level was decreased in the experimental group, productivity continued to increase in both groups. The finding was that it was not the changes in lighting that were affecting productivity. Instead, it was the belief that productivity increased simply because the employees were being studied that is, having an external person interested in them increased their productivity.

In one of the studies, a group of women were asked to join a test group and work in a separate room over a period of five years assembling telephone relays. Productivity was measured by the number of relays each person completed. In the experiment room, a supervisor discussed changes with the participants and used some of their suggestions. The researchers measured how different variables impacted the group's and individual's performance. The variables were; the number and times of breaks and the length of the working day; giving two 5-minute breaks—after discussion with participants over the length of time—and then changing to two 10-minute breaks—not the participants preference. Productivity increased, but then when they received six 5-minute breaks, they disliked it and reduced output. Food was provided for the breaks and the day was shortened by 30 minutes resulting in increased output.

Finally, the schedule was reverted to the original one and again output increased. Researchers hypothesized that the participants worked harder because they chose their own coworkers, worked as a group, were treated as special by having a separate room and because they were consulted by their supervisor. The lessons learned from the landmark Hawthorne Studies have impacted management thinking and contributed to what is known as participative management.

Maslow's Hierarchy of Human Needs

Abraham Maslow suggested that we are motivated by a need hierarchy of five basic human needs known as **Maslow's Hierarchy of Human Needs**.

- *Physiological Needs*—food, shelter, and clothing.
- *Safety Needs*—safe working environment.
- *Social Needs*—a great working environment with quality opportunities for interaction with colleagues.
- *Esteem Needs*—recognition programs, promotion from within, guest comment cards, catch me doing a great job.
- *Self-Actualization*—achieving one's full potential, development and training programs, opportunities for personal growth and development, to be the best that we can be.

Employees work to satisfy the most basic need then work up to the next level need. Once a need is met, it no longer drives our behavior. From a HR perspective, it is important to find out what will motivate an associate to give outstanding guest service.

Maslow's Hierarchy of Human Needs

© Pyty/Shutterstock.com

Herzberg's Motivation-Hygiene Theory

Herzberg's motivation-hygiene theory was proposed by psychologist Frederick Herzberg in the belief that an individual's relation to work is basic and that one's attitude toward work can very well determine success or failure. Herzberg investigated the question, "What do people want from their jobs?" (Herzberg, Mausner, & Snyderman, 1959, as cited in Robbins, 2005). He asked people to describe in detail situations in which they felt exceptionally good or bad about their jobs. The responses were then tabulated and categorized.

According to Herzberg, the factors leading to job satisfaction are separate from those that lead to job dissatisfaction. Therefore, managers who seek to eliminate factors that can create job dissatisfaction may bring about peace but not necessarily motivation (Herzberg, Mausner, & Snyderman, 1959, as cited in Robbins, 2005). Do you agree with these factors? Think about how this relates to you and whether these factors motivate you.

McGregor's Theory X and Theory Y

Douglas McGregor developed a theory of motivation, known as **Theory X and Theory Y**, based on manager's attitudes toward associates and how that affects their level of motivation. McGregor suggested Theory X was a negative management approach where managers thought employees had an inherent dislike for work and had to be coerced into doing anything. On the other hand, the Theory Y approach is where managers think that employees naturally like work and want to be productive. Theory Y is linked to participative management and management involving employees in the decision-making process such as Management by Objectives or Total Quality Management.

McClelland's Acquired-Needs Theory

People tend to be more motivated when they receive good pay for their work

© Robert Kneschke/Shutterstock.com

McClelland's Needs Theory suggests three needs: achievement, power, and affiliation. They are defined as follows (Herzberg, Mausner, & Snyderman, 1959, as cited in Robbins, 2005):

- *Need for achievement:* The drive to excel, to achieve in relation to a set of standards, to strive to succeed.

- *Need for power:* The need to make others behave in a way that they would not have behaved otherwise.

- *Need for affiliation:* The desire for friendly and close interpersonal relationships.

High achievers tend to be the ones who strive most for the needs theory.

Equity Theory

Equity theory is about receiving a fair day's pay for a fair day's work. People tend to be more motivated when they receive good pay for their work. But if the pay were to drop or if another employee were hired to do the same work for higher pay, then the motivation of the first employee would decrease because they are not being treated equally. There are two forms of equity, internal as the example above illustrates and external where an employee in another unit of the same or competing company is paid at a different rate for the same job.

HR professionals strive to maintain external equity by conducting salary surveys amongst similar hospitality operations. For internal equity, they check job analysis and job evaluations. HR professionals also request employees to complete wage and salary surveys to determine the level of satisfaction with their pay for performance.

Expectancy Theory

Psychologist Victor Vroom's **Expectancy Theory** suggests that people won't pursue rewards they find unattractive, or where the odds of success are very low. He says a person's motivation to exert some level of effort depends on three things: the person's expectancy (in terms of probability) that his or her effort will lead to performance (Dessler, 2011); instrumentality, or the perceived connection between successful performance and actually obtaining the rewards; and valance, which represents the perceived value the person attaches to the reward (Dessler, 2011). We can realize that absent any one of these factors, people will not be motivated. Therefore, hospitality managers need to design motivational programs that take these factors into account.

Legalize

While career self-reliance is an important factor in career development, employees must not commit career-sabotage. In January, 2013, an Applebee's server was fired after she posted a photo of a credit card receipt on a social media website. Applebee's, like many restaurants, have an auto-gratuity policy of 18% for parties of 8 or more. The receipt contained the comment "I give God 10%, why do you get 18" and had the auto-gratuity amount scratched out. The receipt was signed by a pastor who subsequently called the St. Louis area Applebee's general manager to complain after the posting went "viral." The server was terminated for allegedly violating the customer's right to privacy and for violating the franchisee's social media policy as set forth in the employee's handbook. While the pastor regrets writing the note, what is done is done. As of early March, 2013, Applebee's was suffering from negative public relations and a possible boycott. Employees must make careful decisions when using technology that could impact their career development and employers need a social media policy.

Workplace Conditions for Optimal Performance

Creating a great working environment is critical in the success of any hospitality enterprise seeking optimal performance. The theories mentioned in this chapter were developed in the United States at a time when the demographics were somewhat different. Today's employees are more multicultural and will have slightly different motivational drivers based on cultural nuances. Managers cannot motivate people but they can create the climate in which employees are more easily able to motivate themselves. Motivation comes from within a person and the person must have an internal drive such as to do a great job or make a better life for their family.

Camaraderie is an important part of creating a great work environment

© Rawpixel.com/Shutterstock.com

Morale: An employee's or group of employee's feeling(s) about his or their job.

Creating a positive work climate is not easy. As one manager said "I am not leading people, I am leading personalities." (Horne 2018) This suggests getting to know the employees and finding out what will motivate them then, create the environment in which it can happen. A critical part of motivation is to be sure that employees know exactly what is expected of them. Ken Blanchard, a famous author and speaker once addressed the National Restaurant Association National Convention with a story about Jo who was not much good at work but was the star of the Wednesday night bowling team. Now imagine Jo bowls and knocks down six pins and his manager says why didn't you knock down ten pins? Then when Jo goes to bowl the next time imagine the manager placing a curtain half way down the alley so Jo cannot see what he is aiming at (Blanchard, 2001). Sound familiar? Yes, it happens all too often, people do not know what is expected of them so they are not motivated to do a great job. Coupled with motivation is **morale** which is an employee's or group of employee's feeling(s) about his or their job. If morale is high then employees are motivated but if morale is low then employees are not motivated.

Developing Management and Employees

Management Development: About enabling managers from all levels to become more effective leaders and to advance within the organization.

Management development is about enabling managers from all levels to become more effective leaders and to advance within the organization. Effective managers are essential for organizational success and management resides between effective leadership and efficient employees, but how do potential managers become managers? There are different paths to becoming a manager—either through the ranks or through outside accomplishments. Managers must have certain knowledge, skills, and abilities to be able to achieve organizational goals and to engage employees. Lacking these skills and abilities, managers will need on-going training to help them be the best they can be. The three major areas that managers need competence are as follows (Bliss, 2010):

- Recognizing and accepting people's individual behavioral differences.
- Verbal and nonverbal communication.
- Conflict management.

Often, managers come out of the hourly paid ranks, having distinguished themselves in individual contributor roles in the organization. Others come into an organization at a management level, with a combination of experience and college degrees. In either case, managers need a formal development program. To facilitate the process, HR professionals can conduct a needs analysis with each manager and each manager can also conduct one for their departmental associates. Once existing skill levels are determined, they can be compared to the required skill set and training needs identified and individual plans for managers and associates are made.

Coaching

Coaching: a part of management and employee development in which a more experienced or skilled individual provides an employee with advice and guidance intended to help develop the individual's skills, performance, and career.

Coaching is a part of management and employee development in which a more experienced or skilled individual provides an employee with advice and guidance intended to help develop the individual's skills, performance, and career. Sometimes managers and supervisors lack necessary people skills, such as in setting goals, providing accountability, delivering effective performance reviews, and even coaching itself (Bliss, 2009).

Examples of coaching include diversity coaching, if an individual was discriminatory or harassing, coaching would help them see things from the other person's perspective. Another topic where coaching can help is with generational differences. Coaching can assist older and younger employees (Baby Boomers, Gen Xers, and Gen Yers) in understanding the different world views and skills of different generations, learning how their different experiences affect the way they view the workplace and discovering how they can most effectively work together to achieve organizational goals. Other areas that managers and employees can be coached on are financial, marketing, employee relations, benefits, and cross-cultural (Bliss, 2009). It is also a good idea to establish a mentoring program that enables younger or newer employees to gain from the knowledge and experience of a mentor.

HR directors can play an important role in encouraging managers and supervisors to be coaches. Coaches educate, instruct, and train employees in job related skills. Coaching is closely aligned with mentoring, which is advising, counseling, and guiding (Dessler, 2011). Coaching and mentoring both require analytical and interpersonal skills. Analytical skills determine what the problem is and interpersonal skills help solve the problem. Good coaches have the knack of explaining what and how to do a job in a way that gets a positive response from the employee.

Coaching draws on the job description and job instructions. The first part of coaching is observing how is the employee doing the job and interacting with others and to use the ABC (antecedents, behavior, consequences) approach (Dessler, 2011). Look at what might have gone on before and does the employee know exactly what is expected of them? Does the employee know the performance standards and does she or he know why they are not being met? (Dessler, 2011). The behavior question is does the person want to do the job or could they do the job if they wanted to? The consequences might be the opposite of rewarding someone for a job well done—or no bonus for you!

Key Points

- Mentoring is a necessary step in career development that is promoted by an organization's HR department.
- Career progression is a direct result of an employee's personal skills, characteristics, experience, work ethic, and planned career path.
- For employee development to be successful, it is important for HR managers to establish effective recruitment and selection strategies.
- Studies have shown that employees respond positively to additional benefits provided by the company that are conditional upon employment.
- Employee development relies on the ability to create a working relationship that motivates and encourages employees to put forth their best effort in return for being provided with desirable benefits and working conditions.

- Employee development is evaluated on three levels of performance within an organization, which include individual, group, and organizational levels.
- Organizational performance refers to an employee's feelings toward the company's principal philosophies, rules and regulations, and overall purpose for existence.
- A person must manage and market themselves in a way that creates demand for them as an employee. Ultimately, self-reliance means that we are in charge of our own destiny and we determine our fate.
- The HR department is also responsible for maintaining records of a company's rules, regulations, and training programs, as well as benefit packages and additional options for employees.
- With the increase of diversity in the workplace, programs are being created that focus on training senior executives to nurture the development of minorities in the workplace.
- Motivation is such a complex topic because we are all motivated by different things and to different extents. We come from diverse backgrounds, tend to be motivated by different things at different life-stages, and have different experiences and abilities.
- Coaching is a part of management and employee development in which a more experienced or skilled individual provides an employee with advice and guidance intended to help develop the individual's skills, performance, and career.

Key Terms

Career development	Individual, group, and	Retention
Career progression	organizational	Self-reliance
Career self-reliance	Management development	The Hawthorne Studies
Coaching	Mentoring	Turnover
Herzberg's motivation-hygiene	Morale	
theory	Motivation	

Discussion Questions

1. Describe a good mentor.
2. Give an example of career progression.
3. Outline the importance of making the right hire.
4. What do you think is the biggest factor in employee retention?
5. What barriers to employment development have you seen?
6. Which motivation theory do you think is most relevant and why?

Ethical Dilemma

The general manager of a prestigious country club was asked by the chairman of the board to hire his daughter for a management position that had recently become available. The general manager's contract is up for renewal along with a substantial bonus. The position has been advertised and two more highly qualified and experienced candidates have applied. What should he do?

References

Adapted from Jerris, L. A. (1999). *Human resources management for hospitality* (p. 200). Upper Saddle River, NJ: Prentice Hall.

Ayres, H. (2006). Career development in tourism and leisure: An exploratory study of the influence of mobility and mentoring. *The Journal of Hospitality and Tourism Management, 13*(2), 113–123.

Blanchard. K. (2001). Gung Ho Restaurants. Address to the National Restaurant Association, May 16, 2001.

Bliss, W. J. (2009, February). Coaching in a business environment. *Society for Human Resource Management.*

Bliss, W. J. (2010, December). Developing management. *Society for Human Resource Management.*

Brooks, Art. (n.d.). How to Select Human Resources Information Technology: Questions to Ask to Determine HR Information Technology Needs. Retrieved January 15, 2013, from http://humanresources.about.com/od/hristechnology/a/assess_needs.htm

Crawford, A., Hubbard, S. S., Lonis-Shumate, S. R., & O'Neill, M. (2008). Workplace spirituality and employee attitudes within the lodging environment. *Journal of human Resources in Hospitality & Tourism, 8*(1), 64–81. Available from http://www.tandfonline.com.ezproxy.lib.usf.edu/doi/pdf/10.1080/15332840802274445 http://books.google.com/books?id=2BWLZTWoAeUC&pg=PA15&lpg=PA15&dq=Recruitment+and+Select ion+Issues+and+Strategies+within+International+Resort&source=bl&ots=mtDeryXJys&sig=1u85MS5iy9wk 5hqvbCxi7iPZs4Y&hl=en&sa=X&ei=E5jrTsq2CsPftgfrxf27Cg&ved=0CCAQ6AEwAA#v=onepage&q=Recr uitment%20and%20Selection%20Issues%20and%20Strategies%20within%20International%20Resort&f=false

Dessler, G. (2011). *Human resource management* (12th ed., p.435), Upper Saddle River, NJ: Pearson.

Heathfield, S. M. (2012). Human Resources Information Systems. Retrieved January 15, 2013, from http://humanresources.about.com/od/glossaryh/a/hris.htm

Herzberg, F., Mausner, B. & Snyderman, B. (2005). *The motivation to work* (pp. 172–173). (New York: Wiley, 1959). As cited in Stephen P. Robbins Organizational behavior. (11th ed.). Upper Saddle River, NJ: Pearson.

Horne (2018) personal correspondence.

Johnson, R. D. & Gueutal, H. G. (2011). Transforming HR through technology: The use of E-HR and HRIS in organizations. *SHRM Foundation's Effective Practice Guidelines Series.* pp. 14, 18–19.

Linda A. J. (1999). *Human resources management for hospitality* (p. 197). Upper Saddle River, NJ: Prentice Hall.

Michelli, J. A. (2008). *The new gold standard: 5 leadership principles for creating a legendary customer experience courtesy of the Ritz Carlton Hotel Company* (p. 148). McGraw-Hill.

Rosen, D. M. (June 28, 2011). Can new technology bolster HR strategy? Retrieved January 15, 2013, from http://www.hospitalitynet.org/news/4052018.html

Schumacher, S. (2011, April, 1). What employees should know about electronic monitoring. *ESSAI, 8*(38). Available from http://dc.cod.edu

Whitelaw, P. A., Barron, P., Buultjens, J., Cairncross, G., & Davidson, M. (2009). Training needs of the hospitality industry. Available from http://www.sustainabletourismonline.com/awms/Upload/Resource/80093%20%20Training%20Needs%20WEB.pdf

© wavebreakmedia/Shutterstock.com

EMPLOYEE COMPENSATION

Introduction

Compensation and benefits for employees is an important factor of any job and thus it is important for employers to thoroughly research options

© Andrey_Popov/Shutterstock.com

Alyssa currently works as a Director of Sales for a large amusement park in California. She has worked with this company for over three years and has an impressive résumé. Alyssa was offered a job with another amusement park in Florida with the same title but with $8,000 more in salary a year. She could use the raise, and she's heard great things about the company. However, after sitting down to compare the pay and benefits of her current job and that of the new job offer, she realizes $8,000 more a year will not make up for the loss in benefits that she has now.

Her current job not only provides an excellent health care package, but more vacation time, employee bonus programs, and even a free gym membership. She decides to turn down the job offer due to the simple fact that the new job would not have the amount and quality of benefits and incentives.

No matter the state of the economy, employers realize that offering benefits to employees is almost and sometimes just as important as compensation. For example, some Americans who cannot afford the kind of health care insurances they want will opt for a lower rate of pay to get better insurance for themselves and their families. Compensation and benefits for employees is an important factor of any job and thus it is important for employers to thoroughly research options.

In Fortune Magazine's "100 Best Companies to Work For," Marriott International was ranked number 32. How does a business in the hospitality industry achieve such a ranking? It starts by focusing on the employee and what they want and need then maintaining that focus. When your employees know they are in good hands, you can be assured your guests are in even better hands.

After studying this chapter, you should be able to do the following:

1. Create a compensation policy for a company.
2. Discuss the importance of the labor market and how you must adjust to survive.
3. Identify what workplace legalities exist in compensation.
4. Identify the difference between exempt and nonexempt employees.
5. Describe unions and the role they play in the work force.
6. Be able to establish the rate of pay for a job.

Compensation Policy

Base Compensation: The fixed pay an employee receives on a regular basis.

Compensation has three components. The relative portion of each is known as the *pay mix* and varies extensively by firm (Milkovich, Newman, & Gerhart, 2012, as cited in Gomez-Mejia, Balkin, & Cardy, 2012). The first and in most cases the largest is **base compensation**, the fixed pay an employee receives on a regular basis, in the form of a salary—a weekly or bi-weekly or monthly pay check (Gomez-Mejia, Balkin, & Cardy, 2012). The second component of total compensation is **pay incentives**, programs designed to reward employees for good performance. These incentives come in many forms (including bonus and profit sharing). The third component of total compensation is **benefits**, sometimes called indirect compensation which can in some cases approach 42% of employee's compensation packages (Martochio, J. J., 2011, as cited in Gomez-Mejia, Balkin, & Cardy, 2012).

> **Pay Incentives**: Programs designed to reward employees for good performance.

> **Benefits**: Programs such as healthcare made available to employees by many employers.

Learning Objective 1: Create a compensation policy for a company

The goal of **compensation policy** is to determine compensation practices and acts as a guide for all employees. Compensation policy includes the benefits, different rates of pay, salary and other incentives a company has to offer to an employee. Compensation policies

> **Compensation Policy**: A policy for compensating employees.

are often strategized to not only attract talent for new positions but retain current employees as well. Compensation policies should be reviewed and adjusted on a regular basis. Companies have found that policies must adjust according the job market and the economy. For example, if a compensation policy is based on a set percentage of sales and sales have dropped for the last two years, the company revises or come up with a new compensation policy.

Since compensation policies also usually include incentives and bonus programs, these factors may also need to be adjusted as the labor market rises and falls. The same way a company may need to adjust when sales are down is relevant to when sales are up. If you offer a quarterly bonus based on a specific sales percentage, and sales have increased consistently over the last 12 months, you may need to raise the sales percentage that needs to be met to remain eligible for the quarterly bonus.

Compensation policies should be company and culture specific. No matter what goals or expectations you have for your company, an effective compensation policy suited for an individual organization can lead toward success in more than one way.

Another term related to compensation is **fringe benefits**, which are the extras given to employees such as hotel room discounts, food and beverage discounts, retail discounts, discounted laundry and dry cleaning, discounted or free parking, discounted or free employee meals, free or discounted cell phones.

> **Fringe Benefits**: Additional benefits given to employees by employers.

Compensation Objectives and Strategies

Before you can establish a compensation policy, HR professionals of a company must outline the goals they want to achieve and the strategies that they need to reach those goals. The goal is the outcome you want to reach for any situation, in this case, compensation goals. What do you want to achieve to be better than your competitors? The strategy is what road map you use to find your destination—how will you accomplish each goal you've set? It seems hard to believe that among all factors that successfully run an operation, compensation for a company is equally important as quality of service. How can you attract and maintain excellent employees? How can you compete with others in the industry while still creating a profit?

The following factors are suggestions for creating compensation goals for any given company:

- To pay in the top 10% of your direct competitive set.
- Pay equity.
- Reward system for superior performance.
- Controlling labor costs.
- Reducing turnover.
- Effective recruiting and retaining of employees.
- Establish rates of pay that are considered fair and equitable to the employee.
- Legal; ensuring the goals and strategies used to reach those goals are within the law and considered ethical and moral.
- Productivity focused.

As a company develops or updates its compensation goals and strategies, a first step is to determine where it stands in comparison to its competitors. By conducting a survey of the competition, they can identify and analyze where it stands with the compensation policies (refer to **Figure 9.1**). If your company is

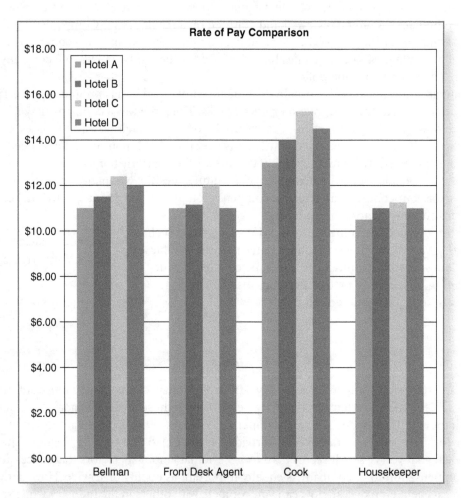

Figure 9.1   Rate of Pay Comparison

Hotel A, and you have just conducted research of your three biggest competitors, you will find that your current compensation is closely in line with all three. You can see that Hotel D offers higher rates of pay for each position you researched. As a competing company, you would want to ensure you are offering the best possible rate of pay for your employees to avoid turnover and low pay equity. However, remember, pay is only part of compensation. A through survey would also look at incentives and benefits.

Learning Objective 2: Discuss the importance of the labor market and how you must adjust to survive

Eric A. Brown, Ph.D. Associate Professor, Department of Apparel, Events, and Hospitality Management, Iowa State University

Educating future hospitality professionals was not my initial career goal. I began working in the hospitality industry over 15 years ago, eventually settling in as a manager in hotel operations. As with most people, my main motivation for growing my career in hospitality was the people. I loved interacting with some of the most passionate employees and doing my part in making a guest's day every day. The favorite part of my job was training and developing employees which lead me down the education path where I now prepare hospitality students for careers in the hospitality industry.

Between recruiting employees and making an offer to a new employee, every manager needs to consider compensation. Even though new employees receive a set compensation when they are brought on, it is something that needs to be constantly evaluated to ensure you are providing adequate compensation to not only retain and motivate employees, but also to ensure you are attracting the best employees.

Practically all hospitality businesses have struggled with retaining good employees and in one of the hotels I managed I ran into an issue where my good employees were leaving. Through conversations with these employees, I found out they were leaving because most of the other hotels in the area were paying more and our hotel was only offering minimal raises each year. Because of this critical issue, I began investigating further and made a proposal on where I believed the compensation at my hotel should be in order to be competitive so we could attract and retain high quality employees.

Hotels have conducted wage surveys where they would call area hotels and ask how much they paid each position in exchange for offering that same information to the other hotel. The problem with this approach was people could choose not to participate or could lie to prevent that information from getting out as many employers saw, and continue to see, their compensation packages as a competitive advantage. An alternative approach I saw was having a current employee apply at another hotel with the main goal of finding out their competition's process as well as how much they were paying.

During my research and proposal development, I used several resources to decide on where I thought compensation should be. One key source I ended up using was O*NET OnLine (www.onetonline.org), a site with extensive occupation level information sponsored by the Department of Labor. Through the site, I was able to see the wage statistics for different positions within a hotel in my area and use that information to justify significant raises for my employees. I highly encourage students to explore this site as you can find a lot of information about careers you intend to pursue. Students can find anything from wage statistics to educational requirements to typical expectations and requirements for jobs. As a manager, I also used this site for ideas when I developed job descriptions or made modifications to current jobs. Compensation is a key resource managers needs to use, and consistently evaluate, in order to ensure success in the hospitality industry.

Contributed by Eric A. Brown. © Kendall Hunt Publishing Company

The Labor Market

Labor Market: A market in which workers find paid work.

Compensation goals and strategies and objectives must be relevant to the labor market. A labor market is a market (whether it be internal or external) in which workers find paid work, pay rates and wages are determined, and an employer can find those able and willing to work. If there is a consistent supply of jobs available, the unemployment rates are low and the labor market is considered healthy. If there is a low demand for work and the unemployment rates are high, the labor market is more than likely struggling. The hospitality labor market is often competing with itself as well as other industries that pay higher wages such as technological, investment, and health care jobs.

To understand a labor market and how it can help determine wages and compensation, look at the state of New York to help you understand their labor market conditions for restaurants (National Restaurant Association, n.d.):

- Every extra $1 million spent in New York's eating and drinking establishments generates an additional 20.2 jobs in the state.
- Every $1 spent in New York's restaurants generates an additional $.86 in sales for the state economy.
- In 2010, there were 41,221 eating and drinking places in New York.
- In 2010, New York's restaurants are projected to register $31.9 billion in sales.
- Restaurant jobs represent 8% of employment in New York.

These facts suggest that the labor market for restaurants continues to be a strong industry in New York. Almost one in 10 working Americans works in restaurants (Restaurant, n.d). Although jobs in restaurants are not typically associated with high salaries, they are jobs that are needed, wanted and necessary for our economy to function. Thus, it is important to compensate a server, a bartender, a chef accordingly and properly for the services they provide.

Learning Objective 3: Identify what workplace legalities exist in compensation

Legal Aspects of Compensation

Beyond the legalities when hiring, firing, and managing employees; companies must always be aware of the most recent laws, and regulations involving employee compensation.

Learning Objective 4: Identify the difference between exempt and nonexempt employees

Exempt and Nonexempt Employee

According to the Fair Labor Standards Act (FLSA) there are two definitive categories in which employees fall into: exempt and nonexempt. The reason for this categorical divide is due to wage and hour laws affecting basic pay rates and overtime hours worked.

Exempt employees are those employees who are not eligible to be paid for overtime work. There are multiple categories in the FLSA, but the one seen most commonly is an employee in a management or supervisory position. They are commonly of at the higher side on a pay grade. To meet an exempt status, an employee must spend at least 50% of their time, supervising two or more employees and is paid at least $250 weekly.

Nonexempt employees are those employees who are eligible for overtime because they are paid at an hourly rate and are covered under the wage and hour laws. Workers earning less than $23,660 per year or $455 per week are guaranteed overtime protection (Wage and Hour Division, n.d.). Nonexempt employees are also called hourly

Nonexempt employees are also called hourly employees and typically do not have managerial roles

© wavebreakmedia/Shutterstock.com

employees and typically do not hold managerial roles in a company. The Fair Labor Standards Act (FLSA) requires that all covered, nonexempt employees be paid at least the federal minimum wage for all hours worked. States also have minimum wages laws where the wages are higher than federal minimum wage rate. The FLSA also provides that covered, nonexempt employees who work more than 40 hours in the workweek must receive at least one and one-half times their regular rate of pay for the overtime hours (hours worked over 40 in a workweek). A workweek, which can begin on any day of the week, is 7 consecutive 24-hour periods or 168 consecutive hours (Dol, n.d.).

> **Exempt Employees:** Employees who are not eligible for overtime pay.

> **Nonexempt Employees:** Those employees who are eligible for overtime because they are paid at an hourly rate and are covered under the wage and hour laws.

Learning Objective 5: Describe unions and the role they play in the work force

Union Influences on Compensation

A trade union or a **labor union** is a group of people who have joined together to achieve a common goal or goals. Goals can include better pay, better work environment, or even better benefits. Through leadership, the unions will frequently negotiate with

> **Labor Union:** A group of employees who have joined together for common goals.

the employer on behalf of a member of that union. This may include the negotiation of promotions, wages, hiring, and firing, safety in the workplace, policies, and work rules.

In December of 2010, Palmer House Hilton, Chicago, workers were set to go "on strike" Workers from the Palmer House Hilton believed the company was taking advantage of the recession by reducing pay or increasing workloads for workers even though they received a bail out from the Government. The decision for a group of workers to go on strike was not a single person's decision or efforts, but the effort of a union. The striking Hilton workers were members of a union called UNITE HERE Local 1. This particular union included housekeepers, dishwashers, cooks, bell staff, food servers, and others.

Union members voted to strike and with 96% in favor, the strike began. Some unions offer other services to their members, such as training, such as a 6-month culinary skills program.

Unions influence employees and companies in many ways. Unions want what is best for the working individual, and typically it results in negotiations and a collective bargaining agreement, which is discussed in Chapter 14.

Sky Chefs, an airline food distributor, workers helped keep the company from going under. They took wage and benefit cuts amounting to as much as 30% of their income. The company decided to raise insurance costs amounting to $500.00 a month for workers who made less than $10.00 an hour. The union representing 7,000 Sky Chefs workers in North America intervened to help the workers negotiate a fair contract.

Compensation Tools

There are two main ways to structure pay decisions: a job-based approach and a skill-based approach (Milkovich, Newman, & Gerhart, 2012, as cited in Gomez-Mejia, Balkin, & Cardy, 2012). The job-based approach assumes that work gets done by people who are paid to perform well-defined jobs and each job is designed to accomplish specific tasks and is normally performed by several people.

Because all jobs are not equally important to the company and the labor market puts a greater value on some jobs more than others, the compensation system's primary objective is to allocate pay so that the most important jobs pay the most (Gomez-Mejia, Balkin, & Cardy, 2012, p. 324).

The skill-based approach is not used nearly as much. Its premise is that employees should be paid not according to the job they hold, but rather by how flexible or capable they are at performing multiple tasks. Under this plan, the greater the variety of job-related skills workers possess, the more they are paid (Gomez-Mejia, Balkin, & Cardy, 2012, p. 324).

Learning Objective 6: Be able to establish the rate of pay for a job

Wage and Salary Surveys

A wage and salary survey is a common method to collect information that offers a comparison of compensation levels across organizations with similar job positions. HR directors either send out a survey themselves about once a year, or have an outside company do it for them. The survey is sent to companies in the area identified as being similar so, for example, a Hilton hotel would want to include a Westin, Marriott, Omni, and Hyatt.

> **Benchmark Jobs:** Anchor jobs around which other jobs are slotted.

Employers use the salary surveys in three ways. First, they use survey data to price benchmark jobs. Benchmark jobs are anchor jobs around which they slot their other jobs, based on each job's relative worth to the company. Job evaluation helps determine the relative worth of each job to the benchmarked job (Gomez-Mejia, Balkin, & Cardy, 2012, p. 324). Second, employers typically price 20% or more of their positions directly in the marketplace (rather than relative to the firm's benchmark jobs), hospitality companies might do this for IT positions. Third, surveys also collect data on benefits such as insurance, sick leave, and vacations to provide a basis for decisions regarding employee benefits (Gomez-Mejia, Balkin, & Cardy, 2012, p. 324). Some companies are using the Internet to check on salary levels for various positions online but they may not as accurate as a real wage survey.

Job Evaluation

Job evaluation as the name suggests, evaluates the worth of a job compared to another and forms the basis of a pay scale. Obviously, jobs that require greater skills, responsibilities, and abilities deserve higher levels of pay then jobs requiring fewer skills, responsibilities, and abilities.

The Equal Pay Act emphasizes four compensable factors: skills, effort, responsibility, and working conditions. The Hay consulting firm recommends three factors: know-how, problem solving, and accountability. When doing a job evaluation, HR directors often make up a committee of HR specialists, employees, and possibly union representatives. After evaluating the various jobs, the committee groups a few similar jobs into **classes** and then **grades** them. The U.S. government's classification system uses the following compensable factors: (1) difficulty of work, (2) supervision received and exercised, (3) judgment exercised, (4) originality required, (5) nature and purpose of interpersonal work relationships, (6) responsibility, (7) experience, and (8) knowledge required. The committee may also select the 10–15 key benchmark jobs that are the ones to set the rates of pay for all other jobs.

> **Classes**: Classes or categories of jobs.

> **Grades**: Grades or classifications of jobs according to certain factors.

Another technique used by HR professionals and job evaluation committees is to award points for the degree of each factor. An example being, using the government's classification above, number one is the difficulty of work and it could have 5 or 10 points for that factor and all the other factors that the committee determines are valid. Consider a housekeeper's job; one of the likely factors would be *effort* and we would probably give 5 or 10 points for that. In addition, don't forget the dishwasher who can make or break an operation. Dishwashers work in hot and noisy conditions so they should receive a lot of points for their *working conditions*.

A **pay grade** is developed based on different factors for an employee that should be taken into consideration when establishing pay rates

© jesterpop/Shutterstock.com

Pay Grades

Pay grade factors include on the job performance, experience, and seniority. Several careers in the hospitality industry require high levels of performance and many years of experience, and thus, the pay rate should reflect those requirements. A pay grade can help you determine the level of pay for each employee based on a points system. A general manager for a hotel would have a higher grade than that of a room service attendant at the same hotel. The higher the overall responsibility of the employee is, the higher the grade and the higher the pay rate will be.

> **Pay Grade**: Pay rate established by taking various criteria into consideration.

Price Range for Each Pay Grade

The price range for a pay grade will be based on the level of job skill and knowledge required for each position at a company. This will be individual for a company, their budget and the number of employees they have. To determine the price range for each pay grade, you must first assign a number of points for a job (**Figure 9.2**). Once you have created a scale of which to grade, you can then determine what rate of pay is appropriate for the given level of points (**Figure 9.3**).

    If you apply both of these figures to a pay grade for an amusement park, you can evaluate the usefulness of pay rates for each grade. A job that may earn a grade of "1," would be a ride attendant. The job does not require a lot of knowledge or experience and earns points in the range of 50–100. A job that may earn a grade of "5," would be a supervisor position inside the park, which requires more experience and knowledge and would earn more points on the grade in the range of 251–300.

Job Evaluation Form		
Job Title:		Evaluation Date 6/23/2019
Name of Employee:		
Name of Supervisor:		
Person Completing Evaluation:		
Date of Employment:	3/1/2019	

1=does not meet expectations
2=barely meets expectations
3=meets expectations and is satisfactory on the job
4=exceeds expectations and shows enthusiasm while doing so
5=makes special efforts to exceed expectations while leading others to do the same

Category of Performance	Evaluation Scale	Comment
Initiative	1 2 3 4 5	
Work ethic	1 2 3 4 5	
Ability to follow instruction	1 2 3 4 5	
Ability to work well with others	1 2 3 4 5	
Appearance	1 2 3 4 5	
Promptness	1 2 3 4 5	
Personal responsibility	1 2 3 4 5	
Dependability	1 2 3 4 5	
Personality	1 2 3 4 5	
Guest relations skills	1 2 3 4 5	

Additional Comments:

Signature of Supervisor	
Signature of Person Completing Review	
Signature of Employee Reviewed	

Figure 9.2

Grade	Job Evaluation Points
1	50–100
2	101–150
3	151–200
4	201–250
5	251–300

Figure 9.3

Bonuses and Merit Pay

Bonuses are paid for good results and from the company's point of view they are good because they are only paid once and not like an increase in salary. Normally, bonuses are paid when the company does well financially or when, for example, a sales manager reaches a certain sales revenue quota.

Merit pay is similar to a bonus and there can be several different elements in the criteria for earning merit pay. Examples are attendance, timeliness, various performance criteria, team spirit, attitude, and guest service.

Many companies pay what is called a "tipped minimum wage" for their employees

© Blend Images/Shutterstock.com

Tips and Service Charges

Many occupations within the hospitality industry take tips and service charge into consideration when establishing pay rates. The minimum wage for a restaurant server is much less than a security guard at a hotel, because the server will receive tips. Obviously, the better service you provide the more you could make; therefore, companies must establish pay rates or follow minimum wage requirements based on an average of tips for an employee who will be relying on tips for the majority of their pay.

The federal internal revenue service defines tips as gratuity given to an employee from a guest for services or tasks provided. Many companies pay what

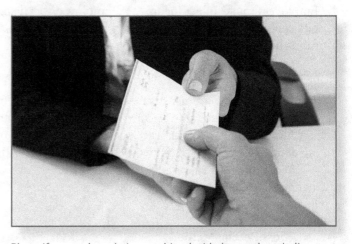

Photo If an employee's tips combined with the employer's direct wages of at least $2.13 an hour do not equal federal minimum wage, the employer must make up the difference (Elaws, n.d.)

© Andrey_Popov/Shutterstock.com

is called a "tipped minimum wage" for their employees. This is a minimum wage established and followed by the Fair Labor Standards Act (FLSA). The FLSA requires payment of at least the federal minimum wage to covered, nonexempt employees. An employer of a tipped employee is only required to pay $2.13 an hour in direct wages; if that amount plus the tips received equals at least the federal minimum wage, the employee retains all tips and the employee customarily and regularly receives more than $30.00 a month in tips. If an employee's tips combined with the employer's direct wages of at least $2.13 an hour do not equal federal minimum wage, the employer must make up the difference (Elaws, n.d.).

Reporting Tip Income—Restaurant Tax Tips (IRS, n.d.)

Tips your employees receive from customers are generally subject to withholding. Employees are required to claim all tip income received. This includes tips you paid over to the employee for charge customers and tips the employee received directly from customers.

Employee Requirements

Employees must report tip income on Form 4070, Employee's Report of Tips to Employer, or on a similar statement. This report is due on the 10th day of the month after the month the tips are received. This statement must be signed by the employee and must show the following:

- The employee's name, address, and SSN.
- Your name and address.
- The month or period the report covers.
- The total tips received.

No report is required from an employee for months when tips are less than $20.

Employer Requirements

Employers must collect income tax, employee social security tax and employee Medicare tax on tips reported by employees. You can collect these taxes from an employee's wages or from other funds he or she makes available.

Allocation of Tips

As an employer, you must ensure that the total tip income reported to you during any pay period is, at a minimum, equal to 8% of your total receipts for that period.

In calculating 8% of total receipts, you do not include nonallocable receipts. Nonallocable receipts are defined as receipts for carry out sales and receipts with a service charge added of 10% or more.

When the total reported to you is less than 8%, you must allocate the difference between the actual tip income reported and 8% of gross receipts. There are three methods for allocating tip income:

- Gross Receipt Method
- Hours Worked Method
- Good Faith Agreement

Employers can request a lower rate (but not lower than 2%) for tip allocation purposes by submitting an application to the IRS. Detailed instructions for computing allocation of tips, reporting allocated tips to employees, and for requesting a lower rate can be found in the Instructions for Form 8027.

Tip Reporting Requirements for Employers

Employers who operate large food or beverage establishments must file Form 8027, Employer's Annual Information Return of Tip Income and Allocated Tips to report employee tip income. A large food or beverage establishment is defined as business where all of the following apply:

- Food or beverage is provided for consumption on the premises
- Tipping is a customary practice
- More than 10 employees, who work more than 80 hours, were normally employed on a typical business day during the preceding calendar year.

A worksheet for determining whether a business meets the criteria listed above is included in the Instructions for Form 8027.

IRS, Reporting Tip Income—Restaurant Tax Tips, 2017

A service charge is another common form of compensation in the hospitality and restaurant business. Country clubs and restaurants inside upscale hotels often include a service charge. A **service charge** or a surcharge is a set fee added to a guest's bill for services or tasks provided that takes the place of tips.

> **Service Charge**: A charge added to guests bills for service.

A service charge can either benefit or hurt an employee of the establishment charging the fee. For instance, if a Country Club charges a 10% service charge on all restaurant services, a guest may assume that a portion of that 10% charge goes to the servers and therefore may only tip 5% to 10% additional. From the guest's point of view, they are tipping the server 20% which is an industry norm, however due to the service charge, the server is actually only receiving 10% of a tip which is much less than an employee relies on for income. On the other hand, if that same club charges a 10% service fee but the entire charge goes directly to the server, it can assure that the server will receive at least 10% tip of the bill versus the change of not receiving any tip at all.

Legalize

Hospitality companies that violate the mandates of the FLSA are risking huge exposure to class action lawsuits especially if they failed to. Employers must maintain accurate time and payroll records. Hospitality companies must be aware that the legal industry has identified this area as a "hot" big dollar class action area with substantial monetary recovery potential.

For example, on September 13, 2012, celebrity chef Mario Batali's eight New York City restaurants were ordered to pay current and former tipped service workers $5.25 million for violations of the FLSA and the New York Labor Law, a record for a multiple restaurant case in New York. New York federal court

Magistrate Judge Ronald L. Ellis approved the settlement of the class action lawsuit, which was filed in 2010. The class consisted of 1,100 members ranging from captains, servers, bussers, runners, bartenders and barbacks who worked at the various restaurants from July 22, 2004 to February 14, 2012.

Gaylord Texan Resort and Convention Center recently agreed to pay 429 service employees a total of $204,329 after a U.S. Department of Labor's Wage and Hour Division launched an investigation and filed a lawsuit against the hotel. Violations of the FLSA included, but were not limited to, paying wages below the federal minimum wage, improperly classifying workers as exempt from overtime compensation, and failing to maintain accurate records of employees' work hours and wages. Gaylord Entertainment Co., the parent corporation, has agreed to promote FLSA compliance by employing stricter oversight with its vendors, providing compliance assistance materials, and improving an employees' ability to complain by establishing a toll-free complaint hotline.

Unfortunately for the hospitality industry, the filing of these class action lawsuits continues at an alarming rate. On March 1, 2012, Darden Restaurants, Inc., and its subsidiaries have been sued in Florida for minimum wage, overtime, and other FLSA violations. Darden owns approximately 1,900 restaurants with brands including Longhorn Steakhouse, and Olive Garden. The Complaint, which was filed in the Southern District of Florida, seeks damages including unpaid minimum wages, overtime pay, spread-of-hours pay, liquidated damages, back pay, front pay, compensatory damages, punitive damages, and attorney's fees. Clearly, the hospitality industry has been targeted by lawyers alleging violations of the FLSA. These lawsuits are very attractive for law firms because if the attorneys can achieve certification of the class from the Court, they can become very profitable.

As these recent settlements and case filings indicate, hospitality industry operators must stay abreast of the latest FLSA mandates. Law firms find these cases very attractive and profitable. Litigation is costly and time-consuming, and a proactive, preventative course of action is the most cost effective means of staying out of court.

Technology in HR—Electronic Compensation

> **Human Resources Management System**: A multipurpose software program that encompasses a range of HR features, including payroll, attendance, benefits, recruiting, training, scheduling, performance reviews, and so on.

Many hospitality organizations, both large and small, use some form of Human Resources Management System to perform their daily HR functions. A Human Resources Management System is a multipurpose software program that encompasses a range of HR features, including payroll, attendance, benefits, recruiting, training, scheduling, performance reviews, and so on. The exact range of features of an HRMS varies between products, as businesses have a unique set of needs based on their differences in size and organizational structure. There are between 50 and 100 producers of HRMS, most of which are software companies or providers (Asu's Estimate., October, 2012). An automated payroll option is the most widely used features of a HRMS. Almost all HRMS include payroll and attendance features, which simplify the employee compensation process.

Using advanced technology to simplify the employee compensation process is useful in minimizing labor, by allowing managers to easily track and control labor hours and overtime pay. Another benefit of automated compensation is the ability of managers to plan incentive programs more efficiently because they have access to more information. Managers can connect their electronic compensation system with other features of the HRMS, such as training, development, and performance reviews. This allows companies to show that the implementation of their compensation structure directly relates to accomplishing a higher level of organizational excellence (Johnson, & Gueutal, 2011).

Merit Increases

A **merit increase** is an increase in wages that is earned through superior performance during the job. It is an important factor in any compensation policy and is often what encourages employees to continuously perform well on the job. A merit increase is one of the simplest concepts that benefit the employee and the employer.

Consider a food attendant for Cedar Point amusement park. If a typical starting wage is $7.50 and there is no merit increases established in Cedar Point's compensation plan, that food attendant will continue to perform only what is required of him or her to keep his or her job and continue earning $7.50. If the food attendant is told that based on a 90-day review he or she may receive a $0.25 increase to his o her hourly pay rate, that employee is going to work more efficiently and perform better so he or she will receive a good review and in turn, receive their increase. Cedar Point is much better off offering a $0.25 raise upon performance with additional incentives for further superior performance than to not have merit increases and have an employee who shows up to work to do the bare minimum.

Other factors such as sales numbers, customer reviews, and other factors involving the job may be taken into consideration when a company determines the basis for a merit increase.

Skill- and Knowledge-Based Pay

Skill- and knowledge-based pay is the amount of compensation an individual will received based on their knowledge, skills, and previous experience involving the job. Skill- and knowledge-based pay is sometimes hard to gage, but many companies have a definitive guideline for basing rate of pay and salary on this concept.

Skill- and knowledge-based pay not only allows an employer to fairly compensate an employee, but it also creates a more efficient operation, see **Figure 9.4**. If employees are aware that the sole substance of their pay is based on their performance, they will not only work harder on a day-to-day basis, but will tend to stay loyal to a company knowing they have the ability to increase their rate of pay.

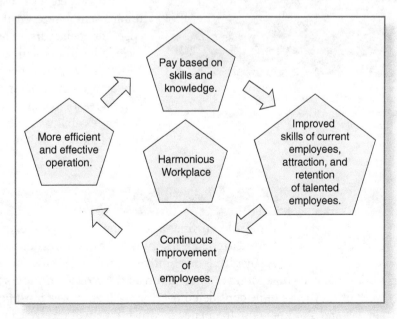

Figure 9.4

Travis Hire applied to work as a banquet and restaurant server at a country club. Travis had worked at three different restaurants while he attended college, and recently graduated with a degree in Financial Planning and Business from a large University. Travis sends his résumé to the country club when he sees the open position for a banquet and restaurant server.

Upon being interviewed, the HR manager explains that the typical starting rate of pay is $7.50 an hour, but because Travis has a background and solid knowledge of serving and a good education, they would like to extend a job offer starting at $8.50 an hour. Travis accepts and begins his employment. A few weeks into the job, Travis cannot help but notice that most of the servers have been working at the club for over three years, something he knows is not common in the restaurant business. He also notices that the work ethic if his fellow employees are strong and everyone works hard through their shifts. Realizing that he needs to meet and even exceed the skills and work of his peers, Travis tries to work harder every day. After 3 months into the job, the HR manager calls Travis into his office to let him know that his skills and hard work have earned him a promotion to banquet captain and assistant restaurant manager.

Comparable Worth and Competency-Based Pay

Pay your employees too little and they may leave, pay your employees too much and you are not operating efficiently as an operation

© ESB Professional/Shutterstock.com

Comparable worth means to pay individuals (usually in the context of men and women) equally for comparable jobs. For example, a company determines that the job of a housekeeper (who are mostly women) is comparable to the job of a facility cleaner (who are mostly men). The company would then ensure that these jobs, although different, have comparable pay.

A Competency Based Pay program rewards employees on their skills, knowledge, or behaviors. These competences include behaviors and skills such as complexity of the tasks, leadership, problem solving, or decision making. Pay levels reflect the degree of competency and reflect an employee's ability to contribute to achievement of the organization's goals and.

The Pay Plan

> **Pay Plan**: A plan for paying employees.

A pay plan defines a company's working week, the day pay is disbursed to employees any bonuses, commissions, or increases in pay.

A pay plan is a definitive guideline for any company. An employee must know if their work week starts on a Monday and ends on a Friday, overtime hours must be accumulated in that 5-day week or they will not be considered overtime. An employee must be able to rely on a paycheck on a certain day and also know the frequency in which they will receive pay. A pay plan must also include a time frame and structure for any bonuses or incentives. Quarterly? Annually? Monthly?

A pay plan can also include the steps necessary to receive a raise in salary or hourly rate. This may require a license to be obtained, training class requirements, a set number of hours in a certain department, and so forth.

Managing Remuneration

Pay your employees too little and they may leave, pay your employees too much and you are not operating efficiently as an operation. Managing remuneration is the process of developing and installing skills in employees to grow the company while making them more valuable to other companies.

The complete concept of management remuneration involves HR efforts to make the compensation for a job more attractive without necessarily directly increasing the rate of pay or salary. One concept of remuneration is fixed pay versus performance driven pay. Fixed pay is a set dollar or salary amount in which a job is to be performed to the full job description. Performance driven pay is based on the efforts an employee puts forth; the harder they work, the more money they will make. Both fixed and performance driven pay plans allow room for bonuses, sales compensation, incentive rewards, and other sources for employee motivation.

> **Managing Remuneration**: The process of developing and installing skills in employees to grow the company while making them more valuable to other companies.

> **Fixed Pay**: A set dollar amount in which the job is performed to the full job description.

> **Performance Driven Pay**: Pay driven by the efforts an employee puts forth.

Key Points

- The goal of **compensation policy** is to design a cost-effective pay structure that will attract, motivate, and retain competent employees (Heneman & Werner, 2005, as cited in DeCenzo & Robbins, 2010).
- Compensation policy includes the benefits, rate of pay, salary, and other incentives a company has to offer to an employee.
- Compensation has three components: Base compensation, pay incentives, and benefit.
- By conducting a survey or comparison of your competition, you can identify and analyze where you stand with your compensation policies.
- A pay grade is developed based on different factors for an employee that should be taken into consideration when establishing pay rates.
- The FLSA requires payment of at least the federal minimum wage to covered, nonexempt employees.
- Employers must collect income tax, employee social security tax, and employee Medicare tax on tips reported by employees.
- The FLSA mandates that nonexempt employees be paid one and a half times the standard wage for each hour worked over 40 hours per week.
- Skill- and knowledge-based pay is the amount of compensation an individual will received based on their knowledge, skills, and previous experience involving the job.

Key Terms

Base compensation	Fringe benefits	Nonexempt employees
Benchmark jobs	Grades	Pay grade
Benefits	Human Resources Management	Pay incentives
Classes	System	Pay plan
Compensation policy	Labor market	Performance driven pay
Exempt employees	Labor union	Service charge
Fixed pay	Managing remuneration	

Discussion Questions

1. What is the difference between exempt and nonexempt employees? Is one better than the other and why or why not?

2. Do you feel wage increases or "raises" should be based on seniority, knowledge of the job, or a job evaluation based on performance? Do you believe one is more effective than another?

3. Why do companies offer bonus programs or incentives that involve monetary rewards? Is this an effective way to motivate employees?

4. Describe the theory behind a pay grade and discuss its legitimacy in determining wages for employees.

References

Anonymous. (n.d.). Available from, http://money.cnn.com/magazines/fortune/bestcompanies/2010/snapshots/82.html

Asu's Estimate. (2012, October). Human Resources Management System. Retrieved from http://www.asuses.net/human-resources-management-system/

David A. DeCenzo, D. A. & Robbins, S. P. (2010). *Fundamentals of human resource management*. (10th ed., p. 264). Upper Saddle River, NJ: Pearson.

Dol. (n.d.). Retrieved August 8, 2012, from http://www.dol.gov/elaws/esa/flsa/hoursworked/default.asp

Elaws. (n.d.). Fair Labor Standards act advisor. Available from https://www.dol.gov/whd/regs/compliance/whdfs15a.pdf

Gomez-Mejia, L. R., Balkin, D. B., & Cardy, R. L. (2012). *Managing human resources* (7th ed.; p.312). Upper Saddle River NJ: Pearson.

IRS, (n.d.). Available from https://www.irs.gov/businesses/small-businesses-self-employed/reporting-tip-income-restaurant-tax-tips

Johnson, R. D. & Gueutal, H. G. (2011). Transforming HR through technology: The Use Of E-HR And HRIS In Organizations. *SHRM Foundation's Effective Practice Guidelines Series*. p. 20–21.

National Restaurant Association. (n.d.). New York Restaurant Industry at a Glance. Retrieved August 10, 2012, from http://waiterpay.com/wp-content/uploads/2010/08/New-York-Restaurant-Industry-at-a-Glance-Report-of-National-Restaurant-Association.pdf

Restaurant, (n.d.). Available from http://www.restaurant.org/pdfs/research/state/newyork.pdf

Wage and Hour Division, (n.d.). U.S. Department of Labor Retrieved August 8, 2012 , from www.dol.gov/esa

© michaeljung/Shutterstock.com

EMPLOYEE BENEFITS AND SERVICES

Chapter 10

Introduction

Starbucks has about 16,000 stores around the world. With stores in diverse locations with a wide range of labor markets, they realize that, when it comes to benefits, one size does not fit all. Perhaps that is the reason why Starbucks employee benefits can be customized, just like their drink menu. Each partner (employee) gets a "Special Blend" of total pay and benefits that is unique to him or her. Benefits include (just for a start) healthcare benefits, a retirement savings plan, life and disability coverage, adoption assistance, domestic partner benefits, and (of course) a pound of coffee each week (starbucks.com, 2011).

Starbucks, with nearly 16,000 stores globally, provides world-class benefits for their employees

© Nils Versemann/Shutterstock.com

Therefore, why do some companies offer different benefits, only certain benefits, or in some cases none at all? The answer is complicated by many factors. Given that benefits can make up to 30–40% of the hourly wage; firms that only employ part-time (currently, less than 30 hours per week) employees who get no benefit may have a competitive edge due to lower labor costs. The dollar amount for only 20 full-time employees quickly adds up. If the average wage is $10 per hour, there would be 20 × $10 = $200 × 40 hours per week = $8,000 per week or $32,000 per month or $41,600 per year (there are 13 accounting periods in a fiscal year) now 40% of $41,600 is $16,640. That is $16,640 that is not going toward profit.

But, what if the labor turnover at the company offering benefits is much lower than the one that is not offering benefits, how would that affect the financials? HR directors suggest that the dollar cost per employee for hourly paid staff to recruit and train is about $5,000. Therefore, if the turnover percent at the nonbenefit company was 70% and at the benefit offering company was 20%, then we can calculate the difference. For the company not offering benefits, 0.7 (70%) × 20 employees is 14 × $5,000 = $70,000. For the company offering benefits, 0.2 (20%) × 20 employees is 4 × $5,000 = $20,000. The difference is $50,000, which is much greater than the cost of $16,640 for offering benefits.

Employee benefits have come a long way from the early days of standard benefits of health insurance, vacation time, and perhaps a retirement plan. Consider the benefits that the search engine Google offers to its employees to differentiate itself from its competitors that want to hire people with the same talents, according to Steven E. Gross, a consultant practice leader at Mercer Human Resource Consulting (Knowledge@wharton, 2007, as cited in Gomez-Mejia, Balkin, & Cardy, 2010, p. 372). One of the benefits that is noticed right away at Google is the food. Google provides 11 free "gourmet" cafeterias at its Mountain View, California, campus that provide a variety of international foods, including a Spanish-style tapa bar and Indian, Chinese, Italian, Thai, and Mexican restaurants (Lashinky, 2007). It also offers a 24-hour on-site fitness center, as well as personal trainers. There are an in-house doctor and nutritionist, a dry cleaner, and a massage service. A biodiesel bus equipped with Wi-Fi shuttles commuters to the office. For employees who drive their car to work, Google supplies on-site carwashes and oil changes. In addition, Google offers employees a $5,000 subsidy to buy a hybrid car (Knowledge@wharton, 2007, as cited in Gomez-Mejia, Balkin, & Cardy, 2010, p. 372). Can you see these benefits coming in the hospitality industry?

However, in a period of economic recession, such as after 2008, many companies that were offering benefits looked to reduce the increasing costs of offering benefits. In 2018, companies had to examine the effects of recent healthcare legislation and what might happen in Congress in the coming years. It is important for employers to establish a benefits strategy and policy that reflects the values and mission of the company. We know that benefits are important to employees and are good recruiting and retention tools. A good benefits package also helps retain

It is important for employers to establish a benefits strategy and policy that reflects the values and mission of the company

© alexskopje/Shutterstock.com

employees. Hospitality companies examine the business environment in which they operate and compete for employees. They also look at the plans offered by competitors and, for example, create a policy of offering total compensation packages that are in the top 10% of their competitive set—or better yet, to offer the best package. When a company offers voluntary benefits, they must be available for all full-time employees and are separate from performance.

This chapter describes the various benefits that companies can offer in detail and the role of benefits as part of a total compensation package. The two main general categories of benefits are those that are legally required and those that are voluntary required. Lastly, important current issues in benefits administration are presented. After studying this chapter, you should be able to:

A good benefits package helps attract and retain employees

© kentoh/Shutterstock.com

1. Describe the four legally required benefits.
2. Explain the two main types of insurance plans and the difference between them.
3. Explain the various voluntary benefits that employers may offer.
4. Identify the characteristics of the different retirement and savings plans.

Learning Objective 1: Describe the four legally required benefits

Types of Benefits

There are six categories of benefits, which are examined in this chapter (Gomez-Mejia, Balkin, & Cardy, 2010, pp. 376–377):

1. *Legally required benefits*: U.S. law requires employers to give four benefits to all employees, with only a few exceptions: Social Security, worker's compensation, unemployment insurance, and family and medical leave. All other benefits are paid by employers voluntarily.
2. *Health insurance*: Health insurance covers hospital costs, physician charges, and the costs of other medical services. Because of its importance, health insurance is usually considered separately from other types of insurance.
3. *Insurance*: Other insurance plans protect employees or their dependents from financial difficulties that can arise as a result of disability or death.
4. *Retirement*: Benefits provide income to employees after they retire.
5. *Time off*: Time-off plans give employees time off with or without pay, depending on the plan.
6. *Employee services*: Employee services are tax-free or tax-preferred services that enhance the quality of employees' work or personal life.

Benefits Legally Required

> **Benefits Legally Required**: Benefits that an employer must offer whether they want to or not.

Benefits legally required are benefits that an employer must offer whether they want to or not. The legally required benefits are Social Security and Medicare contributions, workers' compensation, unemployment compensation, and family and medical leave. The government levies a tax on the employee's earnings for these three.

Social Security and Medicare

> **Social Security**: Provides retired employees, the disabled, and survivors of certain deceased employees, supplementary income to retirement savings so they can maintain a reasonable lifestyle.

Social Security provides retired employees, the disabled, and survivors of certain deceased employees, supplementary income so they can maintain a reasonable lifestyle. Social Security and Medicare are funded by a payroll tax (Federal Insurance Contributions Act or FICA) paid equally by employers and employees at a current rate of 7.65% of the employee's annual earnings on the first $106,800 of income. Therefore, both the employer and the employee pay 7.65% of the employee's income. FICA has two parts: a tax of 6.2% to fund Social Security retirement, disability, and survivor benefits, and a tax of 1.45% to fund Medicare. All income above $106,800 is taxed at a rate 1.45% and paid by both employee and employer (Social Security Administration, 2012a).

Social Security eligibility requirements are that individuals must have worked 40 quarter-year periods, which equates to 10 years of total employment, with a minimum of $1,090 earned per quarter.

Social Security provides retirement income to people who decide to take it at age 65, or for those born after 1950 at age 66 or for those born after 1960 at age 67. The average monthly income provided by Social Security is about $1,250. The amount received is adjusted each year based on the "cost of living adjustment" (COLA), which is calculated by Social Security economists. Projected long-range costs for both Medicare and Social Security are not sustainable under currently scheduled financing and will require legislative action to avoid disruptive consequences for beneficiaries and taxpayers. Options include raising the age when benefits start or limiting the benefits for higher income individuals.

Social Security provides retirement income to people who decide to take it at age 65, or for those born after 1950 at age 66 or for those born after 1960 at age 67

© Kim Reinick/Shutterstock.com

Disability Income is available for those who become disabled and cannot work for at least 12 months. Social Security provides a monthly income comparable to retirement benefits. Unfortunately, the amount of the benefits provided is about 30% of earnings so it is advisable for employees to have additional short- and long-term disability insurance. Social Security disability monthly payments to beneficiaries average about $1,111 per month (Social Security Administration, 2012b).

> **Disability Income:** Available for those who become disabled and cannot work for at least 12 months.

Medicare provides health insurance coverage to those 65 and older, the purpose being to protect them from the high costs of healthcare. Medicare has two parts: Part A covers hospital costs. Individuals pay an annual deductible of about $1,100 and receive up to 60 days of hospital expenses per year covered by Medicare. Part B covers medical expenses such as doctor's fee and the cost of medical supplies for a monthly fee of about $100. The fees are adjusted as costs increase. Part C, Medicare + Choice, is an alternative to the original program (parts A and B) and provides healthcare from different options, such as managed care or private fee-for-service plans. Part D provides coverage for prescription drugs. The retiree pays a $295 deductible, after which Medicare pays 75% of drugs up to $2,700. After that, the beneficiary pays 100% of drug costs from $2,700 to $6,153. Finally, Medicare pays 95% of prescription drug costs above $6,153 (Gomez-Mejia, Balkin, & Cardy, 2010, pp. 376–377).

> **Medicare:** Provides health insurance coverage to those 65 and above, the purpose being to protect them from the high costs of healthcare.

With Social Security **Survivor Benefits**, a deceased employee's surviving family members may receive a monthly income if they qualify. The survivor benefits are related to the deceased worker's primary retirement benefit. Those eligible to receive survivor benefits are (1) widows and widowers age 60 and over, and (2) widows and widowers of any age who care for a child age 16 or younger, an unmarried child or grandchild younger than 18, or a dependent parent age 62 or over (Gomez-Mejia, Balkin, & Cardy, 2010, pp. 376–377).

> **Survivor Benefits:** A deceased employee's surviving family members may receive a monthly income if they qualify.

Workers' Compensation

Workers' compensation is insurance paid for by the employer. It provides cash benefits and medical care for employees who

> **Workers' Compensation:** Insurance paid for by the employer and provides cash benefits and medical care for employees who become disabled because of an injury or sickness related to the job.

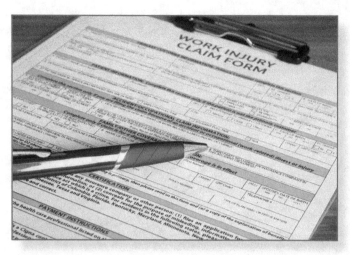

Every state has its own workers' compensation law and commission

© danielfela/Shutterstock.com

become disabled because of an injury or sickness related to the job. Even workers who were wholly at fault for their accidents can still benefit.

Workers' compensation also provides benefits to workers' families for death or permanent disability of an employee resulting from on-the-job injuries (Jerris, 1999). Every state has its own workers' compensation law and commission, and some run their own insurance programs. However, most require employers to carry workers' compensation insurance with private, state-approved insurance companies. Neither the state nor the federal government contributes any funds for workers' compensation (Gomez-Mejia, Balkin, & Cardy, 2010, p. 381). Worker's compensation generally costs about 1% of payroll unless the business is accident prone.

Workers compensation rates depend on the number, frequency, and severity of claims made (called the *experience rating*) and the amount that those claims cost. Unfortunately, hospitality companies tend to have more claims than many other industries. Of course, there is a strong incentive to be accident free. Just walk in the staff entrance and see a large poster on the wall indicating how many days the facility has been accident free.

In most companies, HR professionals with help from line managers create and maintain a safety program. It is vital to gain the cooperation of all employees. Slip-and-fall and kitchen accidents are the most prevalent in the hospitality industry along with strained backs for housekeepers. The HR department should audit workers' compensation claims and challenge any claims they suspect fraudulent or not job related. For example, a manager can ask an injured worker to submit to a drug test. A positive result from the drug test can be a reason for denying a claim. Or, after a serious accident, a safety specialist could conduct an investigation at the scene of the accident. Information gathered from the investigation may reveal inconsistencies in the story that may indicate the employee's claim is fraudulent (Occupational Safety Hazards, 2002, as cited in Gomez-Mejia, Balkin, & Cardy, 2010, p. 382).

Learning Objective 2: Describe the two main types of insurance plans, and the difference between them

Unemployment Insurance

Unemployment Insurance: Provides temporary income for individuals for the time of their involuntary unemployment for a period of 26 weeks. In times of high unemployment, the payments may be extended to 52 weeks.

Unemployment insurance was introduced in 1935 with the passing of the Social Security Act to provide temporary income for individuals for the time of their involuntary unemployment for a period of 26 weeks. In times of high unemployment, the payments may be extended to 52 weeks. It is intended that workers with sufficient income for basic needs and services.

Eligibility for unemployment insurance is dependent upon certain criteria such as:

- The employees lost their job through no fault of their own, for example, because of the closing of the business or due to a layoff.
- Unemployed individuals must have worked a minimum of four quarter periods out of the last five quarter-year periods and have earned at least $1,000 during those four quarter-year periods combined.
- Unemployed individuals must register for available work.
- Unemployed individuals must be ready, willing, and able to accept any suitable employment offered to them through their unemployment office.

The word "suitable" gives an unemployed employee some choice in the selection of a job, for example, a kitchen manager would be right in not accepting a line cook's job. Employees may be disqualified for unemployment insurance benefits for several reasons such as the following:

- An employee who quits voluntarily.
- An employee who is discharged for gross misconduct (e.g., failing a drug test).
- An employee who refuses an offer for suitable work (i.e., a job and pay level comparable to the employee's previous position).
- An employee who participates in a strike (48 of 50 states deny benefits to strike participants).
- A person who is self-employed (Richman, 1995, as cited in Gomez-Mejia, Balkin, & Cardy, 2010, p. 383).

Unemployment insurance is funded by a tax that employers pay for all employees' earnings

© Ditty_about_summer/Shutterstock.com

Unemployment insurance is funded by a tax that employers pay on all employees' earnings. All states give employers an experience rating for comparing the employer's contributions to the unemployment insurance fund against the benefits drawn by the employer's workers from the fund over a period of time. This system allows the state to lower the unemployment tax rate for employers that discharge only a small number of employees, and to raise it for those that discharge large number of employees for any reason (including layoffs) (Gomez-Mejia, Balkin, & Cardy, 2010, p. 383).

Family and Medical Leave

Leaves of absence are generally unpaid, and the amount of time allotted for leave is outlined in the **Family and Medical Leave Act (FMLA) of 1993** (SHRM, 2012b). The leave is for up to 12 weeks.
Additionally, to qualify for leave of absence under the FMLA, an employee must

- Have worked for the company for a full year.
- Have worked a total of 1,250 hours or more during the previous 12-month period immediately before taking leave.
- Be employed by a company that must employ 50 or more employees within a 75 mile radius of the employee's worksite.

> **Family and Medical Leave Act of 1993 (FMLA):**
> A federal law that requires employers to provide up to 12 weeks' unpaid leave to eligible employees for the birth or adoption of a child; to care for a sick parent, child, or spouse; or to take care of their own health problems that interfere with job performance.

Under the FMLA, the leave of absence is available for these reasons:

- Childbirth
- Adoption of a child
- To care for a seriously ill spouse, child, or parent
- To care for one's own serious illness or health condition

The FLMA applies only to businesses that have 50 or more employees and to employers with multiple facilities that have 50 or more workers within a 75 mile radius (Gomez-Mejia, Balkin, & Cardy, 2001, p. 406). The law requires employers to give employees returning from FLMA leave the same job they had before taking the leave or an equivalent job. Employers must maintain coverage of health insurance and other benefits during the time of the employee's leave.

Employees are eligible for FMLA leave after 1 year of service with their employer. A 2008 amendment to the FMLA permits a spouse, son, daughter, parent, next of kin to take up to 26 workweeks of leave to care for a member of the Armed Forces, including a member of the National Guard or Reserves, who is undergoing medical treatment, recuperation, or therapy or illness (U.S. Department of Labor, 2008).

Learning Objective 3: Explain the various voluntary benefits that employers may offer

Legalize

While benefits represent a significant component of an employee's compensation package and a major cost to employers, insurance companies often attempt to deny claims, for example, stating that an injured worker in a worker's compensation claim was an independent contractor rather than an employee or that the injury did not occur during the course of the employee's employment. For example, In August of 2012, a Pennsylvania Appellate Court affirmed an award of death benefits to the widow of a professor who died, apparently from a postsurgical infection associated with the treatment of a broken arm and shoulder that had been sustained in a fall at the salad bar of an off-campus restaurant. The professor had traveled to the restaurant to meet with a doctoral student. The employer contended that the fall and resulting death did not arise out of and in the course of the professor's employment, but the Appellate Court disagreed. The Court acknowledged that injuries sustained during off-premises lunches

The FMLA applies only to businesses that have 50 or more employees and to employers with multiple facilities that have 50 or more workers within a 75 mile radius

© Michail Petrov/Shutterstock.com

were, indeed, ordinarily excluded from workers' compensation coverage. Here, however, the student and professor met for what was anticipated to be a 3-hour meeting over lunch. The two discussed the student's upcoming defense of his dissertation for more than an hour when they decided to go to the restaurant's salad bar to begin their lunch. While at the salad bar, the professor fell. The Court concluded that there was sufficient evidence to support the Board's finding that the professor's injuries occurred while he was furthering the business of the employer at the time of the fall (Pennsylvania State University vs. Worker's Comp. Appeals Board).

Voluntary employer benefits include healthcare plans, supplemental insurance, retirement savings, and pay without work

© Monkey Business Images/Shutterstock.com

Voluntary Employer Paid Benefits

Many companies offer **voluntary employer paid benefits** to employees. These benefits go beyond those mandated by government and include healthcare plans, supplemental insurance, retirement savings, and pay without work. Companies use voluntary benefits to attract and retain employees. Having a reputation for paying good benefits is important in a competitive job market.

> **Voluntary Employer Paid Benefits**: Many companies offer voluntary benefits to employees. These benefits go beyond those mandated by government and include healthcare plans, supplemental insurance, retirement savings, and pay without work.

If a company does offer voluntary benefits, it must offer them within certain legal guidelines. The voluntary benefits must be offered to all employees at the same level and not offer more or better benefits to higher level employees compared to lower level employees. If that were to happen, the company would lose its qualification as tax-exempt compensation, which significantly reduces the value of the benefits. A benefit that meets the regulations necessary for tax exemption status is known as a qualified benefit plan (Stewart & Brown, 2009).

Voluntary benefits can be a constant set of benefits given to all employees or a company can have an approach called a **Flexible Benefits Program**. These programs provide employees with the ability to select some of their own benefits from a bundle of programs that are offered by their employer. This is advantageous to both the employer and its employees for different reasons. While

> **Flexible Benefits Programs**: Provide employees with the ability to select some of their own benefits from a bundle of programs that are offered by their employer.

employees are given a "choice" in regards to the type of benefits they receive, they are also usually responsible for contributing to the cost of these benefits through a deduction in their wages that is taken out before taxes. Employee's advantage from paying for their benefit programs with before-tax income, which increases their overall net income, while the employer gains an advantage from sharing the expense of the benefit programs with the employees. Flexible benefit programs have gained in popularity with employees because they can choose the type of benefit that fits their particular situation.

Paid Time Off

> **Paid Time Off**: This is given so that employees can pursue leisure activities or do personal or civic duties and is distinct from personal leave, holidays, and vacation.

Most employers provide their employees with a certain amount of paid time off (PTO), to pursue leisure activities or do personal or civic duties; it is distinct from personal leave, holidays, and vacation. The amount of time provided to each employee is determined by the employee's status and tenure at the company with which they work. Some companies offer PTO, which traditionally may have been separate from vacation and illness, for associates to use it; however, they see fit (T. Pyburn, personal communication, August 7, 2013).

During PTO, an employee receives an equivalent to their salary or hourly wages for that period of time. An employee may use PTO at any point during the calendar year, and in any way they wish; however, time that is used for situations that would fall under other categories of time off, such as illness, jury duty, bereavement, will not be counted toward PTO. Should an employee leave the company before they are able to use PTO that has been earned, that amount will be paid out after termination (SHRM, 2012c).

Vacations are days of paid leave given to employees under many different schemes for accruing and awarding vacation time. The intention is to give hard working employees time off for rest and relaxation "R&R." In the United States, vacations are generally 2 weeks or 10 paid days plus weekends, but in other countries such as France employees get up to 35 days paid vacation a year. In the hospitality industry, it is fairly common practice for employees to get a vacation after 1 year of service based on the average number of hours worked so, if a person worked an average of 35 hours a week, they would get 1 week of vacation.

Many employees seek out companies that offer healthcare insurance medical expenses including coverage for doctors, hospitalization, testing, and prescription drugs

© Monkey Business Images/Shutterstock.com

Medical, Optical, and Dental

Many employees seek out companies that offer healthcare insurance; medical expenses including coverage for doctors, hospitalization, testing, and prescription drugs. Plans are also sometimes offered for dental and optical care. These insurances help protect employees against the high costs of healthcare from off-the-job accidents or illness. Many employers purchase the insurance from life insurance companies, casualty insurance companies.

The Patient Protection and Affordable Care Act (PPACA) of 2010

The Patient Protection and Affordable Care Act (PPACA) of 2010, also known as Obama Care or the Affordable Care Act, had the intention of making healthcare more affordable to millions of Americans who did not have healthcare coverage, to reduce the cost of healthcare, and to improve the quality of healthcare. There are many provisions in the law, and here are a few.

1. Prohibits denial of coverage for a preexisting condition (excluding tobacco use) nor charge more for a person with one.

2. Makes it illegal for health insurance companies to arbitrarily cancel your health insurance.

3. Protects your choice of doctors.

4. Allows coverage of young adults under 26 years old under their parents policies.

5. Ends lifetime and yearly dollar limits on coverage of essential health benefits.

6. Guarantees the right to appeal.

7. A shared responsibility statement called an individual mandate that requires everyone who is not covered by Medicare, Medicaid, or an employer-sponsored medical plan to get an approved insurance plan or pay a fine.

8. Provides federal subsidies that will be available for low-income families.

The PPACA is paid for increases in a variety of taxes and fees charges to employers and some individuals.

Kinds of Healthcare Plans

There are two main kinds of medical insurance plans Health Maintenance Organizations (HMOs) and Preferred Provider Organizations (PPOs). The HMO is a medical organization consisting of specialists (primary care doctors, surgeons, and so on), often operating out of a healthcare center. HMOs provide full-service medical attention to employees and their families for a fee. The HMO receives a fixed annual fee per employee from the employer (or employer and employee), regardless of whether it provides service to that person (Dessler, n.d., p. 476). HMOs are popular because they can provide medical care for a lower cost but with the disadvantage that the employees can use only providers in the HMO. Blue Cross Blue Shield and United Healthcare are the two largest HMO providers.

> **Health Maintenance Organizations (HMOs)**: An HMO is a medical organization consisting of specialists (primary care doctors, surgeons), often operating out of a healthcare center. HMOs provide full-service medical attention to employees and their families for a fee.

> **Preferred Provider Organizations (PPOs)**: With Preferred Provider Organizations (PPOs), healthcare plans, insurance companies, or employers contract with a group of doctors and hospitals for the provision of services, usually for a higher premium and fee than the HMO.

With Preferred Provider Organizations (PPOs), healthcare plans, insurance companies, or employers contract with a group of doctors and hospitals for the provision of services, usually for a higher premium and fee than the HMO. A list of participating doctors is given to employees so that they can make a selection. In some cases, they must first get a referral from their primary care doctor.

Learning Objective 4: Identify the characteristics of the different retirement and savings plans

Healthcare Cost Control

Due to the ever-increasing cost of healthcare, many companies are searching for ways to contain healthcare costs. Some companies are only allowing HMO plans and others are providing wellness programs in order to help prevent more serious and costly problems later on. Benefit managers are able to modify plans, shop for better rates, bundle groups of employees, and promote healthy lifestyles. Additionally, benefit managers

Now is a good time to seriously consider setting up a retirement plan

© pinkomelet/Shutterstock.com

can (Newton, 2002, as cited in Gomez-Mejia, Balkin, & Cardy, 2001, p. 415):

- *Develop a self-funding arrangement for health insurance*: A company is self-funding when it puts the money that it would otherwise pay in insurance premiums into a fund to pay employee healthcare expenses. Under this type of plan, the employer has an incentive to assume some responsibility for employees' health.

- *Coordinate health insurance plans for families with two working spouses*: Benefit managers can encourage spouses who have duplicate coverage under two different insurance plans to establish a cost-sharing arrangement.

- *Develop a wellness program for employees*: A wellness program assesses employees' risk of serious illness (e.g., heart disease or cancer) and then teaches them how to reduce that risk by changing some of their habits (such as diet, exercise, and avoidance of harmful substances such as alcohol, tobacco, and caffeine) (Reese, 1999, as cited in Gomez-Mejia, Balkin, & Cardy, 2001, p. 415).

- *Offer high-deductible health plans for employees*: A high-deductible health plan (HDHP) is a way that employers can manage the costs of employee healthcare plans. With a high-deductible plan, employees must first pay, out-of-pocket up to several thousand dollars of medical costs each year. The idea behind the HDHP is that people make smarter, less wasteful healthcare decisions when they have a larger financial stake in their own healthcare. Due to the high cost of deductibles, these healthcare plans are less costly for employers, and employees' premiums cost less too (Andrews, 2010, as cited in Gomez-Mejia, Balkin, & Cardy, 2001, p. 415).

Retirement Plans

When we reach retirement, we are not likely to be able to maintain the standard of living that we have enjoyed during our maximum earnings years. Even individuals who will receive Social Security will find that it does not provide sufficient income to meet their need, let alone "extras" such as travel or a new car. Consequently, people who are retired need to have a saving by investing in some additional plan, either personally or through an employer (or both) to accumulate assets to provide additional income after retirement.

Employee Retirement Income Security Act (ERISA) of 1974: Passed into law to prevent employers from preventing employees from getting their duly earned pensions.

Pension Plans: These are set up so that the participants in the plan have money available in their retirement years. Pension plans are contributory versus noncontributory; qualified versus nonqualified; and defined contribution versus defined benefit.

There are many kinds of retirement plans regulated by the **Employee Retirement Income Security Act (ERISA) of 1974**. ERISA was passed into law to prevent employers from preventing employees from getting their duly earned pensions. **Pension plans** usually require a minimum period of tenure before granting pension benefits; this is known as *vesting rights*. In the past, employers required extensive tenure in an organization to be entitled to their retirement benefits.

Pension plans are either contributory or noncontributory. Employees contribute to the contributory plan and employers make all the contribution in the noncontributory pension plan.

Defined Benefit Plans

Defined benefit plans allow employees to know their retirement benefits they will have ahead of time based on a formula that takes the average of the last 3–5 years earnings before retirement. The amount of earnings increases with more years worked. Today, there are unlikely to be any companies offering this type of traditional pension plan because the employer assumes that all the risk in ensuring the amount will be available and is likely to make all of the contributions. Additionally, most employees do not stay with one company for more than 30 years. Rather, they mostly work for a few different companies.

> **Defined Benefit Plans**: Allow employees to know their retirement benefits they will have ahead of time based on a formula that takes the average of the last 3–5 years earnings before retirement.

Defined Contribution Plans

Defined contribution plans are retirement plans where the employer commits to contributing a certain amount for each participant. An example being: an employer who contributes 6%of the employee's salary into the retirement plan. Some defined contribution plans also permit or require employees to make a contribution to the retirement plan. The amount of money available come retirement depends on the success of the investment strategy used. Prior to 2008, retirement plan investments did well, but when the stock market, where much of the money was invested, crashed so did a lot of peoples' retirement plans coining the phrase 201K instead of 401K when selecting this type of retirement plan. Employees are able to choose where their money is invested and the level of risk they want to assume when investing in the plan. Due to needing fewer commitments from employers, more companies opt for defined contribution plans now.

> **Defined Contribution Plans**: Retirement plans where the employer commits to contributing a certain amount for each participant.

401 K Plans

401 K plans are a kind of tax deferred plans that allow participants to accumulate retirement funds while they work. The idea is that when a person has retired they can pay taxes as they withdraw the money from the plan—this lessens the tax burden during the higher income-earning years with participants paying taxes when they are retired and, presumably, earning less. The *Pension Protection Act of 2006* gives participants more flexibility to opt out of investing in company stock into less risky investments such as mutual funds. Some employers now automatically enroll their employees in the company 401K so as to make it easier for them because it was noticed that some were overwhelmed during orientation with so much information that they found it hard to make a decision on retirement plans (Gomez-Mejia, Balkin, & Cardy, 2001, p. 419).There are now Roth 401 (K)s as well that allow people to participate with posttax contributions and enjoy the tax benefit at retirement.

> **401 K Plans**: A kind of tax deferred plans that allow participants to accumulate retirement funds over several years without having to pay taxes on it.

Individual Retirement Plans (IRAs)

Individual Retirement Plans (IRAs) allow people to contribute to a personal savings plan from which the interest is tax-free until the employee cashes it in, usually upon retirement. Employers do not contribute to IRAs and the amount that employees can contribute

> **Individual Retirement Plans (IRAs)**: Allow people to contribute a few thousand dollars to a personal savings plan from which the interest is tax-free until the employee cashes it in, usually upon retirement.

is set by law. The Roth IRA is similar to the regular IRA and all 401 (K) and IRA plans that require participants to reach 59-1/2 years of age before money can be taken out of the savings without penalty. The Simplified Employee Plan (SEP) is similar to an IRA, but is only for self-employed people. Another retirement plan is the profit-sharing Keoh plan, which not only allows the same employee contribution but also allows for an employer contribution that can fluctuate according to the level of profit the company makes.

Disability Insurance

> **Disability Insurance**: Protects employees against the possibility that the hindrance of a mental or physical disability, such as an injury, illness, or pregnancy, may prevent them from being able to perform their necessary work functions for a certain period of time.

Disability insurance protects employees when a mental or physical disability, such as an injury, illness, or pregnancy, may prevent them from being able to work. Disability insurance provides employees with a certain amount of their income for the time they are unable to work as a replacement for the income they lose by being unable to work (SHRM, 2012e). Disability insurance generally does not equate to the full amount of the employee's income, but is instead a certain percentage (between 45% and 66%) that is typically paid out on a monthly basis (Steve, 2001).

Long-Term Care

> **Long-term Care**: Picks up most or all of the expenses for skilled and custodial care for people in their own homes, in adult day care centers, in assisted-living facilities, and in nursing homes.

Medical insurance, even Medicare, does not cover long-term nursing and custodial care that becomes necessary especially for the aged. Long-term care insurance picks up most or all of the expenses for skilled and custodial care for people in their own homes, in adult day care centers, in assisted-living facilities, and in nursing homes. Most employer-sponsored group policies are employee-pay-all, although some do contribute to plans (SHRM, 2012d). There are many LTC plans available with differences in costs and benefits. Differences include:

■ The size of the daily or monthly benefit amount for nursing home care. Many policies offer low, medium, and high options to make premiums affordable to a range of employees. The home-care benefit is a percentage of the DBA and can be as high as 100%.

■ The maximum duration of benefit payouts, usually 3 or 5 years.

■ The so-called elimination period is the time that must elapse between the diagnosis or onset of care and the start of benefits. The choices are usually 30, 60, or 90 days. In older policies, the waiting period may be applicable for each new claim. Newer policies generally impose the elimination period only once—between the policy's effective date and the first claim (SHRM, 2012d).

Introducing Tom Pyburn HR Manager Emeril's Homebase

Benefits and the 21st Century:

. . . the more things change, the more they stay the same.

As a part of the Human Resources planning process it is imperative to take a strategic approach when designing health insurance benefits packages as these plans usually represent the lion's share of a company's total benefits expenditures. Some historical perspective on this volatile market leads us to one certain conclusion—the cost of employer sponsored health coverage will continue to increase. Group health insurance plans for employees began to fully develop as early as the 1930s. As these plans began to expand so did federal regulation. By the 1990s health care reform became one of *the* hot button issues of American politics. Unfortunately, legislators from both parties have debated this issue based on their respective political agendas rather than working on legislation aimed at solving the real problem—the skyrocketing cost of health care. The political struggle culminated in the enactment of Patient Protection and Affordable Care Act (PPACA) in 2010. Although it is impossible to predict exactly what the health insurance landscape will finally look like after all of the regulatory provisions of PPACA are finalized and in force, one thing is clear, employers will still be faced with essentially the same problem. Health insurance benefits for employees will continue to represent a huge cost of doing business.

If PPACA is ultimately successful in ensuring that all (or at least, most) Americans have minimum essential health insurance coverage, companies will have to work even harder to compete for employees using their benefits plans as a point of differentiation to lure candidates. This, plus the increasing cost of providing health coverage, will put even greater pressure on companies to be both strategic *and creative* in designing their overall benefits packages. It will be crucial to make every dollar count. As pointed out in this chapter there must be a positive ROI in terms of attracting and retaining quality employees. Smart companies will survey their employees and create a comprehensive "menu" of benefits tailored to the specific needs of their workforce. While some may value more traditional perks like retirement plans, bonuses and paid time off, other employees may prefer less conventional offerings such as child or elder care services, preventative health and wellness, professional development or even things like dry cleaning allowances, transportation tokens and pet insurance. Businesses should also find ways to communicate the intrinsic benefits inherent their industry. In the hospitality industry, for instance, this might include things such as guest interaction, exposure to great cuisine, opportunity for career advancement, diversity and non-traditional work schedules.

Finally, we should not forget that the most important and often overlooked *"benefit"* we can offer employees is something that is usually not even talked about as a benefit—great management! Which calls to mind the old adage, "the more things change, the more they stay the same". No matter how much we spend on benefits or how creative the ever increasing menu of offerings gets, one thing remains the same—the best way to get and keep great employees is to treat them well. Training managers in effective employee relations must be an ongoing priority if a business wants to stay competitive in today's labor market. A company's reputation as a "great place to work" will do more to improve its recruiting efforts and lower turnover than any PPO or PTO plan ever will. Of course we will always need to provide our employees with competitive wages and benefits they will value. However, we should never lose sight of the fact that what people value above all is having a safe place to work where they are treated fairly and with respect and have the opportunity to provide for themselves and their families while fulfilling their career interests.

Contributed by Tom Pyburn. © Kendall Hunt Publishing Company

Domestic Partner Benefits

A **domestic partnership** can be defined as a relationship between two people of the same or opposite sex, who cohabit but are not married

Domestic Partnership: It can be defined as a relationship between two people of the same or opposite sex, who cohabit but are not married by law according to the state in which they reside.

by law according to the state in which they reside. It is the decision of the company to offer domestic partner benefits to their employees and is not required by law. Many employers will have different policies regarding domestic partner benefits based on state laws, business practices, and personal outlooks; however, when determining domestic partner benefits, it is important for an employer to consider the moral and legal aspects of exercising fair practices in the workplace, as well as the overall needs of their employees (HR.BLR.com, 2012).

There are several things for HR managers to consider when determining domestic partner benefit packages:

- What is the company's definition of a domestic partnership?
- What qualifies employees to receive domestic partner benefits?
- What benefits will the company provide?
- What affects will this have on taxes? (SHRM, 2012a).

Benefits for Part-Time Employees

The definition of what constitutes a part-time employee is typically distinct to each company; however, a traditional definition of a part-time employee would be one who consistently works less than 40 hours in a given workweek (Susan M. Heathfield, 2012). The variety of benefits offered to part-time employees is contingent on an individual company's rules and policies regarding the matter. Some companies only provide the most basic benefits, while others may not provide any benefits at all, unless otherwise required by state law. Under federal law, all companies must comply with the Fair Labor Standards Act (FLSA); however, there is not much legislature that requires companies to provide benefits for part-time employees (Findlaw, 2012). Typically, these benefits are established to increase employee morale and satisfaction.

Technology in HR

There are several benefits that utilize technology in the services offered to employees. Corporate HR systems can be accessed by associates via the Internet from a home computer to update information such as a change of address or benefit. Doctors, dentists, and opticians and even 401K pension plans can also be accessed on-line. Another benefit that is more readily available via the Internet is making requests for complementary room reservations for associates with more than 1 year of employment. Similarly, requests for employee rates at other company hotels can be made via the Internet.

Key Points

- Benefits administration presents HR professionals with the challenge of balancing the needs of the employees and the cost to the employer.
- The legally required benefits are Social Security, workers' compensation, and unemployment compensation. The government levies a tax on the employee's earnings for each of the three required benefits.

- Social Security provides retired employees, the disabled, and survivors of deceased employees, supplementary income to retirement savings so that they can maintain a reasonable lifestyle.
- Medicare provides health insurance coverage to those 65 and above, the purpose being to protect them from the high costs of healthcare.
- Workers' compensation is insurance paid by the employer that provides cash benefits and medical care for employees who become disabled because of an injury or sickness related to the job.
- Unemployment insurance was introduced in 1935 with the passing of the Social Security Act. The purpose of the act is to provide temporary income for individuals for the time of their involuntary unemployment for a period of 26 weeks.
- The FLMA applies only to businesses that have 50 or more employees and to employers with multiple facilities that have 50 or more workers within a 75 mile radius.
- There are two main kinds of medical insurance plans: Health Maintenance Organizations (HMOs) and Preferred Provider Organizations (PPOs).
- With Preferred Provider Organizations (PPOs), healthcare plans, insurance companies, or employers contract with a group of doctors and hospitals for the provision of services, usually for a higher premium and fee than the HMO.
- Flexible Benefits Programs provide employees with the ability to select some of their own benefits from a bundle of programs that are offered by their employer.
- Pension plans are set up so that participants in the plan have money available in their retirement years.
- Disability Insurance provides employees with a certain amount of their income for the time they are unable to work as a replacement for the income they would lose by being away from work.
- Long-term care insurance picks up most or all of the expenses for skilled and custodial care for people in their own homes, in adult day care centers, in assisted-living facilities and in nursing homes.
- The definition of what constitutes a part-time employee is typically distinct to each company; however, a traditional definition of a part-time employee would be one who consistently works less than 40 hours in a given workweek.
- It is the decision of the company to offer domestic partner benefits to their employees, and is not required by law. Many employers will have different policies regarding domestic partner benefits based on state laws, business practices, and personal outlooks.
- Communicating the benefits available to all employees is a huge task. Adding to the challenge is the fact that benefits are becoming more complex and increasingly expensive.

Key Terms

401 K plans
Benefits legally required
Defined benefit plans
Defined contribution plans
Disability income
Disability insurance
Domestic partnership
Employee Retirement Income Security Act (ERISA) of 1974

Family and Medical Leave Act of 1993 (FMLA)
Flexible Benefits Programs
Health Maintenance Organizations (HMOs)
Individual Retirement Plans (IRAs)
Long-Term Care
Medicare
Paid time off

Pension plans
Preferred Provider Organizations (PPOs)
Social Security
Survivor Benefits
Unemployment Insurance
Voluntary Employer Paid Benefits
Workers' Compensation

Discussion Questions

1. List and briefly discuss the six categories of benefits outlined in the chapter.
2. Discuss the difference between disability income and workers compensation.
3. Discuss Social Security; what is it? How is it funded? And who is eligible to receive it?
4. List the qualifications and eligibility requirements for leave of absence under FMLA guidelines.
5. List the criteria necessary for employees to be eligible for unemployment insurance.
6. List the reasons that employees may be disqualified for unemployment insurance benefits.
7. Briefly explain flexible benefit programs.

Ethical Dilemma

1. You are the HR Director of a seasonal ski resort in Vail, Colorado. One of the hourly kitchen employees approaches you and says that he was told by the kitchen manager that he could not receive company benefits because he works part-time hours; however, he informs you that he was hired during the off-season as a full-time employee, and has been working 25 hours per week because currently he is not needed more. At the same time, he claims that one of the front desk staff told him that they were hired as a part-time employee, but receives benefits because they have been working 40 hours per week for the past year. What should you do to resolve this?

2. John is the kitchen supervisor of a small market restaurant property that is part of a well-known chain that operates numerous locations throughout the country. John's boss, the franchisor and manager of the restaurant, calls John into his office one day to inform him that the corporate office has decided to downsize staff at some of their smaller and underachieving properties. The property where John currently works is in a small rural town, and it is the only location within 75 miles. The manager tells John that he is welcome to continue working for the company at a lower position, as they are currently looking for new line cooks. John has a family at home and knows that he will need to maintain a level of income to support them while he looks for a new job; however, he does not want to take a pay cut or regress to a lower position.

   John searches for an open position at other locations within the company and discovers that no new assistant managers or supervisors will be hired for the next few months; however, John would be the first in line for an open position. John then registers for available work through an unemployment office and discovers several opportunities to work as a kitchen supervisor at several local restaurants in the area at a significant pay cut. John's long-term aspirations are to open his own restaurant, and he feels that he is capable of the challenge if provided with temporary income for long enough to locate a financing partner and to get the business running. John knows his options are limited, and he really needs some form of steady income or unemployment insurance while he determines the right move to make? What should John do?

Internet Exercise

1. Explore the internet and search for an outline of employee benefits offered through a particular hotel chain. Print out the benefits and share your results in class. What are the similarities and differences between some of the more well-known chains versus smaller independent hotels or chains?

2. Search the Internet for employee wellness programs and print out your findings to discuss in class. Some helpful websites are www.shrm.org, www.wellnessproposals.com, and www.netwellness.org.

References

Findlaw. (2012). *Part time, temporary, and seasonal employees.* Retrieved May 9, 2012, from http://employment. findlaw.com/hiring-process/part-time-temporary-and-seasonal-employees.html

Gomez-Mejia, L. R., Balkin, D. B., & Cardy, R. L. (2001). *Managing Human Resources* (3rd ed.). Upper Saddle River NJ: Pearson.

Gomez-Mejia, L. R., Balkin, D. B., & Cardy, R.L. (2010), *Managing Human Resources* (6th ed.). Upper Saddle River, NJ: Pearson.

HR.BLR.com. (2012). Domestic partner benefits. Retrieved May 2, 2012, from http://hr.blr.com/HR-topics/ Benefits-Leave/Domestic-Partner-Benefits-Civil-Union

Jerris, L. A. (1999). *Human Resources Management for Hospitality* (p. 177), Upper Saddle River, NJ: Prentice Hall.

Lashinky, A. (2007, January). Search and enjoy. *Fortune,* 70–82.

SHRM. (2012a). *How to design domestic partner benefits.* Retrieved May 2, 2012, from http://www.shrm.org/ templatestools/howtoguides/pages/howtodesigndomesticpartnerbenefits.aspx

SHRM. (2012b). *Leave of absence (non-fmla and non-military).* Retrieved May 8, 2012, from http://www.shrm.org/ templatestools/samples/policies/pages/criticalpersonalleavesofabsence.aspx

SHRM. (2012c). *Paid time off (PTO).* Retrieved May 8, 2012, from http://www.shrm.org/templatestools/samples/ policies/pages/cms_007476.aspx

SHRM. (2012d). Long-term care insurance comes of age. Retrieved June 1, 2012, from http://www.shrm.org/ publications/hrmagazine/editorialcontent/pages/0702agn-compben.aspx

SHRM. (2012e). *Short-Term Disability: Wage Replacement and Leave.* Retrieved May 9, 2012, from http://www. shrm.org/templatestools/samples/policies/pages/cms_008034.aspx

Social Security Administration. (2012a). http://ssa-custhelp.ssa.gov/app/answers/detail/a_id/240/~/2012-social-security-tax-rate-and-maximum-taxable-earnings Retrieved on August 26, 2012.

Social Security Administration. (2012b). http://www.ssa.gov/policy/docs/quickfacts/stat_snapshot/ Retrieved on August 25, 2012.

Steve, C. (2001). *About disability insurance.* Retrieved May 9, 2012, from http://www.about-disability-insurance.com/

Stewart, G. L., & Brown, K. G. (2009). *Human resource management: Linking strategy to practice* (p. 455). Hoboken NJ: Wiley.

Susan M. Heathfield. (2012).*Part time employee.* Retrieved May 9, 2012, from http://humanresources.about.com/od/ glossaryp/g/part_time.htm

U.S. Department of Labor. (2008). *The Family and Medical Leave Act and National Defense Authorization Act for FY 2008.* Available from https://www.dol.gov/whd/fmla/NDAA_fmla.htm, accessed February 14, 2011

© mythja/Shutterstock.com

Chapter 11

LEADING HIGH-PERFORMING EMPLOYEES

Introduction

In this chapter, we will explore what drives *organizational excellence* in high-performance workplaces, as well as the importance of creating and maintaining workplace that stresses not only excellence but also teamwork, motivation, empowerment, and enabling. Furthermore, a workplace that stresses organizational excellence is the one that is both family and employee-centered, uses coaching versus directing, practices ethical decision-making, has equitable policies, celebrates its stakeholders, provides ongoing communications, promotes innovation, stresses service excellence, and is flexible and open to change.

This type of organization will take you closer to becoming an employer of choice, which will result in an organization that serves as a "benchmark" organization of excellence. Let's see how we get there.

After reading and studying this chapter, you should be able to:

1. Explain the importance of coaching and what qualities a good coach should possess.
2. Identify the key points in recognizing performance characteristics.
3. Provide an overview of effective performance evaluations, including possible bias errors that may exist.
4. Describe organizational excellence.
5. Describe the Malcolm Baldrige Award.
6. Describe how to install an Organizational Excellence Program.

Learning Objective 1: Explain the importance of coaching and what qualities a good coach should possess

Performance Leadership, Coaching, and Employee-Involved Goal Setting

Coaching Versus Directing

Coaches develop team members to become the best they can be

© DenisProduction.com/Shutterstock.com

> **Coaching**: A coach is one who not only leads his or her team but also develops the team members to be the best that they can be.

A major force in organizational excellence is leadership style. The leadership style that works best to achieve organizational excellence is coaching. A coach is one who not only leads his or her team but also develops the team members to become the best that they can be. This is accomplished by the coach/manager knowing what motivates each team member, rewarding the behavior that they want to continue in order to accomplish the organization's goals, and then taking action that allows for the employee to grow and develop.

If you played sports when you were younger, think about a coach you remember. What made him or her special? This can also be relevant for a great teacher that you may have had. You remember this person because they possessed effective leadership qualities that helped to develop you as a player or student. That is what coaching is all about; so whether your title is manager, supervisor, director, or employee, think and act like a coach. In the working world, one of the top five things that attract and retain employees is the opportunity to grow and develop, and that is what an effective coach does.

A few additional requirements to be a good coach are:

1. Be there, be assessable, and be active—don't just sit in your office doing paperwork all the time.
2. Be a model for you employees.
3. Focus on each employee's motivational needs.
4. Empower employees to take action and accept mistakes.
5. Provide feedback.
6. Communicate, communicate, and communicate.

In addition, as a coach/manager-leader, it is important to understand motivational theory as postulated by Abraham Maslow (as discussed in Chapter 8 and below) and Frederick Hertzberg (discussed in Chapter 8) to assist in making excellent performance happen. Here is how Maslow's Hierarchy of Human Needs can relate to a coach/manager-leader.

As a coach/manager-leader, you should be concentrating on the top three areas of the triangle. Let's explore each one:

1. *Social/belonging*: This area focuses on building your employees into stakeholders. There is an opportunity to create an environment of belonging and teamwork. This effort will go a long way in creating an employee-centered workplace that can only assist in making your restaurant, hotel, or other type of company successful in both customer service and profit.

2. *Ego/self-esteem*: Consistently and frequently recognizing excellent performance and properly handling performance problems by letting the employee know that you appreciate their work, while building on the employee's strengths, contribute to satisfying this need in the workplace. This can come through concrete actions like cash bonuses, other monetary recognition, or just plain "thank-you". This action will show how much you appreciate the employee.

3. *Self-actualization*: Here is where your role as a coach/manager is really critical. You have an opportunity to assist in helping employees develop into what they want to be. For example, let's say that you are the Food and Beverage Director at a hotel, and you have a dishwasher who is an excellent employee and has told you that their goal is to someday become an executive chef. One thing that you could do is allow the dishwasher to spend 3–4 hours a week "shadowing" the executive chef at your hotel and perhaps even assist the chef in meal preparation. You could then develop a more formal plan to assist the employee in accomplishing their dream.

When managers are reluctant to be good coaches to their employees, company executives should consider adding a measure of how well managers are coaching their employees to the managerial performance appraisal system. Promoting coaching as a dimension in the appraisal of managers signals the importance that the organization places on coaching (Gomez-Mejia, Balkin, & Cardy, 2012, p. 245).

Hiring the Right People

"Hire attitude, train skills" is what Southwest Airlines does. This is good advice for creating an effective high-performance organization and should be part of your recruitment and hiring culture, as recruitment and selection has to be more than just a program. You don't have to necessarily hire

"Hire attitude, train skills" is what Southwest Airlines does

© Chris Parypa Photopgraphy/Shutterstock.com

the smartest but do need to concentrate on who will be the best fit to assist in accomplishing your vision, mission, and goals (Carbonara, 1996).

As you interview and hire, you will also want to build the strength and depth of your "bench" (those employees who could potentially fill roles in the future) for succession planning. For example, if your organization stresses teamwork, you should be asking applicants a question such as "we are very teamwork-centered at this job, so tell me about a time that you were on a team and what was your role on that team." It is important to tailor some of your interview questions to fit your organization's culture. Getting the right people from the start will assist in your quest for excellence in organizational performance.

Participation

You can encourage an organization that stresses participation by involving your team members in the decision-making process, which should include not only decisions that affect your department but also those that affect the organization as a whole. Remember, if you want outstanding results by getting total commitment to decisions, you need to involve those who are going to be affected by the decisions.

For example, let's say that you are the general manager of a medium-sized family restaurant that is only open for dinner on Sundays from 4 p.m. to midnight. In your community, sports bars are popular and sporting events such as basketball and football are in the afternoon on Sunday. You would like to open at noon to capture some of that business, and during the fall, these restaurants generate a lot of revenue during football games in the early afternoon. You can approach this decision two ways: (1) decide by yourself and change your hours of operation on Sundays to 12 p.m. instead of 4 p.m. or (2) you can ask for the staff's input and then involve them in making the decision.

Here are some questions to consider when making the decision to increase the hours of operation on Sunday to include early afternoon service:

1. How many additional labor hours will be needed and will more people need to be hired?
2. Will there be a need to add additional TVs or subscribe to certain sports packages?
3. How will you determine which employees will work the extra hours?
4. Will the selection of menu items need to be changed or increased?

If you choose to include the staff in the decision process, you could ask two to three employees to take each topic, review it, and get back to you with their recommendations. Once you have determined their opinions and recommendations, you will be in a better position to make the decision whether to increase the hours of operation.

Management by Objectives

Management by objectives (MBO) was popularized by Peter Drucker, who was the leading management scholar of the 20th century.[1] MBO provides an opportunity to involve team members in planning for both their individual future, and the future of the organization. During the MBO process, a manager and a team member meet together to resolve an issue and/or plan for a future goal or outcome.

> **Management By Objectives (MBO):** A process where a manager and a team member come together to resolve an issue and/or plan for a future goal or outcome.

MBO can be used to resolve an organizational problem, plan for the individual development of a team member, or resolve a problem that a team member may be having. During the meeting, both sides share ideas and goals with each other on how to move forward and then reach a consensus on what direction to take. The decision is monitored and feedback is provided. Ideally, MBO provides an opportunity to reward success in reaching some or all of the jointly developed goals. Discussion areas to be considered are:

1. Specific details pertaining to what you're measuring and how you're going to measure it.

2. The manager and the employee list goals and objectives and then develop a list based on a consensus.

3. Establish a timetable with specified times set to review each goal/objective. During this time, you will have an opportunity to correct problems and/or praise accomplishments.

4. Interim and final review including review lessons learned.

MBO can be used to resolve an organizational problem, plan for the individual development of a team member, or resolve a problem that a team member may be having

© Santiago Cornejo/Shutterstock.com

For example, let's say that the lead front desk attendant at your resort comes to you and indicates that he or she would like to become general manager of a resort or hotel someday. Your role and responsibility as a coach/manager is to assist in the development of your employees. You ask the employee to come up with a plan that they think will help them achieve their goal. Once they have created a plan, you can sit down with them and come up with a joint plan that will help them work toward their goal, while at the same time benefits the organization as a whole. Some ideas could include the following:

- The employee will spend 8 hours every 2 weeks shadowing the general manager of the resort.
- The employee could enroll in classes toward earning a bachelor's degree in hospitality management. You also adjust their hours so they can attend class.
- The employee could develop a list of what they would like to accomplish in 30, 90, 180 days, etc.
- You will schedule a review session after each period to discuss their progress and provide feedback. During that time, you celebrate and reward achievements and adjust as necessary when things are going as planned.

---

[1] For more information on Dr. Drucker and his many books, please consult your library.

Important Performance Characteristics

> **Performance Characteristics:** Traits needed in an employee to perform a job based on set standards for that job.

Performance characteristics are traits needed in an employee to perform a job based on set of standards for that job. They are observable behaviors and actions that explain how the job is to be done, plus the results that are expected for satisfactory job performance (Indiana University Human Resources, 2015a). Performance characteristics are based on a position, not an individual, available by observation, attainable, and describe the fullest consideration of "adequate" for a job. They are typically expressed in terms of quantity, quality, timeliness, cost, safety, or outcomes (Indiana University Human Resources, 2015b).

Learning Objective 2: Identify the key points in recognizing performance characteristics

As a manager, it is your job to not only establish performance standards, but assess what characteristics each applicant may possess during the recruiting and selection process. Will this person be able to interact with current employees? Do they seem capable of showing up on time? Do they have the basic knowledge of this job? Performance characteristics are also used when assessing a current employee and their eligibility for a promotion. Have they surpassed the bottom line requirements of the job? Have they shown they have knowledge of the goals of the company? Are they able to interact with all of our current employees in a professional and friendly manner? In order to answer these questions, you must first have a way to measure performance characteristics for both potential and current employees.

Measuring Performance Characteristics

There are potential problems that arise from managers not properly conducting the annual performance appraisals with employees

© fizkes/Shutterstock.com

Measuring performance characteristics is the act of comparing what performance is expected out of an employee with that of their actually day to day performance. Take for example, a front desk clerk who has worked at your hotel for a year and is eligible for a promotion for the shift manager position pending a report of her performance characteristics. You have been able to observe her work throughout the year and can accurately measure her performance as an employee. After reviewing the report, you are able to determine that she would be an excellent shift manager, and when a position is available, you will confidently promote that particular front desk clerk.

Not only do performance reports and forms such as these assist you as a manager, but help to define a set of standards that you and your company expect for a position to be relayed to your employees. If a shift manager at the front desks inquiries as to why they have not yet received a promotion, you can easily explain that the characteristics you seek to receive that promotion have not yet been met.

Learning Objective 3: Provide an overview of effective performance evaluations, including possible bias errors that may exist

Evaluations

Formal evaluations of each employee should be done on regular, periodic basis for several reasons:

- *Legal*: You will now have a formal record of performance.
- *Developmental*: One of your responsibilities as a coach/manager is to develop your employees.
- *Feedback*: Although as a coach/manager you should continually be providing employee's information on their performance, the evaluation is a formal and usually at least annual process.
- *Merit pay*: If used correctly, it can be a valuable asset in determining who receives what merit pay increase.

There are three areas that you should consider when evaluating performance and/or a behavior problem:

1. The environment
   - ❏ Has the employee been empowered to do what you asked them to do?
   - ❏ Are the rules and policies too confining?
   - ❏ Does their job description have task identity, significance, autonomy, and feedback built in?
2. Capability
   - ❏ Does the employee possess the necessary skills to perform their job functions?
   - ❏ Has the employee been properly trained for the job that they are assigned?
   - ❏ Is the employee provided with the proper equipment, such as, the most updated computer systems that they need to perform the job they are assigned to?
3. Motivation
   - ❏ Take a look at yourself in the mirror. When is the last time that you complimented the employee for a job well done or just said "thank you"?
   - ❏ Do you know what motivates this particular employee? If yes, act on it. If no, find out.
   - ❏ Is the job designed to be somewhat motivating, that is, task identity, significance, autonomy, and feedback?
   - ❏ Do you involve the employee in any decision-making or at least asked their opinion?

The appraisal method is about developing your employees and is *NOT* a "gotcha" moment. If you are doing your job communicating and motivating employees throughout the year, then the annual performance review should be anti-climactic, that is, there are no surprises because you would have a sense of how well you're doing.

Evaluation Formats

Graphic Rating: A form of evaluation in which each employee is numerically rated according to various characteristics such as quality of work, knowledge, attitude, and so on.

Competency-based Appraisals: A form of appraisal whereby an employee is evaluated on specific competencies, such as how well they plan, prepare, and set up for an event.

BARS: A form of appraisal whereby an employee is rated on various dimensions of the job. It is usually on a vertical scale and may consist of items, such as suggesting or developing new ways of doing things.

Here are three appraisal formats that managers often use as part of the formal performance appraisal:

1. Graphic rating: A form of evaluation in which each employee is numerically rated according to various characteristics such as quality of work, knowledge, attitude, and so on.
2. Competency-based appraisals: A form of appraisal whereby an employee is evaluated on specific competencies, such as how well they plan, prepare, and set up for an event.
3. BARS: A form of appraisal whereby an employee is rated on various dimensions of the job. It is usually on a vertical scale and may consist of items, such as suggesting or developing new ways of doing things.

Whichever appraisal method you choose you must follow a basic appraisal process that typically includes the following:

1. Involve the employee from the beginning, by allowing them to complete a self-evaluation form.
2. Schedule the appraisal interview as least 1 week in advance, so as to give both yourself and the employee time to prepare.
3. Review the employee's personnel file and talk to other managers that the employee may interact with.
4. Set aside the proper amount of time for the appraisal, that is, no phone calls, e-mails. Concentrate on the employee during the appraisal.
5. When the employee leaves the meeting they should have a very clear understanding of their performance and an action plan with objectives for the following year. In addition, ask the employee if you could assist them in meeting their objectives.
6. Follow up with the employee on a regular basis to ascertain how they are doing during the coming year.

Performance Appraisal Problems and Solutions

There are potential problems that arise from managers not properly conducting the formal performance appraisals with employees. This is a subject area that requires constant focus and attention because it is so important to creating and maintaining an effective and efficient organization. Employees are quick to find problems areas within the performance appraisal process because they are being reviewed, critiqued, and possibly reprimanded for their performance. It is important that managers take this process seriously if they want their employees to feel like they truly care, and in return take their review seriously as well.

Employee Handbook: Outlines the expectations and policies that a company requires all employees to know and follow while they are employed with the company, as well as the expectations that an employee can expect from the company.

One of the most beneficial references employees can use to determine the proper way to conduct themselves while on the job is the employee handbook. The employee handbook outlines the expectations and policies that a company requires all employees to know and follow while they are employed with the company, as well as the expectations that an employee can expect from the company in return (U.S. SBA, 2018). If specified performance appraisals are outlined in the employee handbook, they should be expected to take place. While the employee handbook is not a formal contract, one can argue that it is an implied contract.

Timeliness can be a significant problem in the performance appraisal process if employees are not getting their evaluations on time, or even at all. It is important for managers to conduct evaluations at least 30 days before they are due. Holding managers accountable for their performance is a good way to ensure that they are conducting performance appraisals with their employees on a timely basis.

Central Tendency Error occurs when a manager gives most or all of their employees average ratings, regardless of how hard they actually work (Business Dictionary, 2013a). This can be a problem if employees are aware that it is occurring because it decreases the motivation for employees to improve their performance, and could result in employees doing the bar minimum to get by, which decreases efficiency, resulting in a poorly organized department. In order to solve or prevent this from occurring, you need to develop specific core competencies that employees are responsible for achieving and measure those competencies in a genuine manner to show that hard work pays off.

> **Central Tendency Error**: Occurs when a manager gives most or all of their employees average ratings, regardless of how hard they actually work.

Recency Error occurs when you only concentrate on recent performance or something that happened early in the year and not the performance over the entire year (Business Dictionary, 2013b). This is an error on the manager's part that can be prevented by providing ongoing performance feedback, as well as preparing for the evaluation ahead of time by reviewing the record or talking with other managers that the employee may report to. Sometimes the performance appraisal doesn't measure what the employee actually is expected to do. This occurs because the job description may not be accurate in listing the core competencies. To prevent this from occurring, it is important to constantly update job descriptions to make sure the expectations are clear to new employees. One example of preventing this is the use of a combined Position Description-Evaluation Form.

> **Recency Error**: Occurs when you only concentrate on recent performance or something that happened early in the year and not the performance over the entire year.

Performance evaluations should not discriminate against anyone on the basis of age, gender, race, religion, disability, marital status, pregnancy, or sexual preference

© Kaspars Grinvalds/Shutterstock.com

Lack of Follow-Up

Problems can occur if there is a lack of follow up after the evaluation takes place. This sends a message that the evaluation process isn't important and that the manager isn't truly interested in the employees' performance. It is up to the manager to schedule a time to meet with the employee every 30, 60, or 90 days to see how the employee is doing and making necessary improvement. This is an opportunity to correct problems and/or praise progress.

Legalize

When considering legal aspects of performance evaluations it is important to bear in mind the following (Archer North Performance Appraisal System, n.d.): Performance evaluations should not discriminate against anyone on the basis of age, gender, race, religion, disability, marital status, pregnancy, or sexual preference. Evaluations should not be used to punish an employee, they should be correct, fair, and with specific examples. Employees need an opportunity to comment on their evaluation—they can even agree or disagree and even appeal to the next managerial level or an ombudsperson.

Evaluations should be honest—it's no good letting a bad employee get away with things because, if at a later date, the employee was terminated, they could take legal action claiming that they had good evaluations. This would make it difficult for the company to defend the lawsuit. Employees who do not meet the performance standards will need to be counseled as to why and if training will help improve performance. Employees should be given a chance to improve with clear step by step goals. Continuous feedback on performance is critical because it lets employees know how well they are doing toward meeting their goals.

Learning Objective 4: Describe organizational excellence

Organizational Excellence

> **Organizational Excellence (OE):** Measures to what extent an organization's vision, mission, and goals are being met and then taking appropriate action to meet or exceed goals.

> **Total Quality Management (TQM):** A process of continuous quality improvement focusing on guest's needs and expectations.

Organizational excellence (OE) measures to what extent an organization's vision, mission, and goals are being met and then taking appropriate action to meet or exceed goals. OE grew out of Total Quality Management (TQM). TQM is a process of continuous quality improvement focusing on the guest's needs and expectations. TQM means maximizing the organization's potential and assessing how well it meets the vision, mission, and goals, then taking appropriate action to reach any goals where the organization may be lacking (ASQ, n.d.).

The TQM traces its origins back to the 1950s when W. Edwards Deming and Joseph Juran were working on reducing the defects in the production industries, particularly the Japanese automobile industry. It may be hard to believe that there was once a time when the quality of Japanese automobiles was very inferior to American. At that time, Deming and Juran were not very sought after as consultants in America, but in Japan they were in demand (Tuckman, 1994).

The prevailing attitude in America from the 1950s until the late 1970s was that higher quality meant a higher cost, and consumers did not want to pay the additional cost for

Organizational excellence begins with a warm and sincere welcome

higher-end products and services. That attitude began to change when Japanese products with brand names such as Sony and Panasonic almost drove the American consumer-electronics industry out of business. Furthermore, reliable, fuel-efficient Toyotas and Hondas chewed away at the domestic auto industry (Holusha, 1993).

Although the core of their research was to improve quality by using statistics to detect flaws in production processes, Deming and Juran developed a broader philosophy that emphasized managerial problem-solving based on cooperation. Deming urged managers to "drive out fear," so that workers would feel more comfortable making improvements in

Ritz-Carlton has won the prestigious Malcolm Baldrige award twice

© 360b/Shutterstock.com

the workplace. He delighted in telling corporate magnates who asked for help in solving their company's problems that they were a significant part of their own problem (Holusha, 1993).

In order for TQM to be successful, it is often necessary to implement a change in corporate culture. Management has to act in a more cooperative manner with their employees. Leadership and teamwork are critical to an organization's successful installation of TQM. Deming denounced traditionally accepted management practices such as production quotas, performance ratings, and individual bonuses, concluding that they were inherently unfair and detrimental to effectiveness and quality of the workforce. Ultimately, he found that customers would get better products and services when workers were encouraged to use their minds as well as their hands on the job (Holusha, 1993).

In recent past, many companies, especially hospitality companies, embraced the idea of TQM, as they strived to differentiate themselves in a highly competitive market through superior service and guest satisfaction.

Learning Objective 5: Describe how to install an Organizational Excellence Program

Baldridge Award

For a hospitality organization, leading the field has often been the Ritz Carlton, which was initially led under the leadership of Horst Schulze. Ritz Carlton won the Malcolm Baldrige award, not just once, but twice. Each year, the Malcolm Baldrige award is given to the business that meets certain rigorous quality standards (NIST, 2013a).

Service organizations of all types have discovered how to become more successful through the Criteria for Performance Excellence. These organizations serve such diverse groups as luxury hotel companies and other lodging establishment, restaurant establishments, the health care industry, and the oil industry, to name a few. Regardless of the industry or types of customers they service, your organization can benefit from the proven improvement framework that Baldrige offers.

How Baldrige Relates

The Baldrige Criteria can apply equally to all business sectors, including service organizations, and are compatible with other performance improvement initiatives, such as ISO 9000, Lean, and Six Sigma. Using the Baldrige framework, an organization can integrate these approaches, improve productivity and effectiveness, and strive for performance excellence (NIST, 2013b).

Regardless of the type of service your organization provides, the Baldrige Criteria can serve as a valuable framework for measuring performance and planning in an uncertain environment. The Baldrige Criteria helps businesses achieve and sustain the highest national levels of:

- Guest satisfaction and engagement
- Product and service outcomes and process efficiency
- Workforce satisfaction and engagement
- Revenue and market share
- Social responsibility

The requirements of the Education Criteria for Performance Excellence are embodied in seven categories, as follows (NIST, 2013b):

1. Leadership
2. Strategic planning
3. Customer focus
4. Measurement, analysis, and knowledge management
5. Workforce focus
6. Operations focus
7. Results

This provides the framework connecting and integrating the categories. From top to bottom, the framework has the following basic elements.

Organizational Profile

The Organizational Profile (top of figure) sets the context for the way your organization operates. Your organization's environment, key working relationships, and strategic situation including competitive environment, strategic challenges and advantages, and performance improvement system—serve as an overarching guide for your organizational performance management system (NIST, 2013b).

Performance System

The performance system is composed of the six Baldrige categories in the center of the figure that define your processes and the results you achieve.

Leadership (category 1), strategic planning (category 2), and guest/customer focus (category 3) represent the leadership triad. These categories are placed together to emphasize the importance of a leadership focus on students, stakeholders, and strategy. Senior leaders set the organizational direction and seek future opportunities for the organization.

Workforce focus (category 5), operations focus (category 6), and results (category 7) represent the results triad. Your organization's workforce and key operational processes accomplish the work of the organization that yields the overall performance results.

All actions point toward results—a composite of process outcomes, guest-focused outcomes, employee-focused outcomes, leadership and governance outcomes, and budgetary, financial, and market outcomes.

System Foundation

Measurement, analysis, and knowledge management (category 4) are critical to the effective management of an organization and to a fact-based, knowledge-driven system for improving performance and competitiveness. Measurement, analysis, and knowledge management serve as the foundation of the performance management system.

Learning Objective 6: Install an Organizational Excellence Program

Installing an Organizational Excellence Program

Before installing an organizational excellence program, it is best to assess the leadership capabilities of the management from top to bottom of the organization. The reason why this is so important is because organizational excellence will not flourish if effective leadership is not present. Leadership is assessed by asking the manager's subordinates to complete a questionnaire, which is then scored. If the manager scores highly, there is no need for action. However, if the manager scores below average, or low, you can either train or replace that person with someone who displays more leadership qualities. The unsuccessful manager can be offered another position in the organization if they are salvageable. Remember, the success of the organization as a whole is paramount. There is no room for mediocre leadership in organizational excellence. As one leader told the author that he wants "A" grade players on his team not "C" grade players (Col. J. Saputo, personal communication, January 12, 2013).

Once leaders are in place at every level of the organization, the program is ready for installation. All employees need to know what to do, by when to do it, and how to do it, so performance standards are written for each position. The 10 steps to an organizational excellence program are below.

The 10 Steps to Organizational Excellence:

1. Step 1: Form teams of four or five volunteers from each department or area of the organization and train them in problem solving and goal setting.
2. Step 2: Write guest service performance excellence standards.
3. Step 3: Write goals based on guest service excellence expectations.
4. Step 4: Write departmental or area vision, mission, and goals.
5. Step 5: Ensure all necessary resources are available.
6. Step 6: Inspire and empower teams to reach or exceed goals.
7. Step 7: Monitor and record results.
8. Step 8: Note any items not meeting guest excellence expectations and formulate a plan to meet them.
9. Step 9: Recognize and reward teams meeting or exceeding guest excellence expectations.
10. Step 10: Continuously improve the excellence of guest service and then repeat the processes.

Once formed, the teams tend to work well together on selecting the most important guest service topics for scrutiny. One topic, for example, could be at the front desk of a hotel, where guests tend to complain about how long it takes to register for their room. The team considers various suggestions like having additional employees trained and available to register guests at peak check-in times. Another idea is to register guests for conferences at a separate desk and preregister them in order to speed up the process. Yet another suggestion is to set up a registration desk at the airport and to arrange for guest transportation to the hotel. Now that would "wow" some guests. At the London InterContinental at Hyde Park Corner, the front desk agents were trained to escort guests straight up to their rooms upon arrival and check them in there. At another resort, one of the authors personally greeted every guest with a beverage, usually a rum punch, to welcome them and wish them a terrific vacation.

Technology in HR

Technology is very important to the overall effectiveness of a company or organization for many reasons, but especially because of the impact it has on making strategic business decisions, which can heavily influence the path an organization takes, as well as how the organization defines itself in terms of its mission, philosophy, values, goals, and objectives.

Technology in organizational effectiveness within the hospitality industry is described as external and internal, as well as both tangible and intangible. Organizations strive to balance an efficient blend of physical assets (operational equipment), such as POS systems and computer reservation systems, with the process of effectively turning inputs into outputs, such as the elements that make up a restaurant dining experience or hotel experience, which is the external output. The assets used to turn inputs into outputs are thought of as the tangibles, while the software or programs used are thought of as the intangibles. Internally, organizations use online training programs via desktop computers or track and store company and employee information using electronic data collection software to increase their overall effectiveness.

Organizations use technology in many different ways to improve their effectiveness in gaining resources in attempt to create a competitive advantage in the business environment. Through sales and marketing a company is able to differentiate their brand or to increase exposure of their brand, and technology is one of the keys to implementing an effective strategy for differentiation and exposure. For example, a restaurant company may want to advertise different events or menu specials, and the social media platform with which they choose to use can make a world of difference, depending on the restaurant's concept, demographics and location.

Furthermore, a large hotel company may be looking to adapt a new POS software program for all hotels within their brand, which can be an expensive process, but it is essential to the hotel's ability to function and provide exceptional guest service. While it may be significantly cheaper to choose a POS software program that is ranked average compared to some of the more expensive brands, the ease of use, speed of service, and system error may be more efficient, which can influence the way the brand is perceived in the eyes of consumers. In conclusion, more efficient technology can directly relate to an increase in organizational effectiveness both internally and externally.

Key Points

- A workplace that stresses organizational excellence is the one that is both family and employee centered, uses coaching versus directing, practices ethical decision-making, has equitable policies, celebrates its stakeholders, provides ongoing communications, promotes innovation, stresses service excellence and is flexible, that is, open to change.

- A major force in organizational excellence is leadership style. The leadership style that works best with organizational excellence is coaching. A coach is one who not only leads his or her team but also develops the team members to be the best that they can be.

- *Social/belonging*: This area focuses on building your employees into stakeholders. *Ego/self-esteem*: Constantly recognizing excellent performance and properly handling performance problems by letting the employee know that you appreciate their work, while building on the employee's strengths. *Self-actualization*: You have an opportunity to assist in developing employees into what they want to be.

- "Hire attitude, train skills" is good advice for creating an effective high-performance organization and should be part of your recruitment and hiring culture as recruitment and selection has to be more than just a program.

- You can encourage an organization that stresses participation by involving your team members in the decision-making process, which should include not only decisions that affect your department but also those that affect the organization as a whole.

- Management by objectives (MBO) provides an opportunity to involve team members in planning for both their individual future, and the future of the organization. MBO can be used to resolve an organizational problem, plan for the individual development of a team member, or resolve a problem that a team member may be having.

- There are three things that you should consider when evaluating performance and/or a behavior problem, which include the environment, capability, and motivation.

- There are three appraisal formats that managers often use as part of the formal performance appraisal, which include graphic rating, competency-based appraisals, and BARS.

- One of the most beneficial references employees can use to determine the proper way to conduct themselves while on the job is the employee handbook. If specified performance appraisals are outlined in the employee handbook, they should be expected to take place.

- There are potential problems that arise from managers not properly conducting the annual performance appraisals with employees, which include timeliness, recency error, and central tendency error.

- Organizational excellence (OE) grew out of Total Quality Management (TQM). TQM is a process of continuous quality improvement focusing on the guest's needs and expectations. In order for TQM to be successful, it is often necessary to implement a change in corporate culture.

- The Baldrige Criteria can apply equally to all business sectors, including service organizations, and are compatible with other performance improvement initiatives. Regardless of the type of service your organization provides, the Baldrige Criteria can serve as a valuable framework for measuring performance and planning in an uncertain environment.

- The Organizational Profile (top of figure) sets the context for the way your organization operates. The performance system is composed of the six Baldrige categories in the center of the figure that define your processes and the results you achieve.

- Before installing an organizational excellence program it is best to assess the leadership capabilities of the management from top to bottom of the organization. Once leaders are in place at every level of the organization, the program is ready for installation.

Key Terms

BARS	Employee handbook	Organizational excellence (OE)
Central tendency error	Graphic rating	Performance characteristics
Coaching	Management by objectives	Recency error
Competency-based appraisals	(MBO)	Total quality management (TQM)

Discussion Questions

1. As a coach, how would you handle an employee working in your kitchen that was a hard worker, but had trouble getting along with his co-workers? What would you do to try to change his behavior?

2. Why is it important to involve employees in organizational decision-making? Give some examples.

3. It is evaluation time and you have an office manager who is a good worker, but continuously makes mistakes while handling the restaurant cash flow. What kind of plan would you jointly develop with this employee to turn around their behavior?

Ethical Dilemma

You are the Director of Rooms at a large hotel, and the top candidate for becoming next Assistant General Manager. You are committed to creating and sustaining an employee-centered workplace. It comes to your attention that one of your frequent valued guests is sexually harassing one of your front desk attendants. This guest spends a lot of money at your hotel and also brings numerous large meeting groups to the hotel throughout the year. You mention the harassment to the General Manager who tells you to overlook it because the guest in question is "just kidding around". The harassment continues and the front desk employee comes to you again with a complaint. What should you do?

Internet Exercise

Go to the website http://www.nist.gov/baldrige/ and find a topic that interests you then share it with your class.

References

Archer North Performance Appraisal System. (n.d.). *Performance appraisal: Legal and ethical issues in performance appraisal.* Retrieved August 7, 2013, from http://www.performance-appraisal.com/legalaspects.htm

ASQ. (n.d.). *Total quality management.* The American Society for Quality, Inc. Retrieved from http://asq.org/learn-about-quality/total-quality-management/overview/overview.html

Business Dictionary. (2013a). *Central tendency error.* Retrieved February 17, 2013, from http://www.businessdictionary.com/definition/central-tendency-error.html

Business Dictionary. (2013b). *Recency error.* Retrieved February 17, 2013, from http://www.businessdictionary.com/definition/recency-error.html.

Carbonara, P. (1996). Hire for attitude, train for skill. *Fast Company Media Group.* Retrieved February 17, 2013, from http://www.starttogether.org/docs/hiring.pdf

Gomez-Mejia, L. R., Balkin, D. B., & Cardy, R. L. (2012). *Managing Human Resources* (7th ed.). Upper Saddle River, NJ: Pearson.

Holusha, J. (December, 1993). W. Edwards Deming, expert on business management, dies at 93. *The New York Times.* Retrieved February 18, 2013, from http://www.nytimes.com/1993/12/21/obituaries/w-edwards-deming-expert-on-business-management-dies-at-93.html?pagewanted=all&src=pm

Indiana University Human Resources. (2015a). *Define performance standards for each duty, definition, considerations* (part 1). Available from http://www.indiana.edu/~uhrs/training/performance_management/define.htm

Indiana University Human Resources. (2015b). *Define performance standards for each duty, definition, considerations* (part 2). Available from http://www.indiana.edu/~uhrs/training/performance management/define.htm

NIST. (2013a). *Malcolm Baldrige National Quality Award 1992 Recipient: The Ritz-Carlton Hotel Company*. Retrieved February 18, 2013, from http://www.baldrige.nist.gov/Ritz_Carlton_Hotel_Co.htm

NIST. (2013b). Retrieved February 18, 2013, from http://www.nist.gov/baldrige/publications/upload/2011_2012_Education_Criteria.pdf

Tuckman, A. (1994). The yellow brick road: Total quality management and the restructuring of organizational culture. *Organization Studies 15*(5), 727–751.

U.S. SBA. (2013). *Employee handbooks*. Retrieved February 17, 2013, from http://www.sba.gov/content/employee-handbooks

© ne3p/Shutterstock.com

Chapter **12**

EMPLOYEE RELATIONS

Introduction

"I believe there are five major reasons why your employees leave you, and the first three are critical. They don't know what they're supposed to do, they don't know how to do what they're supposed to do, and they don't know how well it's supposed to be done."—David Scott Peters, Restaurant Consultant.

Employee Relations: The relations aspect of management that involves understanding and respecting the concerns and well-being of employees. The goal of employee relations is to prevent and resolve problems in the workplace that could originate from a situation within the company.

> **Employee Relations**: The relations aspect of management that involves understanding and respecting the concerns and well-being of employees.

Dan Simons, a hospitality and restaurant industry consultant says, "Human performance is directly related to human emotion, you simply cannot separate your restaurant's culture from your profitability. If I have a client with a food costs problem, I start with their employee relations. How do they feel? How do they look? Do they have pride in their appearance? The self-esteem and the pride of employees translate in measurable ways" (QSR, 2011).

Good employee relations are not only essential in growing a business, but also for ensuring that the level of policy, communications, and overall expectations are in line with your company culture. A restaurant chain that takes pride in being hospitable, warm, and welcoming should have employee relations that closely mimic those characteristics.

After studying this chapter, you will be able to:

- Discuss the importance of employee relations.
- Explain the concept of communication and the different forms in the work place.
- Provide an overview of communication in written form.
- Explain different methods to enhance employee satisfaction.
- Discuss the reasoning and benefits behind employee assistance programs.

Learning Objective 1: Discuss the importance of employee relations

Why Good Employee Relations are Important

Employees are the most important aspect of an operation. If employees are satisfied, guests will be satisfied, employee turnover will decrease, and total operating costs can go down. Improving employee relations can be a great source of growth that is neither costly nor difficult to implement. So why not put the effort into making sure employees are being heard, understood, and appreciated? There's no reason not to.

Positive discipline, proper delegation, effective communication, grievance programs, and reward programs should be included in an organization looking to form an employee relations program. Larger companies may have an entire department dedicated to employee relations while smaller companies may have an appointed office member or administrator to take on employee relations duties.

During periods of economic stress, many organizations cut back on employee relations programs, recognition, and rewards considering them "optional". But, experts and analysts warn that owners and operators should not only be sparing their employee relations programs during difficult times such as a recession, but they should also be strengthening them (QSR, 2011). If there's a single element of a business that can further your success, it will begin and end with the employee. So, to maintain good employee relations, it is better to be proactive when it comes to critical topics. Let's use sexual harassment as an example. Want to convince managers to report harassment complaints swiftly? Show them a video illustrating—in painful detail—what it's like to sit through a deposition for a harassment lawsuit. "If you show them a manager being cross-examined in a deposition or at trial being questioned about conduct they did or didn't do, then it really comes home" (SHRM, 2013a).

Larger companies may have an entire department dedicated to employee relations while smaller companies may have an appointed office member or administrator to take on employee relations duties.

© Andrey_Popov/Shutterstock.com

The Employee Relations Specialist

An employee relations specialist usually starts with gathering information in the workplace from employees on their opinions and attitudes in the work environment. The specialist then uses this information to construct ideas to resolve any problem. The specialist also has a role in explaining company rules, government regulations, procedures, and policies in the work place and the importance of being compliant.

As part of the job, the specialist in the workplace can gather and distribute employee surveys, organize feedback programs, recognition programs, and employee assistance programs. It is an important position to fill in a large company looking to reduce turnover and increase guest satisfaction. When you have a specialist focusing on the core problems in the workplace, they can put all their efforts into resolving those problems and leading an organization in a positive direction.

Communication

Communication is the process of sending a message to a given receiver through a channel that will effectively deliver the message. Good communication is a vital and necessary feature of good employee relations. Communication forms include emails, memos, reports, Internet chat messages, etc. If the receiver cannot "decode" the message, the form of communication has failed because it was not effectively transmitted. This would be considered "miscommunication." Examples of a message that cannot be decoded by the receiver would be improper use of language and terms not directly identifying subjects or persons in the message. Additionally, the reasoning or motives behind sending the message should be clear.

Communication should always leave room for feedback from the receiver. **Feedback** allows the sender to identify the

> **Communication:** The process of sending a message to a given receiver through a channel that will effectively deliver the message.

> **Feedback:** Allows the sender to identify the effectiveness of the sent message and ensure the interpretation was correctly received.

Noise: Anything within a message or how it was sent that breaks or disrupts the process of sending and receiving.

effectiveness of the sent message and ensure the intent was correctly received. Noise is anything within a message that breaks or disrupts the process of sending and receiving. Distractions in the work place or an inadvertent mistake made by the sender may be considered to be noise. If a message is handwritten and placed on a coworker's desk that is covered in files and papers due to work overload, there is a great chance the handwritten message will not be received due to "noise".

Communication forms include emails, memos, reports, Internet chat messages, and more

Learning Objective 2: Explain the concept of communication and the different forms in the workplace

Two-way Communication: Method of communication that allows feedback. It is considered "two-way" because it allows both the sender and receiver to interact with each other.

Two-way communication is a method of communication that allows feedback. It is considered "two-way" because it allows both the sender and receiver to interact with each other. If there is no way for either a sender or receiver to send feedback, it would be considered one-way communication.

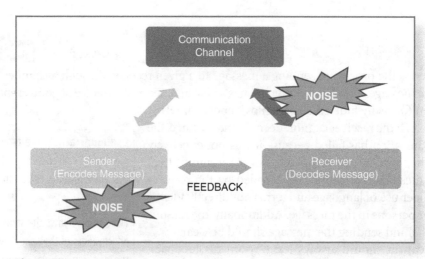

Figure 12.1　Communication Is a Process Impacted by Noise

Types of Communication

Informal communication is any form of sending a message without formal structure. This could include a post-it note left on someone's desk, a text message, or an instant message. Formal communication is any form of sending a message where a format or structure is used. This could include an office memo; a letter with letter head, date, and sign; a recorded conference call; or formal meetings.

Verbal communication is any type of communication using words. Nonverbal communication does not use words and is typically in the form of body language and facial expressions. Both are forms of communication and both can send an effective or uneffective message to a receiver.

In the management of employee relations, there are two important forms of communication: Upward communication and downward communication. Upward communication allows employees at a subordinate level to express their feelings, concerns, or ideas to those at a higher level of supervision or management. This form of communication is useful in an employee relations program that encompasses employee feedback and appeals procedures.

Downward communication gives higher-level management the power to convey their decisions and ideas to lower-level employees in an organization. If an organization's corporate level has information that needs to be communicated to a definite group of people, downward communication is the best form to do so.

> **Informal Communication**: Any form of sending a message without proper structure.

> **Formal Communication**: Any form of sending a message where a format or proper structure is used.

> **Upward Communication**: A form of communication that allows employees at a lower level of management to express their feelings, concerns, or ideas to those at a higher level of management.

> **Downward Communication**: A form of communication that gives higher-level management the power to enforce their decisions and ideas to lower-level employees in an organization.

How Communication Works

It may sound odd, but effective communication is based on listening as much as sending a message. Listening is important because when a sender is sending a message, no matter the size or level of employment, the sender must first understand what it will take for a receiver to understand the message, which in turn, forces a speaker to be able to first listen to the needs of the receiver. What does the receiver already know? What expectations or preconceived notions may they have about you? What type of communication will they benefit from the most?

Effective communication is not just talking back and forth until someone understands, but taking time to find the best route to communicate. Should it be verbal? Written? Should a meeting be held? Sometimes communicating can be a firm handshake when congratulating an employee or a "high-five" for a job well done. Listening to what the receiver knows and anticipates can ensure the sender to choose the best method of communication and also carries out the message.

Learning Objective 3: Provide an overview of communication in written form

Written Communication

> **Written Communication:** Any verbal form of communication in the form of a document that sends a message.

Written communication is any verbal form of communication in the form of a document that sends a message. Written communication includes letters, written statements, employee handbooks, office memos, bulletin boards, and flyers. Today, the most common form of written communication is an email.

An employee handbook provides guidance and information related to the company's history, mission, values, policies, procedures, and benefits in a written format

© designer491/Shutterstock.com

Employee Handbooks

> **Employee Handbook:** A guideline of rules, policies, and procedures for all company personnel to follow and abide by.

An employee handbook can be a valuable communication resource for the employer and the employee. If you've ever worked in the hospitality job or for any company that employs a group of people, you've more than likely signed an employee handbook agreement, a contract stating you have read and understood the policies and procedures as outlined in the handbook representative of that company. A handbook provides guidance and information related to the company's history, mission, values, policies, procedures, and benefits in a written format (SHRM, 2013b).

Employee handbooks typically include topics such as:

- Payroll procedures
- Dress code policies
- Office etiquette and behavior
- Vacation time/personal time
- Hiring and termination policies
- Benefits

Larger organizations will often include many more topics and can be quite lengthy. Small organizations may have a handbook that touches on the basics of the job and company procedures and can be only a few pages. Regardless of the size, employee handbooks give the employee a reference point and employers a written source to fall back on should an employee have an issue regarding company policy.

Companies without employee handbooks can be more liable to legal disputes. Policies that are not in place, but enforced, can be considered misleading and illegal. Companies that use handbooks still must review the verbiage from time-to-time to make sure they are protecting their assets and avoiding legal fees.

For example, a gourmet bakery discharged an employee for stealing a $20 bill out of the cash register. The employee was caught on film doing so and did not deny the fact, however, when that same employee asked why the sibling of the owner was not terminated for taking cash out of the drawer, the owner of the bakery was taken to court for unfair treatment of the firing of one employee over another. The discharged employee won the suit and was rewarded monetary fees for the misunderstanding. How? The bakery owner failed to follow the policies as written in the employee handbook.

The handbook stated: "Any employee caught and/or proved of stealing money or any other item [s] herein belonging to this establishment will be automatically terminated." Including such a statement in an employee handbook is beneficial, however, since the statement read, "*will be* terminated" instead of "*may be* terminated", the owner is legally at fault for not fulfilling the termination of the sibling when it was known the sibling had also taken money from the cashier's drawer.

Memos, Financial Statements, Newsletters, and Bulletin Boards

Memos are a formal, written form of communication that briefly relays a message to a group of individuals. The memo could be from the CEO to all managers, from managers to all shift managers, or managers to all employees. Memos are formal because they are not only specific to the "from" and "to", but the subject of the message, the date it was sent, and the body of the message.

> **Memos:** A formal, written form of communication that briefly relays a message to a group of individuals.

Financial statements are a written, formal form of communication that shows the financial activities of an organization. There are four types of financial statements:

1. Balance sheet
2. Income statement
3. Statement of retained earnings
4. Statement of cash flows

Each statement reports earnings and a given position or "snapshot" of the organization or entity. The most common receivers of financial statements are senior managers, owners, and/or shareholders.

Newsletters and bulletin boards are other written forms of communication that reach a vast group of employees. Newsletters can be emailed, mailed, or passed out to a group of employees. One hotel chain sends out monthly newsletters that highlight new achievements in the company, new hotel openings, company events, and any changes or helpful information for the employee. No matter the level of management, an employee of this chain has a resource for updates and communication. Bulletin boards can be used to post similar information. New job openings, updates for company information can be generated and posted for employees. A deli in Michigan posts all new company information to its bulletin board located inside the break room. It also allows employees to post flyers or notes if they are trying to sell something, looking for a carpool, or even wanted to organize a workplace event.

Learning Objective 4: Describe technology and electronic communications in the employee workplace

HR Technology

Technology has allowed human resource departments to streamline communication. Printers, fax machines, scanners, electronic faxing, Internet, computers, and mobile phones have dramatically increased how communication can be sent.

Lawrence is a HR recruiter for a cruise line that is in season for hiring an abundance of crew of various jobs on the ship. Lawrence receives more than 200 resumes to his email every day. He not only has a system through a job searching website that will filter the best candidates, but an automated response system for candidates who will not fit the position. Of the 200 candidates Lawrence received on Thursday, 20 were automatically disqualified due to a criminal background that the cruise line does not accept, and 10 candidates were disqualified due to their availability and time frames in which they can work. Thus, 30 applicants automatically received an email from the cruise line company stating that management was in receipt of their resume, but after further review their resume would not be reviewed further. It also thanks them for applying and asks to consider the cruise line in the future for employment.

Imagine Lawrence having to do such a task before technology was so readily available. All the 200 resumes not in an electronic format, but paper form, to read, review, and try to narrow down which applicants would not fit the job position or were not qualified. Once he would weed out the bad candidates, Lawrence would then have to call each of those candidates and/or physically mail a letter to a home address stating their resume would not be considered any further.

Emails are electronic forms of mail in which a sender writes and sends a written message to the receiver

As you can see, without technology in today's world, tasks that can be handled by automated filters and communication response would have taken hours and days to do before the existence of Internet and computers. Communication is indispensable and technology has furthered the ability to communicate with sophistication, speed, and quality.

Electronic Communication

Electronic communication has changed the way the world communicates in business today. Before computers, Internet, cell phones, scanners, and instant messaging; businesses communicated on a much simpler level. The holiday office party flyer was posted in the break room instead of email, a marketing campaign was sent in the mail instead of advertised on a business's Facebook page and calling an employee to check on the whereabouts meant picking up a phone and speaking instead of a text message. The rise of different forms of technology and electronic communication also means making sure employees understand how to use each of those forms.

A **voice mail** is one type of electronic communication in which the sender will leave a recorded message for the receiver. Voice mails can be relayed through land line phones or cell phones. **Emails** are electronic forms of mail in which a sender writes and sends a written message to the receiver. Emails are sent through a computer using the Internet or in some cases, company networks.

> **Voice Mail:** One type of electronic communication in which the sender will leave a recorded message for the receiver.

> **Emails:** Electronic forms of mail in which a sender writes and sends a written message to the receiver.

Since the Internet was prominent in 1992, emails have grown to be the most common form of electronic communication. With growth and popularity comes privacy issues; how can a piece of mail being sent over the Internet be protected? If you've ever sent or received an email from an organization that seeks protection in their emails, you may have read the following:

> *This message contains confidential information and is intended only for the intended recipients. If you are not an intended recipient you should not disseminate, distribute, or copy this email. Please notify the Company by email, itdepartment@ABC.com if you have received this email by mistake and delete this email from your system. Email transmission cannot be guaranteed to be secured or error-free as information could be intercepted, corrupted, lost, destroyed, arrive late or incomplete, or contain viruses. Company ABC does not accept liability for any errors or omissions in the contents of this message, which arise as a result of email transmission.*

If an organization plans on reading employee's emails for any reason, whether it be training or quality control purposes, the organization must state that fact in an employee handbook as well as in an email header or footer. An example of such disclaimer would be, "Please note that Company ABC may monitor email traffic data and the content of email for the purposes of security and staff training."

The advantages of email are: It is a written, electronic form of communication that can be easily sent, traced, recorded, and time stamped. Emails can be sent across the country in seconds when the sender has no other form of communicating with the receiver. Emails can be sent from one employee to another, who happens to be sitting right next to them, but wants to have a way to trace their correspondence and ideas on a group project. The disadvantages of emails include information overload, an abundance of personal communication occurring during work hours, and privacy issues as previously mentioned. Even after companies include disclaimers about the parties able to read emails, employees too often view emails in the workplace as private property and forget the consequences that can arise when exchanging information via email.

Email has streamlined the way the hospitality industry operates. Many companies use email as their primary source of communication. Take for instance, booking an airline ticket and hotel to Puerto Vallarta, Mexico through Orbitz.com. During the booking process, you are asked and required to enter an email for contact, you cannot continue to book the trip without this, as Orbitz requires one for communication. Once booked, you are told to check your email for a confirmation. Orbitz will then remind you of your trip as it nears, sends reminders of check in times, and will update you if there is a change in your reservation. Orbitz will then also use your email as a means for marketing; sending you specials and deals for trips, car rentals, plane tickets, and so on. Some hotels will no longer accept reservations over the phone, and if they do, you'll often incur long wait times. If you have a customer service complaint or inquiry, websites are now requiring you send an electronic message explaining your issue or inquiry and you'll receive a response to your email within a given period of time.

Email aside, multimedia technology also growing in popularity and usefulness. **Multimedia technology** is using voice, video, and text to communicate with someone via video images from anywhere in the world.

> **Multimedia Technology:** Using voice, video, and text to communicate with someone via video images from anywhere in the world.

Skype is one form of multimedia being used in the workplace. Skype allows a sender to communicate with a receiver while being able to hear their voice via audio and see them via video. Each subject has a video camera either attached or installed to their computer and, by use of speakers and a connection to the Internet, those subjects are able to communicate similarly to that of face-to-face communication.

Another form of multimedia used in many businesses is on-screen presentations that include still images, video, audio, and text. These presentations can send messages to a single person or group of people can be presented in person or sent in a digital format and ultimately convey one or more messages to the receiver. On-screen presentations often cluster information into graphs, slides, and other forms that represent a summary of information. They are usually projected through a projector onto a media screen or viewed on a computer.

Multimedia's intent is making conveying a message easier and faster. It's also used to enhance the viewer's or receiver's experience by listening and watching or reading. Multimedia has allowed messages to be sent that involve creativity and may spark more interest from the audience than a single source of media.

Take for instance a group of employees at a food distribution company. There are new safety guidelines imposed on all employees working on the "floor" and management must review all new guidelines in a meeting. The HR director puts together a PowerPoint presentation to review the guidelines. Included in the slides are photos, examples of why the new rules are in place, and YouTube videos slip off and fall bloopers that actually add humor to the presentation. When presenting the guidelines to all 35 workers, the director finds the employees are laughing, taking notes, and nodding their heads in agreement. If the director would have taken a more one-source media stance on communicating the required information, would it have been as effective? Take for example a memo, a written form of communication that is completely acceptable in the work place, but how many of the 35 employees would have read the memo and the attached information? And those employees who do take time to read the guidelines, a large portion would not retain the information included, thus making a memo ineffective.

Selecting the best form of communication is a great skill that will help any organization prevail in communicating. Multimedia is one of those ways that allows messages to relay the important information while captivating the audience at the same time.

Legalize

Employers must be careful when employees decide to comment on their job via social medial channels such as Facebook, MySpace, Twitter, YouTube, blogs, podcasts, and the like. A New Jersey District Court recently upheld a jury verdict in which a restaurant was found liable for violating the federal Stored Communications Act (SCA) and invasion of privacy. The SCA is a federal law that creates Fourth Amendment–like privacy protection for email and other digital communications stored on the Internet. (18 U.S.C. Chapter 121) In *Pietrylo v. Hillstone Restaurant Group d/b/a Houston's*, (2009), two restaurant servers were terminated after two of the company's managers accessed a MySpace chat group maintained by one of the servers during their nonwork hours. Further, the Court upheld the jury's finding of malicious conduct, which supported an award of punitive damages.

The chat group's purpose was to vent about work and was intended to be an invitation-only, entirely private outlet. One of the employees accessed the group through her manager's home computer and showed the manager the group's postings. The manager in turn told other managers about the group and coerced one of the employees into relinquishing the group's password. The group's postings included sexual remarks about management, jokes about service standards, and references to illegal drug use. Management deemed these postings to be "offensive" and subsequently fired the two plaintiffs. The jury's finding of malicious intent involved the fact that the password was obtained through implied coercion (give me the password or lose your job). This in turn led to punitive damages which multiplied the award four times.

The jury's award consisted of compensatory damages in the form of back pay—$2,500 and $903, with each plaintiff's amount quadrupled due to punitive damages. While this amount is relatively small due to the minimal amount of ascertainable lost wages, other situations involving employees with higher incomes could warrant much larger jury verdicts. While employers have certain rights and obligations with respect to company-related computer equipment and electronic sites, this case points out the pitfalls of an attempt to extend that authority to nonwork-related equipment and sites. Employers in the hospitality industry should carefully consider the risks of privacy invasion claims associated with obtaining information from social networking sites and weigh the potential liabilities in basing employment action decisions on nonworkplace behaviors.

Meetings

Another form of communication is a meeting. Face-to-face meetings are extremely popular in years because of the communication that is accomplished through sitting with one or more persons to discuss an item. It can provide opportunity for two-way communication.

On-screen presentations often cluster information into graphs, slides, and other forms that represent a summary of information

© vectorfusionart/Shutterstock.com

Imagine you are a catering manager and you have 5–10 events on a weekly basis. Imagine issuing a memo every time a client changed a menu item or imagine sending an email to each employee letting them know their shifts and responsibilities for each event. Such forms of communication would not only be time consuming, but unproductive. Daily, weekly, or monthly meetings are common for most businesses in the hospitality industry. Group efforts mean group communication and the best way to make it effective and positive is a meeting.

Setting up a regularly scheduled day and time for a meeting to discuss operations items is a great way to communicate to a group. Special meetings or calling a meeting to discuss a separate or important item is also a solid form of sending your message to the receiver. Not all meetings need to involve an entire staff or group of people. Some issues deal with an employee or coworker who needs to be addressed as an individual. Ongoing issues in the workplace, attitude problems, or performance reviews are typically discussed in a one-on-one meeting. Meetings are earnest and effective to communicate and ensure that no noise is interrupting the message being sent.

Employee Surveys

Employee surveys can be a way for employees to communicate with management. These are a way for management to find out workers' level of satisfaction with an organization and on specific issues and are typically anonymous. They measure the likes, dislikes, opinions, and attitudes with their job and the organization. An employee survey can help a company to see where they can improve, what areas they are doing well, and what, if any, changes they can make to improve worker productivity and satisfaction. Organization responsiveness to employee feedback leads to higher retention rates, lower absenteeism, improved productivity, better customer service, and higher employee morale (SHRM, 2013c).

HR must get the complete commitment of the organization's top management team before conducting any survey of employees. Once top management is sold on the idea, HR professionals typically facilitate the survey's development, help managers overcome their natural hesitation about employee feedback, develop careful communication plans, and help determine how to interpret and use the data generated (SHRM, 2013c).

> **Employee Surveys**: Measure the likes, dislikes, opinions, and attitudes with their job and the organization to find out workers' level of content and satisfaction with an organization and are typically anonymous.

As a form of employee feedback, surveys give the employees a way to express their feelings and gives the employer measurable facts

© one photo/Shutterstock.com

As a form of employee feedback, surveys give the employees a way to express their feelings and gives the employer measurable facts. If a company told each of its employees to write down on a piece of paper their thoughts, likes, and dislikes in the work place; you'd have hundreds of pieces of paper with rants, personal issues in the workplace, strong opinions, and little positive feedback. When an employee is frustrated, that feeling and situation sticks with them longer than when they feel good about their job or feel well accomplished. This leaves their negative feelings about their job to remain with them as an abundance of opinions and their positive feelings of content to a minimum. A survey outlines specific topics and typically asks for a ranking. With such a system, an employer can measure opinions through a scale rather than reading through individual writings and trying to identify what is "good" and what is "bad".

Employees can also forget about employer efforts on a daily basis and surveys can help remind an individual that there is more to the operation than meets the eye. Employees may look over positive action taken by management when evaluating a company. Including such action and recognition programs reminds the employee that everything happening in an organization is indeed a team effort.

When management analyzes employee surveys, they can bring this information to the next level, whether it is corporate or higher management and express their needs to make change. If a 30-person wait staff at a Tapas restaurant fill out surveys and all 30 indicate their level of dissatisfaction with their immediate supervisors, the general manager of the restaurant will see that they have a serious issue and change needs to occur to reduce turnover and boost employee satisfaction.

The Society of Human Resource Management (SHRM) conducted a study in 2012 to assess the extent to which employees are satisfied with their jobs (SHRM, 2013d). The results indicated that 81% of U.S. employees reported "overall satisfaction" with their current job, with 38% of employees indicating they were "very satisfied", and 43% "somewhat satisfied". Employees' overall satisfaction with their jobs is down five percentage points from its peak of 86% in 2009. How satisfied are you with your job? SHRM also studied employee engagement and found that employees are only moderately engaged (3.6 on a scale of 1–5, where 5 is highly engaged). How engaged are you in your work?

Appeals Procedures

Appeals procedures is a way in which employees of a company can express their views, opinions, and concerns to the management about operations of the organization. Companies without a solid set of appeals procedures are often involved in litigation, legal fees, and turnover.

> **Appeals Procedures**: A way in which employees of a company can express their views, opinions, and concerns of the management, and operations of the organization.

By challenging the way management operates and makes decisions, employees can ensure their concerns are heard. If an employee believes a manager or supervisor is unfair or who is managing in a way that is negatively affecting the company, that employee has the right and is often encouraged to approach the correct outlet and relay their message.

Common Actions Appealed by Employees:

- Unfair performance evaluations
- Expectations and specifications of job duties
- Increase in rate of pay or salaries
- Availability and quantity of employee benefits
- Precautions for workplace safety

Determination of hours worked and overtime hours worked.

There are various types of appeals procedures a company can have. Typically, these are stated in an employee handbook and/or an inconspicuous posting in the workplace. Appeals procedures are encouraged and can more times than not benefit the organization.

Learning Objective 5: Explain different methods to enhance employee satisfaction

A speak-up program suggests specific steps an employee should take in bringing a problem to management. It is a flexible form of appeals procedure as it outlines the way to bring an issue to light. An employee should not fear of

> **A Speak-up Program**: Suggests specific steps an employee should take in bringing a problem to management.

"speaking up" and a speak-up program will ensure that fact is known. This type of program will typically enforce the employee to first speak up to their immediate supervisor and if the issue cannot be resolved or is about the supervisor directly, the next step is allowing for the employee to speak to higher-level management and so forth.

An open-door program is an informal way of allowing any employee at any level to have access to upper-level management when voicing concerns regarding management. The person receiving the complaint has a duty and obligation to thoroughly investigate the issue at hand and resolve or firmly attempt to resolve the situation.

> **An Open-door Program**: An informal way of allowing any employee at any level to have access to upper-level management when voicing concerns regarding management.

> **Ombudsman**: An outside or neutral individual who is brought in to take part in the settling of an employee complaint or dispute.

Even when managers believe they have good communications (in both directions) with their employees, sometimes employees believe they are unable to bring a concern or grievance to management attention. One solution to this is to have a company ombudsman. This person (and it can be a full-time or part-time position) acts as a neutral person or neutral individual who is brought in to take part in the settling of an employee complaint or dispute. The role of the ombudsman is to mediate both parties involving the issue until it is resolved. This method of appeals procedures is also an encouraging program due to the fact that employees will not fear their jobs will be affected by bringing an issue to management's attention or making a complaint against their immediate supervisor.

Ombudsman can and will deem a company in the wrong after an investigation and enforce the repayment of wages and/or proper compensation for the dispute at hand. An Ombudsman office in Australia required a city to pay back more than $39,000 in back pay for more than 250 hospitality workers. Fair Work Ombudsman executive director Michael Campbell said the move followed concerns that junior staff and backpackers were not receiving their lawful entitlements. "While the majority of businesses were compliant, inspectors discovered two employers were underpaying their staff the minimum hourly rate, penalty rates, shift loadings, and allowances", he said (Anonymous, 2011).

> **Grievance Panel**: This is used in a nonunion company and consists of complaining employees, managers, and other active staff and excludes the employee's direct supervisor.

Employee Assistance Programs offer help to employees in need of assistance

© pathdoc/Shutterstock.com

All types of appeals procedures mentioned so far are fairly informal. The most formal types include a grievance panel and union grievance procedure. Grievance panel is used in a nonunion company and consists of complaining employees, managers, and other active staff and excludes the employee's direct supervisor. The panel will investigate the complaints and are usually the last step in solving an appeal. The **union grievance procedure** is similar to a grievance panel, but evolves all employees operating under a union contract. As any company, unions have their own set of procedures in handling appeals. Union grievance procedures almost always include an arbitrator or another neutral party to end the dispute and solve the complaint.

> **Union Grievance Procedure:** This is similar to a grievance panel, but involves all employees operating under a union contract.

Employee Assistance Programs

Dana is a shift manager at a casino bar and is responsible for managing at least 10 cocktail waitresses at any time. Dana has started to notice that over time one of her once stellar employees, Hannah, has not been herself. Dana has seen Hannah lose a significant amount of weight, has been showing up to work looking fatigued, and will not eat any food on her shift breaks. Concerned, Dana speaks to her HR manager to find out the proper course of action to approach Hannah and the situation. She spears to have a problem; it's affecting her work performance and is getting worse. What should she do? For a situation like this, some companies have **employee assistance programs (EAPs)**.

> **Employee Assistance Programs (EAPs):** Programs in place that provide assistance to employees dealing with personal issues that affect their job performance.

An employer-sponsored EAP is a work-based intervention program designed to identify and assist employees in resolving personal problems that may be adversely affecting their performance at work, such as marital, financial, or emotional problems; family issues; or substance or alcohol abuse (SHRM, 2013e).

Employers have a vested interest in the ability of employees to work at or close to their full potential. EAPs are valuable resources that can help employees cope with issues affecting their ability to reach that potential (SHRM, 2013e).

The goal of any EAP is to help an employee get well, solve a personal issue and/or improve a lifestyle condition to improving work ethic and performance. This concept helps the employee and ensures that an organization is getting the best out of that person.

After speaking with the HR manager, Dana decides to approach Hannah with some information about the EAP the company has to offer. She first explains that she's noticed a change in Hannah's work performance and she feels as if it involves something more than her work environment. Making sure she does not offend or attack Hannah, Dana is able to privately offer not only assistance for any issue Hannah is having but to also remind her that her job performance and work environment is affected by her choices.

Learning Objective 6: Discuss the reasoning and benefits behind employee assistance programs

So long a company promotes their EAP, many employees will realize they have a problem and seek help themselves. In essence, an EAP is also the last resort for an employee before disciplinary action or termination takes place. Denial is common in a most addictions, thus problems involving alcohol, drugs, and gambling are often more difficult to rectify than others. Counselors are trained either internally or externally to help the employee deal with their issue. In certain cases, an employee is made to take part in a different form of therapy if medical treatment is required.

After the treatment is completed, a counselor will advise the employer of the status and effectiveness of the employee returning to work. Leave of absences or even termination may be recommended by the counselor depending on the success of the assistance that was provided and the outcome of that assistance.

Employee Recognition Programs

> **Employee Recognition Programs**: Ways to show appreciation to an employee that will prove the organization cares about their performance, ideas, and attitude in the workplace.

Employee recognition programs can be as informal as posting a note on an employee's office door letting them know of a job well done or as formal as a monetary bonus. Regardless of the form of recognition, the benefits an organization can reap from such programs are endless. An SHRM survey (SHRM, 2013f) examined the impact of recognition on employee engagement, satisfaction, and employee performance reviews. The findings confirmed that positive feedback and praise have an impact on employee's performance. When that feedback is coupled with a reward, performance is driven even further.

Human resource departments often develop more in-depth ways of recognizing employees. These may consist of encouraging and assisting with continuing education in a field that would progress the employees' skills in the work place, posting a monthly employee honor roll, or hosting a weekly meeting for suggestions and input. Successful recognition programs encourage evaluation of supervisors and providing suggestions for ways for the organization to improve.

Recognition Awards

> **Recognition Awards**: Awards giving credit to employees, teams, or departments that have made contributions to improve the organization.

Recognition awards are awards giving credit to employees, teams, or departments that have made contributions to improve the organization. A front desk manager received "employee of the month" and their name was added to a perpetual plaque and the employee's photo was hung for other employees and guests to see. A server at a country club received "employee of the month" and received 2 tickets to an NFL football game. An event planner received a $500 bonus check for exceeding the company's goal for events booked.

Recognition awards can be monetary or nonmonetary. Some of the most effective awards are the ones that cost barely anything, but the message of recognition is strongly relayed. Some organizations keep a constant "stock" of awards, that is, tickets to sporting events, gift certificates to restaurants, movie passes, and more. Other awards may require a high authority such as a corporate office or advance supervisor for approval. Awards can also be given by coworkers and do not necessarily have to be from a direct manager or superior. Whatever encouragement, praise, and recognition an organization can spread to its employees will surely be reciprocated by the employees back into the source.

Key Points

- The goal of employee relations is to prevent and resolve problems in the workplace that could originate from a situation within the company. Employee relations are not only essential in growing as a business, but for ensuring the level of policy, communications, and overall expectations are in line with your company culture.

- An employee relations specialist gathers information in the workplace from employees on their attitudes in the work environment; the specialist then uses this information to construct ideas to resolve any problems.

- Communication is the process of sending a message to a given receiver through a channel that will effectively deliver the message. If the receiver cannot decode the message, the form of communication has failed because it was not effectively transmitted.

- Verbal communication is any type of communication using words. Nonverbal communication does not use words and is typically in the form of body language and facial expressions.

- In the management of employee relations, there are two important forms of communication; upward communication and downward communication.

- Today, the most common form of written communications in companies takes place in that of an email, financial or written statements, and letters.

- Electronic communication has changed the way the world communicates in business today. Before computers, Internet, cell phones, scanners, and instant messaging; businesses communicated on a much simpler level.

- Multimedia technology is using voice, video, and text to communicate with someone via video images from anywhere in the world.

- Though there are many successful forms of communications, one of the most prominent and productive ways is through a meeting. Face-to-face meetings are extremely popular and have been for many years because of the communication that is accomplished.

- Employee surveys are a way to find out a worker's level of content and satisfaction with an organization and typically anonymous. They measure the likes, dislikes, opinions, and attitudes with their job and the organization.

- There are various types of appeals procedures a company can have. Typically, these are stated in an employee handbook and/or an inconspicuous posting in the workplace.

- Companies without a solid set of appeals procedures are often involved in litigation, legal fees, and turnover. The most formal types include a grievance panel and union grievance procedure.

- Employee assistance programs (EAPs) are programs in place that provide assistance to employees dealing with personal issues that affect their job performance.

- The goal of any EAP is to assist, help an employee get well, solve a personal issue, and improve a lifestyle conditional to improving work ethics and performance.

- Employee recognition can mean posting a note on an employee's office door letting them know of a job well done or rewarding a monetary bonus for stellar performance.

- Recognition awards can be monetary or nonmonetary. Some of the most effective awards are the ones that cost barely anything, but the message of recognition is strongly relayed.

Key Terms

An open-door program	Employee assistance programs	Feedback
Appeals procedures	(EAPs)	Formal communication
A speak-up program	Employee handbook	Grievance panel
Communication	Employee recognition programs	Informal communication
Downward communication	Employee relations	Memos
Emails	Employee surveys	Multimedia technology

Noise   Two-way communication   Voice mail
Ombudsman   Union grievance procedure   Written communication
Recognition awards   Upward communication

Discussion Questions

1. Internet messages, text messages, and multimedia communication are increasing in the workplace as acceptable forms of communicating. Do you feel that social network sites such as Facebook or LinkedIn are acceptable forms of communicating in the workplace? For what purposes?

2. If you were responsible for distributing the company picnic invitation for 500 employees at a large hotel management company, what source of communication would you choose and why?

3. List three programs you feel are important for an organization's employee relations.

Ethical Dilemma

Eagen works as a ferry driver and bartender that transports tourists from Michigan's Upper Peninsula to Mackinac Island and tends bar while the ferry is not running. The tourists that visit the island do so from April through September. Since the season is short, work is usually sparse and competitive. One of Eagen's coworkers, Jeremiah, has been working all through the season and has been asking to pick up overtime hours when possible, offering to wash dishes and mop floors at the bar and even asking around to other employers on the island for work. Knowing the work is coming to an end, Eagen believes there's a reason Jeremiah has been scurrying for additional funds so he decides to confront him.

When Eagen sits Jeremiah down to see what's going on in his life, Jeremiah breaks down. His wife was recently diagnosed with cancer and he does not have health insurance or enough money to pay for all of the up and coming treatments she will need. Jeremiah's been losing sleep, his daughter's grades have been dropping in school and he's lost a significant amount of weight due to the stress he's going through.

Eagen tells Jeremiah he should seek help through the EAP program their company has for all their employees. He explains it's confidential but can really help him in the situation he's facing. Not wanting to ask for help, Jeremiah turns down Eagen's suggestion but thanks him for listening and being a trust-worthy friend.

As concerned co-worker and friend that cannot disregard the situation, Eagen decides to tell the HR supervisor about what Jeremiah's going through. When the supervisor sits Jeremiah down to confront him about his wife's illness, he is furious that Eagen would divulge information to another co-worker, especially HR when he specifically stated he did not want any assistance.

1. Why do you think Eagen approached HR with Jeremiah's situation? Would you do the same in a similar situation?

2. Why do you think Jeremiah does not want to take part in the employee assistance program that his employer offers?

3. If you were the HR supervisor speaking to Jeremiah about his situation, how would you explain the EAP and the positive benefits it has to offer?

Internet Exercise

Many successful organizations are the ones that focus the most on the employee first. Use an Internet search engine to search for Fortune Magazine's or CNN's "top employers to work for". Find the top two companies that are members of the hospitality industry. Try to research each company and see what they are considered to be "top employers".

References

Anonymous. (2011, January). *Fair work ombudsman targets Darwin employers.* Available from http://www.hospitalitymagazine.com.au/article/Fair-Work-Ombudsman-targets-Darwin-employers/527079.aspx

QSR. (2011, February). *Maintain relations.* Available from http://www.qsrmagazine.com/articles/what_matters_most/139/relations-1.phtml

SHRM. (2013a). *Anti-harassment training following the Supreme Court's Vance ruling.* Retrieved August 13, 2013, from http://www.shrm.org/hrdisciplines/employeerelations/articles/Pages/Anti-Harassment-Training-Following-SupremeCourt-Vance-Ruling.aspx

SHRM. (2013b). *Developing an employee handbook.* Retrieved August 13, 2013, from http://www.shrm.org/templatestools/howtoguides/pages/developemployeehandbook.aspx

SHRM. (2013c). *Managing employee surveys.* Retrieved August 13, 2013, from http://www.shrm.org/templatestools/toolkits/pages/managingemployeesurveys.aspx

SHRM. (2013d). *2012 State and local employee job satisfaction survey.* Retrieved August 13, 2013, from http://www.shrm.org/legalissues/stateandlocalresources/stateandlocalstatutesandregulations/documents/12-0537%202012_jobsatisfaction_fnl_online.pdf

SHRM. (2013e). *Managing employee assistance programs.* Retrieved August 13, 2013, from http://www.shrm.org/templatestools/toolkits/pages/managingemployeeassistanceprograms.aspx

SHRM. (2013f). *SHRM/Globoforce survey: Employee recognition programs, Spring 2013.* Retrieved August 13, 2013, from http://www.shrm.org/research/surveyfindings/articles/pages/globoforce-employee-recognition-program.aspx

© ndoeljindoel/Shutterstock.com

HEALTH AND SAFETY

Introduction

Ensuring a healthy and safe working environment is a key aspect of fostering a productive, efficient workforce that effectively produces satisfied guests. In a hospitality operation, there are many safety hazards that one can and will inevitably encounter. Sharp knives and hot surfaces in the kitchens, loading and unloading heavy cartons of goods, balancing cumbersome loads of breakable dishes, and handling potentially corrosive cleaning materials are only a few of the various hazards that workers and supervisors need to be prepared for on a daily basis.

After studying this chapter, you should be able to:

- Discuss the legal and governmental effects of the Occupational Safety and Health Act (OSHA).
- Explain the Hazard Communication Standard.
- Describe the Americans with Disabilities Act (ADA).
- Describe workplace injuries and workers' compensation.
- Discuss workplace safety.
- Know how to recognize and confront sexual harassment.
- Recognize the signals of substance abuse and the actions to be taken.

Legal Aspects of Safety and Health Practices

The Occupational Safety and Health Administration (OSHA): The basic purpose of OSHA is to administer the Occupational Safety and Health Act of 1970.

The Occupational Safety and Health Administration (OSHA) was established within the U. S. Department of Labor in 1971 in order to "assure so far as possible every working man and woman in the nation safe and healthful working conditions and to preserve our human resources" (OSHA, 2013a).

The basic purpose of OSHA is to administer the Occupational Safety and Health Act of 1970, which was major legislation meant to assure a safe and healthy working environment for employees. The act describes mandatory safety and health standards that apply to all employers and employees in the United States, with a few exceptions such as self-employed individuals, family farms that employ only family members, workplaces already covered by other statutes, and state and local governments. OSHA enforces the standards under the act by providing assistance and support to states through research, information, education, and training in the field of occupational safety and health.

OSHA enforces the standards under the act by providing assistance and support to states through research, information, education, and training in the field of occupational safety and health

© Jamesilencer/Shutterstock.com

The act requires employers to comply with occupational safety and health standards by providing a place of employment that is free from known hazards that are likely to cause death or serious physical harm. Employees, in turn, must adhere to the same standards and all rules, regulations, and orders stated under the act.

An important feature of the act is inspections of workspaces by OSHA representatives. OSHA normally conducts its inspections without prior notice although employers have the right to request an inspection warrant before proceeding with the inspection. Since the OSHA cannot realistically police each and every workplace in the country, the common practice is to conduct "situational inspections" based on (OSHA, 2013a):

- Information of impending danger.
- Hospitalization or death of three or more company employees.
- Complaints.
- Referrals from federal, state, or local agencies.
- Follow-ups.
- Planned investigations, aimed at high-hazard workplaces.

Additionally, OSHA has begun "virtual" investigations to a company via mobile phone, email, and fax. The subject employer has 5 business days to respond with a disclosure of problems found and corrective actions taken. If the response is satisfactory, then no on-site inspection needs to take place. Otherwise, OSHA compliance officers will conduct an on-site inspection. Prior to going on-site, the officers will research various data sources to ascertain the history of previous inspections of the employer.

Hazard Communication Standard

It is estimated that over 30 million workers are exposed to one or more chemical hazards each year (OSHA, 2013a). The Hazard Communication Standard, also known as the *Employee Right-to-Know Law*, was developed by OSHA in the 1980s to require chemical manufacturers to evaluate the hazards of their products, label them accordingly, and provide data sheets explaining these hazards. Though the labels' formats may differ from one manufacturer to another, they must contain similar types of information. The Material Safety Data Sheet (MSDS) contains information such as the maker of the chemical, the hazardous ingredients used, the physical and chemical characteristics of the product, physical and health hazards, the stability of the product, precautions for safe handling, and storage instructions. A sample MSDS is found in Figure 13.1.

> **Hazard Communication Standard**: Also known as the Employee Right-to-Know Law, this standard requires chemical manufacturers to evaluate the hazards of their products, label them accordingly, and provide Material Safety Data Sheets (MSDS).

> **Material Safety Data Sheet (MSDS)**: An information sheet produced by the manufacturer of a hazardous product that explains what product it is, why it is hazardous, and how it can be stored and handled safely.

Employers that use these hazardous chemicals must ensure that their employees know how to read the labels and accompanying MSDS, are adequately trained to handle the chemicals correctly, and are well versed in relevant emergency procedures in the case of a spill or if a person comes in contact with the chemical.

MATERIAL SAFETY DATA SHEET - 9 SECTIONS

SECTION 1 - PRODUCT INFORMATION

Product Name
Product Use
Manufacturer's Name
Physical and Mailing Address
Emergency Contact Phone Number

WHMIS Classification (optional)

Supplier's Name
Physical and Mailing Address
Emergency Contact Phone Number

SECTION 2 - HAZARDOUS INGREDIENTS

Hazardous Ingredients (very specific)

SECTION 3 - PHYSICAL DATA

Physical State (What does it look like? Is it a liquid, gas, or solid?)
What happens to it under a variety of circumstances? (i.e. heat, freezing, dropping, etc.)
Flammability and how to extinguish. Includes a wide variety of details concerning how easily this product

SECTION 4 - FIRE AND EXPLOSION DATA

will ignite / explode and how to deal with it.
How stabile is this product?

How it reacts under various conditions.

SECTION 5 - REACTIVITY DATA

Incompatibility with other substances.　　　　Hazardous Decomposition Products
Information about how the product affects and enters the body. Immediate affect. Long term toxic affect.

SECTION 6 - TOXICOLOGICAL PROPERTIES

Exposure limits. In summery, immediate and long term affects to the human body.

SECTION 7 - PREVENTIVE MEASURES

Personal Protective Gear; ventilation, etc.; leak and spill info; waste disposal; handling and storage;
special shipping instructions

SECTION 8 - FIRST AID MEASURES

Information for immediate first aid treatment. Usually always ends with "contact a Doctor"

SECTION 9 - PREPARATION INFORMATION / *Who prepared this and contact info*

Figure 13.1 Sample MSDS

Source: From www.firesafetraining.com. Copyright © 2016. Reprinted with permission

The standard covers most U.S. businesses and gives the employees the right to know the risks involved in handling hazardous products as well as what measures they can take to mitigate these risks. Hazardous products include common everyday items such as laundry chemicals, swimming pool chlorine, and toner for copiers. The risks may involve physical hazards such as fire and explosion, and/or health hazards such as irritation, burning, nausea, and headaches.

To summarize, the Hazard Communication Standard requires employers to do the following (S. Ruckl, personal communication, May 14, 2012):

1. Post a list of hazardous substances found in their establishments.

2. Post MSDSs for each hazardous product in their possession.

3. Explain to employees how to read and use the MSDS and the labels of hazardous products.

4. Train employees in the proper handling of hazardous chemicals and in emergency procedures.

The *Material Safety Data Sheet (MSDS)* contains information such as the maker of the chemical, the hazardous ingredients used, and the physical and chemical characteristics of the product

The Americans with Disabilities Act

The **Americans with Disabilities Act (ADA)** prohibits discrimination against employees in all job-related policies and procedures, including hiring and firing, promotions, compensation, training, and other terms and conditions of employment. Those with either physical or mental impairments are included in the definition of persons with disabilities.

> **Americans with Disabilities Act (ADA):** An act that makes it unlawful to discriminate in employment matters against Americans with a disability.

Since there are some disabilities that would prevent a person from performing the requisite tasks of the job, the ADA defines a "qualified employee" as one who has such an impairment but that, with or without reasonable accommodation, can perform the essential functions of the job. The law requires employers to make **reasonable accommodations** to disabled employees. Reasonable accommodation is defined as those changes or adjustments to a job or work environment that will enable someone with a disability to perform essential job functions without inflicting "undue hardship" to the employer's busi-

> **Reasonable Accommodation:** Any change or adjustment to a work environment that will enable someone with a disability to perform essential job functions.

ness. Undue hardship is defined as actions requiring significant difficulty or expense considering the employer's size, nature, and financial resources. For example, a reasonable accommodation would be when a person in a wheelchair requires a desk tall enough so that the arms of the wheelchair go under the desktop. An example of an undue expense would be the installation of an elevator in an old (historic) building so a single employee in a wheelchair could access the second floor.

Workplace Injuries and Diseases/Illnesses

According to the U.S. Department of Labor Bureau of Labor Statistics, sprains and strains account for over 42% of all reported occupational injuries

© thodonal88/Shutterstock.com

An occupational injury is defined as any injury resulting from a work-related event or a single instantaneous exposure in the workplace. According to the U.S. Department of Labor Bureau of Labor Statistics, sprains and strains account for over 42% of all reported occupational injuries. These, combined with bruises and contusions, cuts and lacerations, and fractures, account for almost two-thirds of reported occupational injury cases (CDC, 2013). An occupational illness or disease, on the other hand, is defined by OSHA as, "any abnormal condition or disorder, other than one resulting from an occupational injury, caused by exposure to factors associated with employment."

It is estimated that one in twenty full-time workers in the United States is injured at work every year. Occupational diseases are much harder to identify than occupational injuries and, as such, tend to be underreported in statistical surveys. The complications lie in the fact that first, diseases in general have no fixed timeframe for symptoms to occur. Symptoms can take years after exposure to develop, and once they are apparent, tracing the cause to an isolated incident at work becomes difficult. Second, occupational diseases are difficult to isolate from lifestyle-related diseases. Employees who live less than healthy lifestyles may be more susceptible to disease at the workplace, and once these employees develop illnesses it becomes difficult to pin down the cause between the workplace and their general lifestyle.

Workers' Compensation

Workers' Compensation: Insurance paid by the employer that gives medical care, income continuation, and rehabilitation expenses for people who sustain job-related injuries or sicknesses.

Before the idea of workers' compensation was developed in Germany in 1884, employees who got injured on the job were responsible for their own medical care and were not paid their wages until they could return to work. Those who bothered to take legal action against their employer had the odds stacked against them since the common notion was that being paid a salary meant employees assumed the risks of a job as part of a fair exchange.

By the early years of the 20th century, after many workplace disasters had occurred, public opinion had pressured state legislatures to remedy the matter and by 1949 all states in the United States had passed some form of workers' compensation law. The new legislation represented a shift in the perception of workers' injuries: where once they were thought of as a risk to be undertaken by employees in exchange for a salary, now they were thought of as a cost of doing business to be borne by the employer (Gomez-Mejia, Balkin, & Cardy, 2010, p. 512).

Employers were now required to provide workers' compensation to their employees, which entailed providing insurance that gave medical care, income continuation, and rehabilitation expenses for people who sustain job-related injuries or sicknesses. With some exceptions depending on the circumstances, the tradeoff for employees that claim workers' compensation is that they forfeit the right to sue for negligence.

The compensation is mandated by the state and provides insurance for employees injured on the job regardless of fault. Employers typically purchase the required insurance through workers' compensation insurance companies although exemptions are sometimes granted to smaller companies and to large companies that can shoulder the insurance responsibility in-house.

According to state-approved laws, the employer pays medical and disability benefits. Each state is different. For example, below is an example of what occurs in Florida, where a Bureau of Employee Assistance and Ombudsman Office was created to inform and educate injured workers of various benefits (CFO, 2013):

- An authorized primary doctor and specialist(s) when medically necessary
- All authorized medically necessary care and treatment related to your injury such as
    - doctor's visits
    - hospitalization
    - physical therapy
    - medical tests
    - prescription drugs
    - prostheses

- Mileage reimbursement for travel to and from your authorized doctor and the pharmacy
- Vocational rehabilitation benefits including
    - on-the-job training
    - schooling
    - job placement assistance

The U.S. Department of Labor requires employers to maintain an on-site log of work-related injuries and illnesses that result in any of the following (OSHA, 2013b):

- Death
- Loss of consciousness
- Days away from work

- Restricted wok activity or job transfer
- Medical treatment beyond first aid
- Any work-related injury diagnosed by a physician/healthcare professional
- Any work-related case involving cancer, chronic irreversible disease, a fractured or cracked bone, or a punctured eardrum
- Employers should also post a year-end summary of work-related injuries and illnesses for employees to review.

Safety

> **Safety Program**: A plan made up of elements such as a safety committee, safety rules, training, and incentives, all of which are geared toward keeping a workplace safe.

A safe working environment can be fostered through the development of a thorough safety program. This is done through the participation of all levels of the company. Though concern for safety should begin with top management setting the tone for the rest of the organization, no one knows the job, its risks, and what could be improved better than the employees. The input and participation of line workers is therefore critical to an effective safety program (Gomez-Mejia, Balkin, & Cardy, 2010, p. 529).

Some types of accidents happen more often than others. The most common types of workplace accidents are:

- Slips and trips
- Improper handling (lifting, lowering, pulling)
- Traffic accidents (being hit by a moving vehicle, objects falling from a moving vehicle)
- Electrical accidents/burns

The responsibility of minimizing risks associated with workplace accidents falls on the shoulders of the employer

© Andrey_Popov/Shutterstock.com

The responsibility of minimizing risks associated with workplace accidents falls on the shoulders of the employer. Most accidents can eventually be traced to employer negligence. As such, employers need to have workplace prevention strategies in place at all times. The "General Duty Clause" of the Occupational Safety and Health Act of 1970 states that "each employer shall furnish to each of its employees a place of employment which is free from recognized hazards that are causing or likely to cause death or serious physical harm to its employees." Though there are laws such as this in place, a workplace survey conducted by the Society for Human Resources Management found that over 50% of respondents expressed a level of concern that workplace violence might occur at their organizations (Denning, 2006).

In order to increase safety awareness and to prevent accidents, most hospitality operations have safety programs in place that include the following components (Denning, 2006):

- They establish a safety committee with participation by all departments within the company. Both managers and employees participate in safety decisions with management being especially attentive to employee suggestions for improving safety. (See further details on safety committees below.)

- They communicate safety with a multimedia approach that indicates safety lectures, films, posters, pamphlets, and computer presentations.

- They instruct managers and supervisors how to communicate, demonstrate, and require safety, and they train employees in the safe use of equipment.

- They use incentives, rewards, and positive reinforcement to encourage safe behavior. They reward employee complaints or suggestions about safety. They must also provide rewards to employees with exceptional safety records.

- They communicate safety rules and enforce them. OSHA obligates employees to adhere to safety rules, and in good programs managers are willing to use the disciplinary system to penalize unsafe work behavior.

- They use safety directors and/or the safety committee to engage in regular self-inspection and accident research to identify potentially dangerous situations, and to understand why accidents occur and how to correct them.

Since supervisors oversee day-to-day operations and enforce the safety rules, report and correct unsafe conditions, train employees, maintain safety records, and in general act as role models for their workers, it makes sense that they are very involved in the safety program. If the supervisor is safety-minded, he or she is more likely to create a safe working environment where safety is practiced and respected.

Safety policies and procedures outline the basic behaviors that are expected from employees in order to prevent accidents. They also include descriptions of safety training that employees will be given, the frequency of safety inspections, and guidelines for how to act when accidents do happen.

Because the accident rate for employees is higher during their first month at work than for any subsequent month, safety training should start at the very onset of a worker's employment during basic orientation, and this information should be included in the employee handbook. Employees should be evaluated for what they have learned at the end of training, rewarded for working safely, and required to undergo repeated and updated training at least once a year.

As noted above, most hospitality companies have a safety committee. These committees are made up of various representatives within the company and meet regularly to discuss general safety matters as well as to review data on accidents that have occurred, to inspect the facility, to oversee training, and to suggest new and revised policies and procedures.

> **Safety Committee**: A committee that meets regularly to discuss and perform safety-related functions such as inspections and training.

Photo Safety Committees perform useful work in helping maintain a safe working environment

© Photographee.eu/Shutterstock.com

Conducting periodic safety inspections may also be part of the role of a supervisor. Inspections involve checking for and correcting unsafe conditions such as frayed wiring, overstocked crates, and unsanitary conditions. Responsibility for inspections may also pass beyond the supervisory level and onto the employees themselves to encourage them to take a more active role in accident prevention.

When accidents do happen, accident reporting and investigation is the responsibility of the supervisor regardless of how minor the injury appears to be. Prompt reporting is beneficial to all concerned. The supervisor can quickly correct the unsafe condition that caused the accident to protect the other employees, the injured person can receive the proper care and compensation without delay, and the company can prepare itself in case the possibility of legal action is on the table.

Constant vigilance and supervision in the form of regular safety audits help assess the safety conditions of the workplace. This will minimize the risk of accidents as it helps assess the effectiveness of existing prevention plans and activities. OSHA conducts safety audits in all industries. Audits include the following:

- Worker compensation document analysis
- Work area inspections
- Interviews with on-site staff and employees
- A review of the company's health and safety program
- A review of work procedures
- A review of the operation of the safety committee (if applicable)
- A review of accident investigation reports
- A review of the emergency action plan

It is the responsibility of management to provide employees with the appropriate safety training to allow them to effectively perform their duties in a safe manner. In addition to general safety rules to provide guidelines for all employees to follow, there should be specialized safety rules for each unique role in the workplace.

Though safety incentive programs are becoming more popular, there is some controversy associated with them. The controversy stems from the theory behind such programs, which suggests that accidents in the workplace are caused by negligence and unsafe behaviors on the part of the employee, as opposed to the existence of unsafe conditions that endanger them. Providing rewards to employees with good safety records incentivizes them to simply not report injuries rather than curing the unsafe condition that caused the injury in the first place (USW, 2013).

A study by OSHA on safety incentive programs found no basis for employer claims that programs providing incentives to employees who don't report injuries actually makes workplaces safer. OSHA also noted that such programs actually result in a "chilling effect" on injury and illness reports. OSHA fined USA Waste Management $65,000 for having a safety incentive program that provided employees with a "bonus pool," which rewarded employees that had excellent safety records but which also included reward for good attendance and work practices. The fine implies that the company induced the falsification of records through under-reporting of incidents. It is the position of OSHA that "Traditional Incentive Programs" that link reward to reduction of injury "can provide an inducement for workers to under-report injuries and illnesses…" (Sims, 2013).

Costs Associated with Unsafe Work Environments and Accidents

Apart from the pain and suffering inflicted on the injured or ill worker, there are several direct and indirect costs associated with unsafe work environments and accidents to consider whenever an accident occurs.

For workers some of the *direct costs* of an injury or illness are (OSH, 2013):

- the pain and suffering of the injury or illness;
- the loss of income;
- the possible loss of a job;
- health-care costs.

It has been estimated that the *indirect costs* of an accident or illness can be four to ten times greater than the direct costs, or even more. An occupational illness or accident can have so many indirect costs to workers that it is often difficult to measure them. One of the most obvious indirect costs is the human suffering caused to workers' families, which cannot be compensated with money.

The costs to *employers* of occupational accidents or illnesses are also estimated to be enormous. For a small business, the cost of even one accident can be a financial disaster. For employers, some of the *direct costs* are (OSH, 2013):

- payment for work not performed;
- medical and compensation payments;
- repair or replacement of damaged machinery and equipment;
- reduction or a temporary halt in production;
- increased training expenses and administration costs;
- possible reduction in the quality of work;
- negative effect on morale in other workers.

Some of the *indirect costs* for employers are (OSH, 2013):

- the injured/ill worker has to be replaced;
- a new worker has to be trained and given time to adjust;
- it takes time before the new worker is producing at the rate of the original worker;
- time must be devoted to obligatory investigations, to the writing of reports and filling out of forms;
- accidents often arouse the concern of fellow workers and influence labor relations in a negative way;
- poor health and safety conditions in the workplace can also result in poor public relations.

Overall, the costs of most work-related accidents or illnesses to workers and their families and to employers are very high. On a national scale, the estimated costs of occupational accidents and illnesses can be as high as 3–4% of a country's gross national product. In reality, no one really knows the total costs of work-related accidents or diseases because there are a multitude of indirect costs that are difficult to measure besides the more obvious direct costs.

Sexual Harassment

The Equal Employment Opportunity Commission (EEOC) issued guidelines on sexual harassment in 1980, indicating that it is a form of gender discrimination under Title VII of the 1964 Civil Rights Act. According to the EEOC (EEOC, 2013), sexual harassment consists of "unwelcome advances, requests for sexual favors, and other verbal or physical conduct of a sexual nature when: (1) submission to such conduct is made,

There are thousands of sexual harassment charges every year costing millions of dollars

© Tomasz Guzowski/Shutterstock.com

either explicitly or implicitly, a term or condition of an individual's employment, or (2) submission to or rejection of such conduct by an individual is used as a basis for employment decisions affecting the person." The EEOC deals with approximately 76,000 cases each year—around 27,000 of these cases are based on race, 23,000 based on sex, and 22,500 based on retaliation. In addition to this, 12,500 sexual harassment charges and 5,000 pregnancy discrimination charges are made, and $274 million in monetary relief was gained by the parties making the charges (Robins & Grinberg, 2007).

> **Quid Pro Quo Sexual Harassment**: A type of sexual harassment where submission to or rejection of a sexual favor is used as the basis for employment decisions regarding that employee.

There are several types of sexual harassment. The definition given by the EEOC refers to **quid pro quo sexual harassment**. Sexual harassment of this nature involves making the submission to or rejection of a sexual favor the basis of an employment decision regarding that employee. This is committed by managers and supervisors when they give or promise to give something, such as a pay raise or promotion, in exchange for sexual favors. For example, when a manager asks a female employee to come to his residence for a drink and she refuses, and, in response, he tells her that he could make sure she gets a promotion if she changes her mind, then the quid pro quo kind of sexual harassment has occurred.

> **Environmental Sexual Harassment**: A type of sexual harassment where comments and innuendos or a sexual nature, or physical contact, interfere with an employee's work performance or create an intimidating, a hostile, or an offensive working environment.

A second type of sexual harassment is called **environmental sexual harassment**. In such cases, the harassment in the form of sexual comments, innuendos, or physical contact is persistent and severe enough that it affects an employee's well-being and, in effect, creates an "intimidating, hostile, or offensive working environment." For example, when the men in a workplace constantly make crude, sexually oriented comments and jokes, and leave their pornographic magazines in full view, this can make a female coworker feel intimidated and ill at ease. If the situation persists and creates an environment where she cannot continue working, then environmental sexual harassment has occurred.

> **Third-party Sexual Harassment**: A type of sexual harassment involving a customer or client and an employee.

The third type of sexual harassment is **third-party sexual harassment**. This involves an employee and a customer or client. The customer or client may be the one harassing the employee or it may be the other way around. For example, if a female customer is a regular at a bar and constantly showers the bartender with excessive, unwanted attention, the bartender may feel like he cannot do anything about it since she is the customer. In this case, third-party sexual harassment has occurred.

The manager is responsible for identifying, confronting, and preventing the sexual harassment of both female and male employees by other people they encounter at work. Failure to do so can cost a company in terms of lost productivity, low morale, a tainted reputation, as well as legal costs and punitive damages in case of lawsuits.

Here are some specific actions that can be taken in order to deal with the issue of sexual harassment effectively:

- *Know the company sexual harassment policy*: The policy should include a formal complaint procedure as well as provisions for investigations and prompt disciplinary action against those found guilty of sexual harassment. Guidelines for harassers who retaliate against their accusers should also be included.

- *Educate employees*: Employees need to know how to recognize harassment and know what to do once they see it occur. They also need to be aware of the investigation procedure and the consequences for an employee found guilty of sexual harassment.

A company sexual harassment policy should include a formal complaint procedure as well as provisions for investigations and prompt disciplinary action against those found guilty of sexual harassment

© Sinart Creative/Shutterstock.com

- *Investigate thoroughly and promptly*: When an incident of sexual harassment is brought to a manager's attention he cannot assume guilt of innocence. The situation must be investigated immediately according to the company's policy.

- *Provide follow-up*: After the investigation and ensuing company response, the manager needs to verify with victims and witnesses that the harassment has stopped and that no retaliation is taking place.

- *Prevent harassment*: The manager can help accomplish this by being visible in the work area, being a solid role model, taking all reported incidents seriously, and acting on them swiftly.

Legalize

Restaurants are particularly susceptible to sexual harassment claims. According to the EEOC's suit, Missoula Mac violated federal civil rights laws at its Reedsburg, Wisconsin McDonald's by permitting male employees to create a hostile work environment of sexual harassment against female coworkers, some of whom were teenagers, and by retaliating against those who complained about sexual harassment. The EEOC's complaint alleged that since at least 2006, several male employees subjected female coworkers to sexual harassment, including sexual comments, kissing, touching of their private areas, and forcing their hands onto the men's private parts. Despite being notified of the situation, Missoula Mac failed and refused to take prompt and appropriate action to correct the harassment and the resulting hostile environment, forcing at least one of the harassed employees to quit. Further, the company fired other harassed employees after they complained repeatedly about their coworkers' behavior. Three women previously employed at the Reedsburg McDonald's filed discrimination charges with the EEOC that led to the lawsuit.

Sexual harassment and retaliation for complaining about it violate Title VII of the Civil Rights Act of 1964. The EEOC filed its suit (EEOC and Dunse, Brown, and Gay v. Missoula Mac, Inc. d/b/a McDonald's Restaurants, .No. 3:11-cv-00267-bbc) in April 2011 after first attempting to reach an out-of-court settlement through its conciliation process. Missoula Mac, Inc., the owner and franchisee of 25 McDonald's restaurants, has agreed to pay $1,000,000 and provide substantial injunctive relief to resolve a class sexual harassment lawsuit filed by the U.S. Equal Employment Opportunity Commission (EEOC), the agency announced pursuant to a consent decree and order filed in July 2012.

"This is a sad case, demonstrating again that sexual harassment is still a challenge for women at some of our most successful, best known brands," said John P. Rowe, district director of the Chicago District Office of the EEOC, which conducted the investigation that led to the lawsuit.

John Hendrickson, the EEOC regional attorney in Chicago, added, "The ongoing sexual harassment in Reedsburg, and the company's refusal to stop it, devolved into a culture of oppression, retaliation and fear. Women who work in restaurants have it tough enough without having to put up with sexual harassment."

EEOC General Counsel P. David López commented that "sexual harassment in the restaurant industry remains a problem nationwide." López added that "harassment no longer can be accepted as simply 'part of the culture' of the restaurant industry." "As seen in this case," he stated, "many younger workers' first experience with the workplace is in this industry and it is important that harassment of these workers not be tolerated" (www.eeoc.gov retrieved March 2013).

Other Types of Harassment

Workplace **harassment** is not limited to sexual harassment. All forms of harassment based on national origin, race, color, religion, disability, or age are illegal. The term harassment refers to behavior that is intimidating, hostile, or offensive toward someone, or to the act of creating an intimidating, a hostile, or an offensive environment for someone, based on that person's national origin, race, color, religion, gender, disability, or age.

> **Harassment**: Any behavior that creates an intimidating, hostile, or offensive working environment for someone based on that person's national origin, race, color, religion, gender, disability, or age.

Intimidating behavior may involve threatening someone with harm of some kind. Hostile behavior could include asking something completely unrealistic of an employee. Offensive behavior generally involves ridiculing or taunting someone. An employer should be vigilant for such behavior as it is detrimental to the creation of a safe working environment.

Substance Abuse

Substance abuse is often defined as working under the influence of, using, or being impaired by alcohol or any drugs. Drugs are not limited to illegal substances and can include legal, over-the-counter, or prescription medication such as painkillers that alter consciousness. Substance abuse is a pervasive workplace problem. Some estimate that 15% of the U.S. workforce has been hung over at work, been drinking shortly before showing up for work, or been drinking or impaired while on the job at least once during the previous year (Anonymous, 2006, as cited in Dessler, 2011, p. 606).

Some experts estimate that as many as 50% of all "problem employees" are actually alcoholics (Strazewski, 2001, as cited in Dessler, 2011, p. 606). Drug-using employees are more than three and a half times more likely to be involved in workplace accidents (Nighswonger, 2000 and Claussen, 2009, as cited in Dessler, 2011, p. 606). The U.S. Department of Labor estimates that around 6.5% of full-time and 8.6% of part-time workers in the United States are currently illicit drug users. The estimate is even higher for the hospitality industry in particular (Walker & Miller, 2010, p. 367).

Drug abuse has a higher profile when talking about substance abuse in general. Alcohol abuse, however, is actually more extensive in the workplace than that of all illegal drugs combined. Substance abuse can have very serious effects on job performance and safety of employees and guests. Aside from the immediate health risk to the employee, a supervisor must concern himself with the behavioral repercussions of the abuse. These behaviors will sometimes be visible in the workplace. These employees will often have difficulty meeting performance standards and getting along with coworkers. Employees who are engaged in substance abuse tend to be late for work more often, take more sick days, are more often involved in accidents, and are more likely to file for workers' compensation claims.

The U.S. Department of Labor estimates that employee substance abuse has cost American businesses around $81 billion in lost productivity, lost time, accidents, breakage, healthcare, and workers' compensation. Substance abuse at the workplace can also have other consequences such as lower workplace morale when other workers have to pick up the slack of the abusive employee, and a tarnished company image (Walker & Miller, 2010, p. 367).

Several government initiatives have been put in place to deal with the concern of substance abuse in the workplace. The Drug Free Workplace Act of 1988 is among them and it requires most federal contractors and anyone who receives federal grants to provide a drug-free workplace by complying with the following major requirements (DOL, 2013):

- Inform employees that they are prohibited from doing any of the following in the workplace: unlawful manufacture, distribution, dispensation, possession, or use of a controlled substance. Inform employees, in writing, what actions they can expect if they do.
- Give employees a copy of the policy and ask them to abide by it as a condition of continued employment.
- Inform employees of the dangers of drug abuse at work and available counseling, rehabilitation, and employee assistance programs.
- Make a good faith effort to maintain a drug-free workplace.

Beyond these major requirements, a supervisor has several responsibilities when it comes to dealing with substance abuse in the workplace. Among these are

- *Any disciplinary action taken should be based on observable, job-related factors*: Substandard job performance or inappropriate workplace behavior are acceptable factors rather than taking action merely on the basis of the existence or suspicion of a substance abuse problem. Since substance abuse is regarded as a health problem or disease, taking disciplinary action based solely on the substance abuse is illegal. There must be focus on the inability to meet the requirements of the job for the action to be legal.
- *Managers must know the company policy on substance abuse*: A substance abuse policy generally covers the following topics (Walker & Miller, 2010, p. 367):
  - Rules regarding alcohol and drug possession and use.
  - Penalties for rule violations.
  - When employees may be subject to drug testing.
  - Programs available for counseling, education, and rehabilitation, such as employee assistance programs.
  - Drug testing of job applicants and employees is becoming an increasingly common practice. The most common is for-cause testing, where an employee is asked to take a drug test if the person's supervisor has a reasonable suspicion that the employee may be impaired due to substance abuse. Random testing is another way companies monitor their workers for drug use.

- *Managers need to identify and constructively confront employees who are substance abusers*: Early intervention is important so that the abusive employee can seek professional help when the problem can be more easily resolved. The longer the abusive behavior goes on the more difficult it will be to change. Intervention is also most effective when it occurs before the situation has called for disciplinary action on the part of the employer.

When performing an intervention, the supervisor needs to strike a balance between being firm and being empathic. On the one hand you are asking the employee to step up his job performance or face appropriate sanctions; on the other hand you are expressing concern for his situation and are offering a referral to professionals that can help. The probability of the employee accepting the intervention is maximized when he or she appreciates both facets of the intervention.

- *Managers should not try to diagnose or give advice on employees' substance abuse problems*: Becoming too involved complicates the situation and may lead you open to manipulation. The employee may also become angered when they feel that the intrusion is not warranted. The supervisor needs to focus on workplace behaviors that are relevant and observable since the workplace is where he has recognized authority. The actual issue of substance abuse is best left to trained professionals who will be able to appreciate and give insight to issues that the manager may not be equipped to handle.

Guest Safety

It is tempting to believe that the guests of an establishment face far fewer hazards than do workers and employees. Though they may not come into constant proximity to hot surfaces in the kitchen and heavy boxes in storage, guests still do face slippery surfaces, hot drinks, as well as potential allergic reactions and food poisoning. Ignoring these potential threats to guest safety can prove very costly when your business faces legal action.

The manager is already heavily involved in the safety program that we discussed earlier. As such, they are already familiar with safety policies and procedures; they train the employees, take part in safety committee meetings and inspections, report accidents, and perform general supervisory duties with safety as a priority. To protect guests as well as employees, managers should be aware of the following:

- *Slips, trips, and falls*: Steps are the most common culprits behind slips, trips, and falls. Stairs and steps, whether outside or inside, need to be well lit, to contain sufficient traction, and to have handrails. Wet floors are another hazard. Mopping during off-peak hours with an accompanying "Wet Floor" sign is a good idea. Parking areas for guests should be clear of trash and ice during winter.
- *Burns*: Hot beverages are dangerous when not handled with care. Your particular operation may have guidelines in place regarding temperature of beverages prepared and method of serving to prevent burns.
- *Food allergies*: Anaphylactic shock occurs when the throat swells up to the point where air cannot pass into the lungs. This type of reaction occurs in some people in response to the ingestion of certain kinds of food. To prevent such occurrences, policies and procedures should be in place to tell servers how to handle a guest's inquiry regarding allergic ingredients. First-aid kits with "EpiPens" need to be on hand to suppress anaphylactic shock symptoms and employees need to be trained to use them.

- *Foodborne illness*: Foodborne illnesses make millions of Americans sick each year and kill almost 10,000 people annually. Outbreaks can be prevented by maintaining high sanitation standards and well-supervised food preparation procedures.

- *First aid*: To protect both guests and employees who are injured or ill, it is crucial to have at least one person per shift who is trained in the administration of first aid, emergency treatment given before providing regular medical care, and cardiopulmonary resuscitation (CPR), a procedure used in case of cardiac arrest.

Security

The National Restaurant Association Educational Foundation states that the purpose of a security program is to protect the assets of a facility from incidents such as theft, violent crime, and burglary. These assets could include the building, the grounds, equipment, furnishings, supplies, and cash on hand, as well as employees and guests of the business. Much of a manager's work involves securing these assets by conducting such activities as reference checks on applicants, following cash handling procedures, restricting access to keys, and handling various kinds of emergencies as they arise. In the interest of the security of employees, guests, and the company in general, supervisors need to familiarize themselves with all procedures and enforce them without hesitation.

Hospitality Employees and AIDS

Acquired Immunodeficiency Syndrome, better known as AIDS, is an illness that harms the body's ability to fight infection. AIDS is caused by the human immunodeficiency virus (HIV), which is spread through the sharing of body fluids that can occur via tainted blood transfusions, unprotected sexual intercourse, or the sharing of needles with someone who is HIV positive. Studies have shown no evidence that food handling or casual contact can spread HIV.

Persons who are HIV positive tend to take time, sometimes several years, before they start showing symptoms. Eventually the HIV infection manifests itself through such symptoms as fatigue, diarrhea, weight loss, and wounds that don't heal. Once serious infections or cancers are developed, the infected person is then diagnosed with AIDS.

The Americans with Disabilities Act has made it illegal to fire an HIV-positive employee or to discriminate against them in employment matters. As long as they can perform the essential functions of their job with reasonable accommodation (i.e., flexible work hours), they should be allowed to work. Among an HR director's and line manager's responsibilities when dealing with an HIV-positive employee are as follows:

- HIV-positive employees tend to fear the loss of their jobs and their benefits, so it is important to be supportive. The HR director needs to explain that the company's existing policies on medical and other benefits still applies to him or her. If the company offers other forms of support such as counseling or emergency loans, then the supervisor needs to explain this also.

- Make reasonable accommodations. Reasonable accommodations need to be made to allow the employee to perform the essential functions of their job. The HR director needs to discuss the precise nature of such accommodations.

- Review the basics of the Family and Medical Leave Act.

- Keep the employee's medical information confidential.
- Educate your employees about the nature of AIDS. To reduce the stigma of having AIDS, employees need to be aware of the way that the disease affects and does not affect the lives of those living with it.

If the company has a formal, written policy on AIDS, then the HR director and line managers should use that as a guideline. Constant updating of sanitation standards and safety training is also a must to ensure that the employee's condition does not affect the health and safety of the workplace as a whole.

Key Points

- The Occupational Health and Safety Act of 1970 was signed on December 29, 1970.
- The Act created the Occupational Safety and Health Administration (OSHA), which developed the first workplace safety and health guidelines for companies in the United States.
- OSHA developed the Hazard Communication Standard in the 1980s. Also known as the Employee Right-to-Know Law, it established guidelines for labeling hazardous materials.
- The Americans with Disabilities Act was created to combat discrimination against the disabled in work-related matters.
- Occupational disease is difficult to identify. The SENSOR program was created to enhance the monitoring of occupational disease at both the local and state levels.
- Workers' compensation is mandated by the state and provides insurance for employees that are injured on the job, regardless of fault.
- Safety programs are a common way to increase awareness and to prevent accidents. They contain the following elements: the formation of a safety committee, a multimedia communication approach, training of employees, incentives, communication and enforcement of rules, and a mechanism for inspection and research.
- Workplace accidents have direct and indirect costs for both workers and employers.
- Managers need to identify, address, and prevent workplace sexual harassment in all its different forms (quid pro quo, environmental, and third-party).
- There are nonsexual forms of harassment that are based on factors such as gender, ethnicity, race, religion, age, and disability that must also be identified, addressed, and prevented by the manager.
- Substance abuse is a pervasive workplace problem that can involve both illegal and legal drugs and medication.
- Among a manager's responsibilities when dealing with substance-abusive employees are to base disciplinary action on observable, job-related factors; to know and follow company policy on substance abuse; to constructively confront the offending employee; and to avoid diagnosing and giving advice on the substance abuse problem in particular.
- The manager needs to be wary of threats to guest safety such as slips, burns, food allergies, and foodborne illnesses. The manager must also ensure that there is adequate first aid training on site to address these dangers when they arise.
- The Americans with Disabilities Act makes it illegal to discriminate against employees with HIV/AIDS. It is the manager's responsibility to make reasonable accommodations for infected employees and to generally create a supportive workplace environment.

Key Terms

Americans with Disabilities
   Act (ADA)
Environmental sexual
   harassment
Harassment
Hazard Communication
   Standard

Material Safety Data Sheet
   (MSDS)
Quid pro quo sexual harassment
Reasonable accommodation
Safety committee
Safety program

The Occupational Safety and
   Health Administration
   (OSHA)
Third-party sexual harassment
Workers' compensation

Discussion Questions

1. What is the role of OSHA? How has it changed the way health and safety are treated at the workplace?

2. What does the Hazard Communication Standard require employers to do?

3. Why are occupational diseases more difficult to deal with than occupational injuries?

4. How has the perception of workers' compensation changed over the years?

5. Discuss the Americans with Disabilities Act. To what extent does it prohibit discrimination in workplace decisions?

6. What are the basic components of a safety program?

7. How does one differentiate between the different types of sexual harassment?

8. How can a manager deal with sexual harassment effectively?

9. How does substance abuse manifest itself in the workplace?

10. What are the responsibilities of a manager in dealing with substance abuse in the workplace?

11. What are the responsibilities of a manager when dealing with HIV-positive employees?

Ethical Dilemma

You are the HR manager of a high-end hotel that is known for excellent, round-the-clock service. Your hotel staff caters to your guests' every whim and endeavors to make their stay with you a truly memorable experience. Guests are pleasantly surprised that they can make odd requests even in the wee hours of the morning and have them granted. Because of this level of attentiveness and enthusiastic service, the hotel does brisk repeat business. Operationally the hotel is profiting handsomely because they avoid costly overstaffing by retaining only high-performing, driven employees that work long hours.

One day you find out through a fellow employee the secret behind this high performance from your staff. Apparently, most of your hotel staff smoke marijuana on the rooftop during breaks to get them through the long and hectic hours. Your source tells you that there are rumors that a few take other kinds of substances to keep themselves energetic. As the HR manager, what do you do?

Internet Exercise

1. Go to the website www.osha.org and find a publication that relates to the hospitality industry. Print out your findings to discuss in class.

2. Go to the webpage:
   http://www.ncagr.gov/cyber/kidswrld/foodsafe/foodquiz.html

Test your basic knowledge on food safety by taking this quiz. Print your results to discuss in class.

References

CDC. (2013). Retrieved January 26, 2013, from www.cdc.gov/niosh

CFO. (2013). *Brochures guides and posters.* Retrieved January 16, 2013, from http://www.myfloridacfo.com/wc/employee/benefits.html

Denning, P. (2006, March). *Workplace violence: Trend and strategic tools for mitigating risk* [White Paper]. Society for Human Resources Management.

Dessler, G. (2011). *Human Resource Management* (12th ed.). Upper Saddle River, NJ: Pearson.

DOL. (2013). *Drug-free workplace advisor.* Retrieved January 18, 2013, from http://www.dol.gov/elaws/asp/drugfree/screenr.htm

EEOC. (2013). *Sexual harassment.* Retrieved January 18, 2013, from http://archive.eeoc.gov/types/sexual_harassment.html

Gomez-Mejia, L. R., Balkin, D. B., & Cardy, R. L. (2010). *Managing Human Resources* (6th ed.). Upper Saddle River, NJ: Pearson.

Health, Safety & Environment Department, United Steelworkers (USW). (2013). *Safety incentive and injury discipline policies: The bad, the even worse and the downright ugly.* Retrieved January 17, 2013, from http://assets.usw.org/resources/hse/resources/safety-incentive-and-injury-discipline-policies-final-4-07.pdf

OSH. (2013). *Workers' activities.* Retrieved January 18, 2013, from http://actrav.itcilo.org/actrav-english/telearn/osh/intro/inmain.htm

OSHA. (2013a). *Congressional findings and purpose.* Retrieved February 2, 2013, from https://www.osha.gov/pls/oshaweb/owadisp.show_document?p_id=3356&p_table=OSHACT

OSHA. (2013b). *Employment law guide—Safety and health standards: Occupational safety and health.* Retrieved January 16, 2013, from http://www.dol.gov/compliance/guide/osha.htm

Robins, C., & Grinberg, D. (2007, February). *Job bias charges edged up in 2006, EEOC Reports.* The U.S. Equal Opportunity Commission.

Sims, B., Jr. (2013). *Effective motivation: A wake-up call from OSHA last year has many safety managers thinking hard about their incentive programs.* Retrieved January 17, 2013, from http://www.rewardandrecognizenow.com/articles/oshmag2.htm

Walker, J. R., & Miller, J. E. (2010). *Supervision in the hospitality industry: Leading human resources* (6th ed.). Hoboken, NJ: Wiley.

WORKING WITH ORGANIZED LABOR

Introduction

In 2007, the *U.S. Department of Labor's National Labor Relations Board (NLRB)* accused Starbucks of being in violation of the law in trying to prevent workers in some of its New York shops from unionizing. Among other things, the NLRB accused managers in those stores of retaliating against workers who wanted to unionize by firing two of them and illegally interrogating others about their union inclinations. A Starbucks spokesperson said the company believed the allegations are baseless and that the firm would vigorously defend itself (Greenhouse, 2007, as cited in Dessler, 2008, p. 595).

This chapter will offer important information necessary to deal effectively with unions and grievances. After discussing why employees join unions and what unions want, we briefly discuss the history of unions in the United States, union membership, labor relations and the legal environment, the process of unionization, collective bargaining, the types of strikes, and the impact of unions on human resources.

After completion of this chapter, you should be able to:

- Describe the purpose for a union's existence and be able to explain why they are attractive to certain individuals.
- Explain the details of each of the main pieces of labor legislation.
- Outline how a union drive and election takes place.
- Discuss collective bargaining.

Learning Objective 1: Describe the purpose for a union's existence, and be able to explain why they are attractive to certain individuals

Why Employees Join Unions

How employees feel about their workplace and particularly about the leadership and work climate determine if they will likely join a *union*. Employees need someone in their corner when rogue managers go after them. With union membership, they feel more secure knowing that someone will stand up for them if they are mistreated or if management does not abide by the contract, known as the collective bargaining agreement. Consider this although it was written a few years ago—it offers insight into unionization:

It's 7.30 on a cool December evening in Las Vegas, and 105 off-duty hotel maids, cooks, and bellhops are waiting for their monthly union meeting to start. It had been a long day working at MGM the big casino hotel, but still the room buzzes with energy.

One by one, a dozen or so members recount their success in recruiting, 2,700 new colleagues at the MGM Grand, the world's largest hotel. After a 3-year campaign of street demonstrations, mass arrests, and attacks on the company's HR practices, which helped oust a stridently anti-labor CEO, MGM Grand recognized the union a year later without an election. Another group reports on the victory at New York, a new hotel that agreed to the unionization of 900 workers.

Much of the credit for these successes lies in the spirited rank and file. Indeed, the day after the meetings, some members gathered—on their day off—to sign up recruits outside the New York, New York hiring office. Says Edelisa Wolf, an $11.25-an-hour server at the MGM Grand: I spend a day per a week volunteering for the union, because otherwise we would earn $7.50 an hour and no benefits (Sweeny's blitz, 1997, as cited in Dessler, 2008, p. 595).

Some might think that employees join a union solely for higher wages; it's not so. There are deeply held values and dignity involved. Additionally, benefits and seniority are also very important.

A **union** is an organization that represents employees' interests to management on issues such as wages, work hours, and working conditions. Employees participate in running the union and support it with union dues. Laws protect employees' rights to join and participate in unions. The law also requires employers to bargain and confer with the union over certain employment issues that affect unionized employees (Gomez-Mejia, Balkin, & Cardy, 2007, p. 473).

Employees in the United States seek union representation when they are (1) dissatisfied

Unions represent employees' on wages, working hours, and working conditions

© a katz/Shutterstock.com

with certain aspects of their job, (2) feel that they lack influence with management to make the needed changes, and (3) see unionization as a solution to their problems (Brett, 1980, as cited in Gomez-Mejia, Balkin, & Cardy, 2007, p. 473). The union's best ally is bad management. If managers listen to employees, give them some say in the policies that affect their jobs, and treat them fairly, employees will not usually feel the need to organize (Gomez-Mejia, Balkin, & Cardy, 2007, p. 473).

> **Union**: An organization that represents employees' interests to management on issues such as wages, work hours, and working conditions.

Union workers generally receive significantly more holidays, sick leave, unpaid leave, insurance plan benefits, long-term disability benefits, and various other benefits than do nonunion workers. Unions also seem to have been able to somewhat reduce the impact of (but obviously not eliminate) downsizings and wage cuts in most industries (Belman and Voos, 2004, as cited in Dessler, 2008, pp. 597–598).

Unions and What Do Unions Want?

We can generalize by saying that unions have two sets of aims, one for *union security* and one for *improved wages, hours, working conditions,* and *benefits* for their members (Dessler, 2008, p. 598).

The **American Federation of Labor and Congress of Industrial Organizations (AFL-CIO)** is a federation of about 100 national and international labor unions in the United States. The AFL and CIO merged in 1955 and, for many, the AFL-CIO has become synonymous with the word union (Dessler, 2008, p. 598). The AFL-CIO is organized into three levels. One, the employee joins a local union, where they pay their dues and where the **collective bargaining** takes place and the labor contract is signed. The local chapter is one chapter of many that form a national union (the second level). The third level is the national federation such as the AFL-CIO. The mission of the AFL-CIO is to bring social and economic justice to our nation.

> **The American Federation of Labor and Congress of Industrial Organizations (AFL-CIO)**: is a federation of about 100 national and international labor unions in the United States.

> **Collective Bargaining**: Negotiation between a group of employees (and their representatives) and their employers on the terms of an agreement that outline all aspects of working conditions, benefits, and other aspects of work.

In the hospitality industry, **UNITE HERE,** a part of AFL-CIO, is the main union. UNITE HERE has represented hotel and restaurant employees for more than 100 years. Membership includes over 90,000 food service workers employed in corporate cafeterias, airports, universities, school districts, sports stadiums and event centers, amusement parks, cultural institutions, and national parks. In addition, UNITE HERE represents tens of thousands of restaurant workers inside hotels and casinos (UNITEHERE, 2013).

A Brief History of U.S. Labor Relations

Labor relations in the United States has a varied past. The guilds of the early 1800s were *forerunners of unions.* Beginning with the industrialization of America when the working conditions were unacceptable by today's standards, people often worked 10 or 12 hours a day for very low wages. At that time, labor in America was considered a commodity to be bought and sold, and the prevailing political philosophy of laissez faire (leave things alone) resulted in little action by governments to protect the workers from exploitation (Dulles, 1960, as cited in Cascio, 2003).

Until the early 1900s, the court system generally saw employment relationships as private agreements between an employer and an individual laborer. Unfortunately, many large employers took advantage of this relationship and forced employees to work in unsafe conditions for long hours at minimal wages. Gradually, labor unions formed and gained strength, and the federal government responded with laws and regulations that significantly influenced the evolution of organized labor in the United States (Stewart & Brown, 2009, p. 489).

The American Federation of Labor (AFL) was formed by Samuel Gompers in 1886. It focused on practical, bread-and-butter gains for its members. Gompers aimed to increase both wages and working conditions. The AFL grew rapidly until World War 1, at which point its membership exceeded 5.5 million people (Dessler, 2008, p. 597).

The American Federation of Labor and Congress of Industrial Organizations in Washington, DC on November 26, 2016

© Mark Van Scyoc/Shutterstock.com

Between the 1950s when union membership was at its peak (still below 50% of the workforce) and today, there has been a steady decline in union membership to a current level of about 8% of the workforce. Given that unions get their income solely from the dues of members, it is not surprising that unions have intensified their efforts to attract new members. Due to the decline of the manufacturing sector, unions have to look to the government and yes, even the hospitality industry, which makes a particularly attractive target due to its large size and the number of low paying jobs. Additionally, the hospitality industry is one which cannot be exported or handled offshore (Mitchell, 2013).

Union Membership in the United States

The life cycle of union membership in the United States has functioned not unlike the traditional life cycle of an everyday commodity, such as a product or service. It begins with an introduction into the market. After some time, the commodity gains interest in the eyes of consumers, resulting in a growing increase in demand. Eventually, the demand hits a peak and then for whatever reason, it begins to decline.

The idea that sparked union membership was introduced in the late 1800s; however, widespread interest did not take flight until after the passing of the National Labor Relations Act (NLRA) in 1935, which we will discuss in further detail later in the chapter. Between the years of 1935 and 1954, union membership saw significant growth in the United States, from approximately 8.5% of employed workers to an unparalleled peak of 28.3%. This gradual increase spanning 19 years was the result of high demand for work in a flourishing agricultural industry that was stricken with an amass of low-paying jobs and strenuous working conditions. Union membership remained heavily manned through 1979, at which time, the number of members in the United States peaked, at an estimated 21 million; however, this is also due to the population increase of employed workers in the United States, as the percentage of union representation in the labor force had dropped to 21.2% (Gerald, 2013).

In recent decades, union membership has significantly declined as a result of various economics factors, which include but are not limited to the decline of the agricultural industry, changes in other commercial industries, types of occupations available and newly arising occupations, as well as the increase in HR management. From 1979 to 2011, we have seen a gradual decline in both the number of union members as well as the percentage of union representation in the labor force.

In 2017, there were approximately 14.8 million union members in the United States, totaling 10.7% of the labor force. Within these numbers, the union membership rate of public-sector workers (34.4%) continued to be five times higher than that of private-sector workers (6.5%). Among states, New York continued to have the highest union membership rate (23.8%), whereas South Carolina continued to have the lowest (2.6%) (United States Department of Labor: Bureau of Labor Statistics 2018).

Wages of union workers are traditionally 20% higher on average than comparable wages of non-union workers. In 2011, among full-time and salaried workers, union members earned a median weekly income of $209 more than the comparable income of nonunion members, a number that is significantly greater. The trend of union membership has been a steady decline that appears to begun leveling off. It goes to show that the benefits of union representation remain attractive to individuals in certain occupations, industries, and regions throughout the United States. The question is whether unionization will continue to decline, remain stagnant, or begin to increase in future years. We look to the changing nature of economic and industrial relations in the United States to determine where future trends may take us.

Union Tactics (UNITEHERE, 2013)

UNITE HERE defected from the AFL-CIO to form their own organization called "Change to Win". The main tactic of Change to Win was the Labor Peace Agreement. Unions pressure ownership and management from top-down to agree to union demands before even approaching employees. There are several variations of these so-called *Labor Peace Agreements*. One type is called a Neutrality Agreement, where the company agrees not to oppose future unionization efforts, either at a particular property, or perhaps nationwide. These neutrality agreements can be "strict", requiring the company: 1) do nothing at all during the union organizing campaign; 2) affirmatively allow union organizers access to the property; or 3) give union spokespeople a forum from which to persuade employees to support the union.

Change to Win: UNITE HERE defected from the AFL-CIO to form their own organization.

Labor Peace Agreement: The main tactic of Change to Win.

Neutrality Agreement: The company agrees not to oppose future unionization efforts, either at a particular property, or perhaps nationwide.

Some labor peace agreements go so far as to require the company to recognize the union on the basis of authorization cards alone. These are referred to as Card Check Agreements. There is no campaign and no secret ballot election. Some locations in the country (e.g., San Francisco, Chicago, and New York) are much more prounion than other parts of the country. There may be politicians at either the local or national who are able to put pressure on employers to deal favorably with unions. City councils often become useful tools for unions and may pass local ordinances requiring employers who do business with the city, or who do business in a certain area of the city to recognize unions or deal favorably with them.

> **National Labor Relations Board (NLRB):** A five-member board appointed by the president of the United States to enforce the Wagner Act.

Unions traditionally organize employee workplaces from the ground up. A several weeks long period of persuading employees to sign authorization cards, usually low key and sometimes secretive, would result in an election petition with the National Labor Relations Board (NLRB), the government agency in charge of labor management relations.

Under current law, if union organizers collect signatures from 30% of workers, then the NLRB is brought in to supervise a secret-ballot election

© Kzenon/Shutterstock.com

Under current law, if union organizers collect signatures from 30% of workers, then the NLRB is brought in to supervise a secret-ballot election. If the majority votes to organize, the union is certified (UNITEHERE, 2013). When hospitality companies resist union's attempts at organizing, union tactics can get very aggressive; for example, the union will see to it that various complaints go to government agencies. These complaints may or may not have any foundation but because the government is involved, the company must spend many hours answering the complaints. Unions will also pressure employees to join the union by waiting outside the staff entrance, passing out leaflets, and talking to employees as they come and go.

Industrial Relations System

> **Industrial Relations System:** The working relationship between employees and their employers, through active management practices that are regularly applied throughout the company.

An industrial relations system is determined by the working relationship between employees and their employers, through active management practices that are regularly applied throughout the company. These practices include implementing standard operating procedures, managing conflict resolution among employees, and implementing motivational techniques in the workplace. A successful industrial relations system results in continued organizational effectiveness and operational efficiency.

Labor relations should be viewed as the central theme of managing a successful industrial relations system. Each industrial relations system is unique, and must take into consideration a company's district cultural environment. A sound industrial relations system fosters positive labor relations between employees and management, as opposed to a relationship that is exclusively beneficial to one over the other. This creates an environment that encourages active employee participation in management decisions concerning the company's labor relations policy and procedures. A sound system maintains a constructive cooperation among employees, as well as between employees and managers (De Silva, 2013).

Introducing Eric Centazzo, Area Director of Human Resources Starwood Hotels and Resorts Worldwide, Inc. The Sheraton Chicago Hotel & Towers.

"As many people seem to have done, I fell into the hospitality industry over 20 years ago. I was offered a front desk position at a large property in New York City and the rest is history. That first front desk position also happened to be a unionized job, so I not only got my first exposure to hospitality, but also to unions. In all honesty, I don't recall that I ever met with any representatives from my then union, and looking back now I am thankful. I mean no offense, but have come to learn that in many cases when you need to meet with your union representative it is typically due to an issue or problem you are encountering that you need assistance with.

I was lucky enough to spend many years in operations in hotels before transitioning into Human Resources. As such I was able to obtain firsthand knowledge about what our associates experience and what we as leaders ask of our employees. This knowledge has really assisted me in my transition to Human Resources, especially as it relates to managing issue. With respect to conflict resolution or issue management I have come to view myself as a mediator. I am not there to represent management, or be the advocate for the associate per se. My role is to view the issue, investigate who seems to be in the right, and then move in that direction regardless of whether management, the associate, or even the union is right.

Early on, as I became an operational manager I had always been told how difficult working with unions can be. In all honesty, I came to view it completely different. The way I look at it, you are given, or you negotiate a set of rules (a Collective Bargaining Agreement) and all you need to do is follow the rules and everything will be fine. Sounds simple I know . . . You don't have to necessarily agree with the rules, but you do need to respect and follow them. I have seen it time and time again where managers do not agree with, or blatantly thumb their nose at the rules (provisions of a CBA) and this is what gets them into trouble. People often tell me that they feel it intrusive that a third party (union) has the ability to question how they manage their associates or run their department. I tell these individuals that they have a choice. They choose to work, lead, in a union environment and if they can't follow the rules or understand that we are governed by a CBA, then they may need to rethink if they are right for the environment.

I have always viewed the relationship we maintain with the unions that govern our hotels as a partnership. Let's face it, many of our hotels are unionized and are likely to always remain so. Thus, my feeling is that every attempt should be made to foster a positive and amicable working relationship with the union. I can never understand where companies continue to perpetuate the stereotypical antagonistic approach to dealing with unions, essentially treating them like an intruder that has no right to be there. This does nothing but creates animosity between the company and the union, and work to ill affect moral among the associates. Until someone can show that maintaining the antagonist union / management relationship provides them with a lower cost of doing business and better associate culture, I will choose to continue to work to foster a positive and respectful relationships with the unions that have our associates as their members. While there are many times where we as a company will agree to disagree on various issues, both sides always understand that this is business, not personal, and our dealings always remain professional and respectful."

Contributed by Eric Centazzo. © Kendall Hunt Publishing Company

Learning Objective 2: Explain the details of each of the main pieces of labor legislation

Labor Relations and the Legal Environment

Laws pertaining to labor relations were established at the federal level starting with the Norris LaGuardia Act in 1932

© Mark Van Scyoc/Shutterstock.com

Over time, Congress has become involved in labor relations to redress the balance as it tilted too far one way of the other. If too much power is with employers or the unions, Congress seeks to make the balance even or tip the scale in the political favor of whichever party is in power. For many years, the political establishment regarded labor relations as something between the employer and employee. Eventually, legislation was necessary and among the early labor bills was the Norris–La Guardia Act.

The Norris–La Guardia Act

The Norris–LaGuardia Act, 1932, outlawed the use of injunctions to stop union activity. Until that time, if group of employees were trying to start a union and called for a strike or some other activity, the company could go to court and get an injunction there by stopping the union activity. This law changed that and served as a bridge to the Wagner Act.

The Wagner Act

Wagner Act: Formally known as the National Labor Relations Act (NLRA), Wagner Act is a federal law passed in 1935 that created the National Labor Relations Board and provided employees the right to organize unions.

The most important legislation related to unions is the Wagner Act, which is actually titled the National Labor Relations Act (NLRA). This federal law was passed in 1935 against a background of union activities that sometimes escalated to physical violence. Union organizers were trying to recruit members and management was resisting. The main purpose of the Wagner Act was to ensure employees have the right to participate in labor unions (Stewart & Brown, 2009, p. 490).

The Wagner Act specifically gives employees the right to form and join unions and to assist unions in recruiting members. Employees also have the right to bargain collectively, which means electing representatives who bargain for the interests of the group. Employees also have the right to strike, collectively refuse to work and to protest unfair labor practices (Stewart & Brown, 2009, p. 490).

Unfair Labor Practices: Employer labor practices that are against the law including prohibiting employees from joining unions, firing employees because of their union membership, or establishing a company-dominated union.

The Wagner Act also stipulated that when striking, union members had the right to form picket lines but not to block access to the business or to threaten violence against nonstriking employees or to attack management representatives. This provision was also coupled with another that prohibited employers from engaging in unfair labor practices that interfere with the union rights of employees. Unfair labor practices include prohibiting employees from joining unions, firing employees because of their union membership, or establishing a company-dominated union. In addition to requiring employers to bargain collectively with the union duly selected by the employees, the act setup procedures for establishing appropriate bargaining units (homogeneous groups of employees) where employees can elect a bargaining agent (a representative for labor negotiations) by a secret ballot (Wagner Act, 2013).

The Wagner Act created the *NLRB*; the board has five members appointed by the President of the United States, subject to Senate approval, to serve 5-year terms. The president also appoints a General Council which has a prosecutor, the board, the judge, and jury. The NLRB has two main functions: One to oversee employee elections that determine whether a union can be formed at a particular workplace and, two, to investigate allegations of unfair labor practices and to provide remedies, if necessary. Currently, 33 regional offices located in major cities across the country carry out the work of the NLRB and the General Council (Stewart & Brown, 2009, p. 491).

The five-member NLRB is appointed by the President of the United States

© Ken Wolter/Shutterstock.com

The NLRA proved to be an effective tool for labor unions. Union membership and economic power grew so rapidly between 1935 and 1945 that the business community complained that unions were abusing their new strength. As a result, in 1945, Congress passed the Taft–Hartley Act.

The Taft–Hartley Act

Congress passed the *Taft–Hartley Act*, also known as the Labor–Management Relations Act, because many business organizations complained that the Wagner Act had shifted power too far toward unions. This act amended the NLRA by prohibiting certain union practices as unfair labor practices. These activities include **secondary boycotts** (boycotts against the employer's customers or suppliers), jurisdictional strikes over work assignments, and strikes to force an employer to discharge an employee on account of his/her union affiliation or lack of it. The act also bans **"featherbedding"**, which occurs when the union requires a company to pay employees' wages even though the employees are not performing any services (Stewart & Brown, 2009, p. 491).[1]

> **Secondary Boycotts**: A boycott by unionized employees that is designed to pressure a company to not purchase goods and services from another company that is engaged in a labor dispute with a union.

> **Featherbedding**: A practice where a union requires an employer to pay employees' wages for work that is not performed.

---

[1] The First Sixty Years: The Story of the National Labor Relations Board 1935–1955. American Bar Association. Can be found online at www.nlrb.gov/About_Us/History/the_first_60years.aspx

Closed Shop: A from of union security in which the company can hire only union members. This was outlawed in 1947 but still exists in some industries (such as printing).

Union Shop: A form of union security where the company can hire nonunion people, but they must join the union after a prescribed period of time and pay dues. (if they do not, they can be fired).

Agency Shop: Employees who do not belong to the union must still pay union dues on the assumption that the union's efforts benefit all workers.

Open Shop: From the union's point of view, probably the least attractive type of union. The workers decide whether or not to join a union; and those who join must pay dues.

Right to Work Laws: A term used to describe state statutory or constitutional provisions of union membership as a condition of employment.

Union Security—there are several types of union security (Stewart & Brown, 2009, pp. 598–599):

1. **Closed Shop**: The company can only hire union members. Congress outlawed this in 1947, but it still exists in some industries (such as printing).

2. **Union Shop**: The company can hire nonunion people, but they must join the union after a prescribed period of time and pay dues. (if not, they can be fired).

3. **Agency Shop**: Employees who do not belong to the union still must pay union dues on the assumption that the union's efforts benefit all the workers.

4. **Open Shop**: In an open shop, the workers decide if they want to join a union—those who do not join do not pay dues.

The Taft–Hartley Act specifically made closed shops illegal. In addition, it provided states with the authority to enact **right-to-work laws**—laws allowing open-shop agreements. In essence, right-to-work laws create open shops where employees are not required to join or contribute to a union. Currently, there are 22 states that have right-to-work laws. Naturally, unions are not in favor of right-to-work laws. However, they are in favor of the Employee Free Choice Act (EFCA) which is discussed later in this chapter.

The Taft–Hartley Act allowed employees to decertify a union they no longer want and the NLRB must regulate the decertification process. The Taft–Hartley Act created a new agency, the *Federal Mediation and Conciliation Service,* to help mediate labor disputes so that economic disruptions due to strikes and other labor disturbances would be fewer and shorter (Gomez-Mejia, Balkin, & Cardy, 2007, p. 476).

The Landrum–Griffin Act

The Landrum–Griffin Act of 1959 resulted from a highly publicized investigation of union corruption and racketeering. Unions and other groups had taken union funds for private use and that the Teamsters union was clearly under the influence of organized crime. One result of the probe was the expulsion of the Teamsters and two other unions from the AFL-CIO. The AFL-CIO is the largest U.S.

Taft-Hartley created a new agency, the *Federal Mediation and Conciliation Service,* to help mediate labor disputes

labor organization, a federation of autonomous labor unions that is dedicated to enhancing and promoting unionism (Landrum-Griffin Act, 2013).

The Landrum–Griffin Act includes the following provisions:

- Unions must have a constitution with bylaws that are filed with the U.S. Secretary of Labor.
- Unions must have a bill of rights for union members to ensure minimum standards of union democracy.
- Unions must report their financial activities and the financial interests of their leaders to the Department of Labor.
- Union elections are regulated by the government, and union members have the right to participate in secret ballot elections.
- Union leaders have a fiduciary responsibility to use union money and property for the benefit of the membership and not for their own personal gain (Gomez-Mejia, Balkin, & Cardy, 2007, p. 477).

Following a long period of decline in union membership, the climate for union membership will likely increase dramatically in the next few years for two main reasons: the continuing economic situation, and President Obama's intention to pass the EFCA. It is not a matter of if but when, if he gains re-election.

The Employee Free Choice Act

The Employee Free Choice Act amends the NLRA to require the NLRB to certify a bargaining representative without directing an election if a majority of the bargaining unit employees have authorized designation of the representative (card-check) and there is no other individual or labor organization currently certified or recognized as the exclusive representative of any of the employees in the unit (CONGRESS. GOV, n.d.).

Union Avoidance Strategy

Many companies are reluctant to have unions representing their employees; so, they formulate a strategy to avoid the disruption of work and a loss of control over its workforce. For example, an employee may not do the work of another employee even in an emergency. Companies that choose an avoidance strategy are likely to be, at best, in an *armed truce* with unions and, at worst, in open conflict with them. There are two different approaches to union avoidance: union substation and union suppression (Gomez-Mejia, Balkin, & Cardy, 2007, p. 516).

The best union avoidance policy is to have a proactive employee relation

© ESB Professional/Shutterstock.com

Learning Objective 3: Outline how a union drive and election takes place

The Process of Unionization

At the time of writing, the EFCA is pending in Congress but, its chances of becoming law seem doubtful at this time. If it does become law, then the previous section above will take the precedent over what are currently the steps in union organization.

Organizing

When employees feel that their employers' or managers' labor practices are unfair or their labor relations are not in the employees' best interest, they are likely to seek alternative means to achieve a more improved arrangement, especially when direct confrontation with employers does not produce the desired outcome. As the word spreads throughout the organization, the group of employees "in the know" increases, creating a larger consensus of disgruntled employees. This is typically the time when union organizations will begin organizing drive.

To organize a union for a particular unit of employees you must have 30% of those employees' sign union authorization card. Once that has been completed, the National Labor Relations will review the card for authenticity and then schedule a vote on the employer's site. As the employees come to vote, they are checked in by an NLRB representative, a member of the union trying to organize them, and a member of management. Only those authorized can vote. Once the voting has been completed, the votes are counted by the NLRB, the union, and management. For the union to win, they must obtain 51% of all votes cast. For example, if there are 200 potential voters and only 130 voted, all that is needed to win the election is 65 votes. The election of the union is then certified.

Initial Contact

Union organizations will designate an individual "organizer", or a group of "organizers" to target a company's employees to attract new member representation to increase their strength within the company.

Obtaining Authorization Cards

"Authorization cards" are the key to success for union representatives when they infiltrate a company. The organizers will dispense "authorization cards" to employees, which denote their authorization to participate in the union. Organizers use a variety of tactics to convince employees to sign authorization cards, which includes forcible encouragement, conformity, and persuasion by stressing the benefits of unionization. Once the union successfully recruits at least 30% of the employees, they will contact the employer to ask for union recognition within the company. If the employer refuses the request, then the union can petition for representation within the company through the NLRB (Hunter, 1999).

Certification

Once *certified*, the union cannot be voted out until 1 year has passed. Legally, the union and the company must now bargain in good faith to reach an agreement. If the employees become dissatisfied with the union after a year; they, can call for a *decertification* election. The decertification process is the same as the certification process just in reverse.

Union and Management Union Election Tactics

Both sides are going to try to convince the employees of their point of view. You cannot promise anything if they vote or don't vote for the union, that is pay increases, etc. The best approach for you is to have a proactive employee relations record with your nonunion employees. You CANNOT WAIT for a union organizing campaign to take action. It will be too late.

Bargaining Unit

A **bargaining unit** consists of a group of people with mutual interests who are recognized as both employees of a company, as well as members of an official labor union in dealing with ongoing labor relations with their companies' management agency. The bargaining unit is first established upon the union's organizing drive tactics for acquiring representation within the company. Bargaining unit members are solely distinct from union members. All employees of a company represented by a union are considered members of the bargaining unit; however, only those who pay dues to the labor union are considered union members (Anonymous, 2013).

> **Bargaining Unit:** A group of people with mutual interests who are recognized as both employees of a company, as well as members of an official labor union in dealing with ongoing labor relations with their companies' management agency.

The Decertification of a Union

The **Decertification of a union** essentially means to officially get rid of the union's recognition or bargaining power within an establishment. Because a union acts as the "exclusive bargaining representative" for a company's employees, they have the right to elect the union's dissolution. There are certain rules established by the NLRB's governing body, which determine when employees can petition for union decertification:

> **Decertification of a Union:** To officially get rid of the union's recognition or bargaining power within an establishment.

- Petitions must be filed no less than 1 year after a union has won an NLRB-directed election for continued representation.
- Petitions cannot be filed throughout the first 3 years that a collective bargaining agreement is employed, except during a "window period" which arises 60–90 days before the CBA's expiration date (the "window Period" may vary depending on the industry).
- If the employer and union enter into a new contract after the previous contract expires, a petition must be submitted during the previous contract's "window period", or else a petition cannot be filed until the next "window period".
- Employers cannot participate in or influence the decertification process.
- If more than 50% of employees represented by a union sign the petition for decertification, an election is not necessary, and the employer can remove union acknowledgement (National Right to Work, 2013).

The process of union decertification is a several step process, which begins with "filing a petition" at the NLRB's regional office. In order for decertification to be considered by the NLRB, the petition must be signed by at least 30% of the employees. Next, a decertification election is held to determine if the majority of employees vote for or against union representation. A union will only remain if the election results in a majority ruling. If a tie vote occurs, the union will be removed from the workplace (Society for Human Resource Management, 2013).

Learning Objective 4: Explain the issues pertaining to collective bargaining

Collective Bargaining

Collective Bargaining: The process of negotiation between labor (the employees), a union, and an employer leading to a contract.

Distributive Issues: Cover areas where rewards and benefits must be divided among parties. Dividing current profits between employees and owners is a distributive issue.

Integrative Issues: Can result in mutual gains, increasing the overall level of rewards and benefits for everyone.

When a unionization drive results in certification, then the union and company representatives prepare for collective bargaining which leads to a labor contract. Most contracts last for 2–3 years, after which renegotiation takes place.

For good collective bargaining, a climate of trust and respect is necessary. However, sometimes that is easier said than done, anything less will add to the already complex situation. Negotiators that seek a win-win agreement help not only the process but also the labor management relationship.

There are two sets of interests important in collective bargaining: Distributive and Integrative. Distributive issues cover areas where rewards and benefits must be divided among parties. Dividing current profits between employees and owners is a distributive issue. Integrative issues, in contrast, can result in mutual gains, increasing the overall level of rewards and benefits for everyone. Improving employee safety, for instance, can result in greater benefits for management and employees (Stewart & Brown, 2009, p. 508).

The union contract is a legal document that contains provisions related to workers' rights and benefits

© Bacho/Shutterstock.com

The union contract is a detailed description of the rights of both employees and management. It typically contains the following information (Stewart & Brown, 2009, p. 508):

- Time limits of the agreement
- Management rights
- Employee rights
- Job classification and pay
- Grievance procedures
- Hours of work
- Overtime and vacation pay
- Seniority issues
- Employee benefits *(in the public sector in certain cases benefits are not included bargaining)*

Unions and management hold negotiations to agree upon the terms of a contract.

Negotiations

Unions and management gather information during prenegotiations. Information on how many employees there are in each job classification, current wages, overtime, demographic information, and the cost of benefits such as lunch, breaks, vacations, health insurance, and perhaps childcare provisions.

Both unions and management try to get the best terms for them. Unions want a good deal for their members and management wants a reasonable return on investment for owners. Unions and management realize that they are in a competitive market, meaning that if the costs are significantly higher at a union property compared to a nonunion then more guests will likely go to the lower cost hotel and the union hotel will not be able to compete.

The teams for the *negotiations* generally include on the management side, a chief negotiator who may be a company person or someone hired as a consultant, the HR director, the general manager, and/or nonunion management. The union negotiators include national union negotiators, local union members, shop stewards, and the local union president. The respective teams meet before the negotiations to decide on their game plan of which topics are the most important on their agenda for the negotiations. Management may, for example, be most interested in containing wage increases whereas unions may be more interested in healthcare and other benefits.

During the negotiating, both sides sit across a table and work their way through an agenda of items for discussion. The bargaining process can last weeks, even months, and if a contract is agreed upon, it is scrutinized by both parties a few times to ensure it is correct. Then the contract is sent to all union members for ratification by a formal vote. If a majority of members agree, the contract can then be signed.

The NLRB and the courts classify bargaining topics as mandatory, permissive, and illegal. *Mandatory* topics are wages, hours, and employment conditions. *Permissive* topics are those that both parties agree to discuss, although neither is obliged to bargain on them. Examples of permissive topics include pensions or retirement benefits and participative management. *Illegal* topics include closed shop agreements, featherbedding, and discriminatory employment practices (Jerris, 1999, p. 267).

Legalize

The union should abide by all applicable labor laws; but, if it does not, management can request a cease and desist order from a judge. If management does not keep to the law and any agreements, the union can also request an injunction from a judge. It is in the best interest of both sides to try and work things out instead of taking more drastic actions. The Collective Bargaining Agreement (CBA) is the legal agreement document that governs the working relationship between the union and the management. If the union feels that management has wronged a member, it will conduct an investigation and if necessary file a grievance. In this case, management representatives will hold a hearing with the union representatives in step one. If the matter is not resolved at step one, it goes to step two, where a more senior level of management reviews the grievance.

Bargaining Impasses and Mediation

Generally, the negotiations end with an agreement and a contract. However, if there is no agreement, and an impasse is reached, where neither the union nor management is willing to concede, then one of four events can occur (Jerris, 1999, p. 238). The employees might call a strike where they refuse to work until management grants the concessions they want.

Unions that may not want to go as far as a strike can opt for a *boycott* where union members picket the company entrance with posters about the *labor dispute*. Union members also encourage other union members not to cross the picket line and patronize the company. They will also contact suppliers to encourage them to suspend doing business supplying the company. Unions call for boycotts when hospitality companies resist union organizing efforts with avoidance tactics or a stagnation of the negotiations or there are serious grievance issues.

Successful labor management relations often include involving the union in various decisions affecting the organizations

© Take Photo/Shutterstock.com

Another response to an impasse is a *lockout* where management closes the operation or runs it with a few nonunion employees and perhaps others brought in to help. The reason for management doing a lockout is to force the union to accept their demands or to counter work slow-downs by employees. Because hospitality operations are open 24-hours a day, seven days a week, lockouts don't happen very often.

If unions and management fail to agree they can opt for *third-party mediation*. Usually, a professional, trained mediator or arbitrator is engaged to help both sides reach an agreement by listening to both sides and facilitating an agreement. The arbitrator then makes a decision which is binding on both management and unions.

Remember both sides need to reach an agreement that both sides can live with as it could be in place for 3 years. Remember to never "run up the score".

The Agreement

Once the agreement is in place, it is important for both sides to abide by it. The contract could be for 3 years and it is essential for labor peace for both sides to make every effort to make the contract work. Successful labor management relations often include involving the union in various decisions affecting the organizations. This action can help create a feeling of stakeholders/partners on part of the union members. Southwest Airlines does this successfully.

Strikes and Types of Strikes

A *strike* is a withdrawal of labor, and there are four main types of strikes:

1. An *economic strike* that results from a failure to agree on the terms of a contract.
2. Unions call *unfair labor practice strikes* to protest illegal conduct by an employer.
3. A *wildcat strike* is an unauthorized strike occurring during the term of a contract.
4. A *sympathy strike* occurs when one union strikes in support of another (Jerris, 1999, p. 238).

There are far fewer strikes today than say 40 years ago. Both unions and management have come to realize that no one really wins a strike as heavy losses are incurred on both sides. In addition, both management and unions are working closer together with unions having more of a say in the running of companies along with profit sharing deals which mean part ownership of the company and a lesser likelihood of striking against it.

Once a strike is called, one of the first activities is for union members to picket, meaning to carry signs at the workplace announcing the concerns of the union and its members. The intention is to inform others of the labor dispute and to persuade people from using the business of the struck employer.

Employers, on the other hand, can shut down the struck area until the strike is over or, to contract work out to diminish the effects of the strike. Another measure employers can take is to use supervisors and non-striking employees to carry on the business. Or, they can replace the striking workers with others who are not union members.

Union victories like the one at the Boathouse are rare. Almost everywhere

Both unions and management have come to realize that no one really wins a strike as heavy losses are incurred on both sides

© EQRoy/Shutterstock.com

else in the labor movement, the news is bleak. A three-decade assault on workers' rights to organize has been worsened by high unemployment, outsourcing to low-wage nations, ever more aggressive anti-union tactics by management, and rising health-care costs—all of which make wage increases a distant memory. Today, collective bargaining is mostly about concessions, not new benefits, and collective bargaining itself is the exception, with union representation in the private sector down to just 7% of workers.

Lockouts

A **lockout** is a labor-relations strategy implemented when an employer refuses unionized employees permission to work for a certain period of time, while denying them the right to pay during that time. This usually occurs during the midst of labor disputes between unionized employees and management. This is usually management's solution to

> **Lockout:** A labor-relations strategy implemented when an employer refuses unionized employees permission to work for a certain period of time, while denying them the right to pay during that time.

a union strike, and typically results in either a suspension in a company's work production or continued production using temporary non-unionized workers (Josh, 2013).

Employers implement lockouts in a number of ways including banning employees from coming on property, which is enforced by changing the locks, hiring security personnel or administering harsh fines and penalties for coming onto the premises. Sometimes, employers simply do not allow locked out workers the ability to clock in to work. Strikes and lockouts are essentially battles between employees and employers to win the upper hand of a dispute and gain leverage over the other. Lockouts are used to convince unionized employees to back down and agree to the company's terms or conditions. On many occasions, the lockout amounts to a lose-lose for all parties involved.

For example, in one of the more extensive labor-relations disputes of recent years, members of UNITE HERE employed by Multi Employer Group in 14 hotels throughout the San Francisco Bay area initiated a 2-week strike to refute the duration of their new labor contract agreement. The strike resulted in a lockout of 4,300 employees that lasted well beyond the strike's end, which aimed to pressure the union into accepting the contract length as is and bypass the loss of work wages. However; the workers took drastic measures and formed massive picket lines which lasted for weeks. The hotels suffered extensive losses in business and revenue throughout this time, while the union acquired significant political support from the local government and others as well. Eventually, the lockout was discontinued and the picket lines dissolved. The workers returned to their jobs, but the contract agreement dispute remained unresolved (David, 2013).

Grievance Procedures in the Unionized Company

The labor contract is the formal document by which both sides should conduct themselves. In the event that an employee feels that he or she has been unfairly treated, they can begin grievance proceedings. An example would be a manager disciplined an employee for excessive tardiness or refusing to do a normal job duty request. If the employee felt that the discipline was outside the labor contract, they could initiate grievance proceedings by filing a grievance.

Grievance procedures follow procedures laid down in the contract. They normally begin with the employee bringing the matter to a higher level manager. Most grievances are solved at this level. However, if the employee and the more senior manager cannot agree, the employee would then take the grievance to the union shop steward. The shop steward is an employee who is a union member that advocates for employees. Some unions have a grievance committee who deal with more complex issues. On the employer's side, the next level is senior management and /or the HR director, who may play a direct or supporting role in the grievance.

> **Shop Steward**: A representative of the union who acts as an advocate for employees.

> **Arbitration**: A process where an independent *and impartial* person *listens to both sides in* a labor relations dispute and makes a binding determination.

If the two parties cannot agree by this time, the final step in the process is arbitration. Only a small percentage of grievances reach arbitration and when they do, the arbitrator is like a judge. She or he hears both sides of the issue—from management and the union, then makes a generally binding decision. Grievances typically happen when managers and companies are too profit driven and forget the importance human relations and a positive work climate.

The Future of Labor-Management Relations

About 7–8% of the private section workforce are now union members. During the 1950s, the number was about 35%. One of the reasons for the decrease is that most employers are treating their employees better thereby reducing the need for a union. Many of the benefits and protection that we take for granted were initiated by unions, that is child labor laws, equal pay, workplace safety, health care, etc. to name a few areas.

The future of union management relations must be inclusive and collaborative to resolve workplace issues. This is normally called interest-based bargaining. There are a number of organizations doing this successfully. Unionized employers can be quite successful such as Southwest Airlines and others. If your organization is unionized, I would suggest involving the union members in various employee committees and in certain decision making. Remember your employees not you are the front line people representing your organization to your customers. You can become an employer of choice with or without unions. It's about *your* leadership.

Key Points

- A Union is an organization that represents employees' interests to management on issues such as wages, work hours, and working conditions.

- Employees in the United States seek union representation when they are dissatisfied with certain aspects of their job. Or, employees feel they lack influence with management to make needed changes or see unionization as a solution to their problems.

- Unions want union security and improved wages, hours, working conditions, and benefits for their members.

- The American Federation of Labor and Congress of Industrial Organizations (AFL-CIO) is a federation of about 100 national and international labor unions.

- Unfortunately, many large employers took advantage of the fact that until the early 1900s, the courts saw employment relationships as private agreements between an employer and an individual. Many employees worked long hours 10–12 a day in poor conditions for low pay.

- The American Federation of Labor (AFL) was formed by Samuel Gompers in 1886.

- UNITE HERE defected from the AFL-CIO to form their own organization called "Change to Win". The main tactic of Change to Win is the Labor Peace Agreement. Unions pressure ownership and management from top down to agree to union demands even before approaching employees.

- There are several variations of a Labor Peace Agreement, one is called a Neutrality Agreement, where the company agrees not to oppose future unionization efforts.

- The National Labor Relations Board (NLRB) is the government agency in charge of labor management relations. It has five members appointed by the president, subject to Senate approval, to serve 5 year terms.

- If ever the Free Choice Act is passed, it would allow a majority signature drive to form a union without the need for a secret ballot.

- In 2011, there were approximately 14.8 million union members in the United States totaling 11.8% of the labor force.

- The wages of union members are traditionally 20% higher on average than comparable wages of non-union workers.

- An industrial relations system is determined by the working relationship between employees and their employers.

- The main purpose of the Wagner Act was to ensure employees have the right to participate in labor unions.

- The Taft–Hartley Act was passed because many employers said that the Wagner Act had shifted power too far toward unions. This act prohibited certain union practices as unfair labor practices, including secondary boycotts and featherbedding.

- The Taft–Hartley Act made closed shops illegal and provided states the authority to enact right-to-work laws.

- Collective bargaining takes place when a union is certified and leads to a labor contract which generally lasts 2–3 years.

- A strike is a withdrawal of labor and there are four main types of strikes: Economic, unfair labor practice, a wildcat, and a sympathy strike.

- A lockout is a labor-relations strategy implemented when an employer refuses unionized employees permission to work for a certain period of time.

Key Terms

Agency Shop	Integrative issues	The American Federation
Arbitration	Labor Peace Agreement	of Labor and Congress of
Bargaining unit	Lockout	Industrial Organizations
Change to Win	National Labor Relations	(AFL-CIO)
Closed Shop	Board (NLRB)	The union contract
Collective bargaining	Neutrality Agreement	Unfair labor practices
Decertification of a union	Open shop	Union
Distributive issues	Right to work laws	Union Shop
Featherbedding	Secondary boycotts	Wagner Act
Industrial relations system	Shop steward	

Discussion Questions

1. Discuss the history of U.S labor relations. What were the major trends throughout history? How does the hospitality industry fit into the history of labor relations?

2. What is the most important legislation related to unions, and what did it accomplish?

3. Do you agree or disagree with Steve Joyce of Choice Hotels that the Free Choice Act will be a disaster leading to a 20% drop in profitability?

Your Call

As HR Director, you become aware that some employees are trying to persuade others to join the union. What should you do?

Ethical Dilemma

You are a blue-collared person who works hard to provide for your family. As an active member of the union that represents the employees of your company, you regularly attend the monthly union meetings. At this month's meeting, your new labor agreement with the company will be unveiled. You wait patiently as the union president approaches the podium to make the announcement.

When the news is finally disclosed, to everyone's dismay, it seems that all employees will receive minimal increases in pay, but will undergo changes in their benefits package that are less attractive than in the previous agreement. The new benefits package includes medical and vision insurance, but the medical insurance provider has changed from a Preferred Provider Organization (PPO) to a Health Maintenance Organization (HMO). Also, under the previous agreement, employees were covered with medical and dental insurance instead of medical and vision insurance.

There is outrage amongst the group for several minutes. Finally, when the group settles down, the union president asks for volunteer discussion in attempt to remedy the situation. One person suggests that the employees go on strike for several weeks' time in order to force a new labor agreement from their employer. Another person argues that a strike will most likely result in a lockout, and the employees will forfeit pay for an extended period of time. The union president calls for a vote to determine if the group should strike against their employer.

1. How should you vote in this situation?
2. What factors play into your decision?
3. Are there other possible solutions to this dilemma that you could propose before a vote takes place?

References

Anonymous (2013). *Bargaining unit*. Retrieved January 20, 2013, from http://cpol.army.mil/library/permiss/411.html

Cascio, W. F. (2003). *Managing human resources* (6th ed., p. 508). New York: McGraw-Hill Irwin.

CONGRESS.GOV. (n.d.). Available from https://www.congress.gov/bill/111th-congress/house-bill/1409

David, B. (2013). *San Francisco hotel lockout boxed employees*. Retrieved January 21, 2013, from http://labornotes.org/node/852

De Silva, S.R. (2013). *Elements of a sound industrial relations system*. Retrieved January 16, 2013, from http://www.ilo.org/public/english/dialogue/actemp/downloads/publications/srseleme.pdf

Dessler, G. (2008). *Human resource management* (11th ed.). Upper Saddle River, NJ: Pearson.

Gerald, M. (2013). *Union membership trends in the United States*. Cornell University ILR School. Retrieved January 12, 2013 from http://digitalcommons.ilr.cornell.edu/cgi/viewcontent.cgi?article=1176&context=key_workplace

Gomez-Mejia, L. R., Balkin, D. B., & Cardy, R. L. (2007). *Managing human resources* (5th ed.). Upper Saddle River, NJ: Pearson.

Hunter, R. P. (1999, August). *The union organizing drive*. Retrieved January 20, 2013, from http://www.mackinac.org/2318

Iverson, K. M. (2001). *Managing human resources in the hospitality industry* (p. 236). Upper Saddle River, NJ: Prentice Hall.

Jerris, L. A. (1999). *Human resources management for hospitality* (p. 267). Upper Saddle River, NJ: Prentice Hall.

Josh, E. (2013). *The employer strikes back*. Retrieved January 21, 2013, from http://prospect.org/article/employer-strikes-back

Kuttner, R. (2013). *A more perfect union*. Retrieved January 21, 2013, from http://prospect.org/article/more-perfect-union-1

Landrum-Griffin Act. (2013). *Landrum-Griffin Act*. Retrieved January 16, 2013, from http://law.jrank.org/pages/8069/Landrum-Griffin-Act.html

Mitchell, M. S. (2013). *Union organizing trends in the hospitality industry*. Retrieved January 12, 2013, from hospitalitynet.org/news/4032340.search?query=hospitality+industry+unions

National Right to Work. (2013). *Decertification election*. Retrieved January 20, 2013, from http://www.nrtw.org/decertification-election

Society for Human Resource Management. (2013). *What is the process to decertify a union?* Retrieved January 20, 2013, from http://www.shrm.org/TemplatesTools/hrqa/Pages/decertifyaunion.aspx

Stewart, G. L., & Brown, K. G. (2009). *Human resource management: Linking strategy to practice*. Hoboken, NJ: Wiley.

United States Department of Labor: Bureau of Labor Statistics. (2018). *Union members summary*. Retrieved January 12, 2018, from http://www.bls.gov/news.release/union2.nr0.htm

UNITEHERE. (2013). *100,000 food service members—And growing!* Retrieved January 12, 2013, from http://unitehere.org/industry/food-service/

Wagner Act. (2013). *Wagner Act—Further readings*. Retrieved January 16, 2013, from http://law.jrank.org/pages/11179/Wagner-Act.html

INDEX